THE CITY TAKE-OVER CODE

THE CITY TAKE-OVER CODE

BY
Sir Alexander Johnston

OXFORD UNIVERSITY PRESS
1980

Oxford University Press, Walton Street, Oxford OX2 6DP
OXFORD LONDON GLASGOW
NEW YORK TORONTO MELBOURNE WELLINGTON
KUALA LUMPUR SINGAPORE JAKARTA HONG KONG TOKYO
DELHI BOMBAY CALCUTTA MADRAS KARACHI
NAIROBI DAR ES SALAAM CAPE TOWN

Published in the United States by
Oxford University Press, New York

© Sir Alexander Johnston 1980

All rights reserved. No part of this publication may be reproduced, stored in a retrieval system, or transmitted, in any form or by any means, electronic, mechanical, photocopying, recording, or otherwise, without the prior permission of Oxford University Press

British Library Cataloguing in Publication Data

Johnston, Sir Alexander
   The City Take-over Code.
   1. Consolidation and merger of corporations—
   Great Britain
   2. City Working Party. City code on take-overs
   and mergers
   338.8'3'0941   HD2848   80–40065
   ISBN 0–19–828424–1

Film-set in 11/12 point Baskerville
Printed and bound in Great Britain
by W & J Mackay Limited, Chatham

PREFACE

THE City Code on Take-overs and Mergers has now been in existence for more than ten years and this seems to be an appropriate time to recount the history of an interesting experiment in self-regulation. This book is a record of the experiment as seen by a member of the Take-over Panel: a practitioner in the field of take-overs would have written an account which was different in various respects. As regards the scope of the book, it has to be remembered that the Code is concerned with the procedures by which take-over bids are conducted. It deals with ways and means, The Code is not concerned with whether take-overs generally or individually are good or bad. I have added to the history of events some notes on the interpretation of the general principles and rules that constitute the Code.

I wish to record my indebtedness to present and past members of the Panel executive for the help they have given me, particularly Mr Peter R. Frazer and Mr T. Peter Lee. I have tried to avoid obtruding personal views, but no doubt at various points these views have influenced my presentation of the subject. The book should not be regarded as expressing the views of the Panel or of the Panel executive, save where these views are being stated.

A.J.
31 December 1979

CONTENTS

HISTORY OF THE CODE AND PANEL

I.	Self-Regulation	3
II.	Before the First Attempt at Regulation	8
III.	First Efforts at Regulation	19
IV.	First City Code and Panel	30
V.	Revision of Code and Reorganization of Panel	51
VI.	Panel Establishes Itself	58
VII.	Recession and Afterwards	82
VIII.	Further Revision	98
IX.	Future of the Code	115
X.	Panel Organization	125
XI.	Government and the Code	137
XII.	Law and the Code	147
XIII.	Insider Dealing	155
XIV.	Securities and Exchange Commission	170
XV.	European Economic Community	179

NOTES ON THE CODE

Introduction	189
Definitions	191

CONTENTS

General Principles   195
Rules   214

APPENDIX A   288
APPENDIX B   297
INDEX   305

History of the Code and Panel

I
SELF-REGULATION

AT one time self-regulation referred to the habits of individuals, much as we still speak of self-discipline, but it is now widely used to refer to disciplines accepted by members of professional and other voluntary bodies. This book describes a form of self-regulation which has been developed in the securities industry over the last twenty years. Much has been said and written about self-regulation versus state regulation. In the field of securities regulation, there are some things that clearly fall within the province of the State. It is accepted that the State should impose conditions designed to secure a minimum standard of conduct: and only the State can impose and enforce requirements of general application to all and sundry. The normal instrument of state regulation is statute law and, where more detailed provisions are required, use is made of statutory rules made under statutory powers. Latterly, less rigid instruments have been used in the shape of codes of conduct—as with the Highway Code or the codes authorized by legislation dealing with industrial relations and with fair trading. In form, there is now considerable flexibility in the instruments at the disposal of the State.

Where the State has endeavoured to exercise control, directly by a Government Department or through a statutory board, it would be wrong to say that the supervision is necessarily slow, cumbrous, and complicated. There are, however, tendencies in that direction which are not easily countered. Licensed dealers in securities are supervised by the Department of Trade under the provisions of the Prevention of Fraud (Investment) Act 1958. The Department made rules for the conduct of business by licensed dealers in 1939 under an earlier Act and substantially revised them in 1960. Any substantial amendment of the rules is calculated to take at least six months to effect and this is one of the reasons why, in a fast-moving situation, the rules remained unchanged over a great number of years in spite of a real desire to bring them up to date. The Insurance Brokers Registration Council, set up by an Act of Parliament of 1977, has been able to promulgate a code of conduct for insurance brokers with commendable speed, but the code and rules on other aspects have to be submitted to the Minister for approval and laid before both Houses of Parliament and the Council's disciplinary procedure is closely regulated. All this may slow down the operations of the Council in the long run. And the more complicated and fast-moving the commercial and financial operations that are being regulated, the more difficult it is to create a satisfactory governmental supervisory body. The governmental body may not be close enough to the operations to know what is happening and it may not move quickly enough. At the same time, a state body has substantial powers to get at the facts and to enforce its decisions.

It is often said that state regulation can distinguish only between black and white. What is not prohibited is permissible. Not only does this fail to deal with a grey area between bad practice and good practice but it encourages some citizens to find ways round the specific statutory prohibitions although what they are doing may be entirely contrary to the intention of the legislation. All this is true, subject to the qualification that most laws depend on the observance of certain general ethical standards in the community. The tax laws are framed on the assumption that most people are honest and the same is true of commercial law. In so far as there has been a decline in moral standards, much of our legislation in its present form becomes less effective. Self-regulation deals with the grey area in conduct between black and white and, because it can insist on the need to observe the spirit of its precepts, it can ensure that they are applied fairly and flexibly in individual situations and changing circumstances. As it has been put, the law is concerned with what is lawful: self-regulation seeks to enforce what is fair.

Self-regulation is seen in its simplest form when a body of men, often members of a profession, agree to observe certain standards of conduct in their work. They may originally have come together for quite different reasons—say, to share common services as a measure of economy—but by self-regulation they endeavour to achieve a certain standard of conduct in all their members. We are concerned in this book with a form of self-regulation which aims at securing higher ethical standards than can be secured by state regulation. Those administering a scheme of self-regulation may set out rules of conduct and then trust to all concerned to observe them, or they may decide to interpret the code and supervise its operation. Self-regulation exists in the fullest sense when a group agrees upon a code and interprets and administers it without external interference.

Self-regulation is usually simple in operation and flexible in its application to individual cases. In practice, it makes much fewer demands on resources than do state organizations. It is also better adapted to deal with quickly moving developments. It may suffer from a lack of powers—both in investigations and in the exercise of discipline; but the extent to which this is a disadvantage in practice has to be examined in each field in the light of experience. A self-regulatory system may get into difficulties if it endeavours to extend its regulatory functions beyond those who have submitted themselves to its jurisdiction. To be fully effective, self-regulation has to be self-policing. It is not enough for those who subscribe to a code of conduct to sit back and leave those who administer the code to do all the work. This is recognized in the European code of conduct relating to transactions in transferable securities, adopted by the EEC Commission in July 1977. Dealers in securities are expected not only to thwart any attempt at market manipulation but also immediately to inform the competent authorities and the companies concerned. In relation to the City Code on Take-overs and Mergers and its administration by the Panel, it is accepted that merchant banks and others subscribing to the Code have a duty to assist the Panel in discovering the whole truth of any matter under examination.

Self-regulation has flourished in the City of London, because, as a matter of convenience, activities are often carried on under one roof—such as The Stock Exchange, Lloyds, the

Baltic Exchange, and so forth—and those who agreed to work in the same place and to share common services came to expect a certain standard of behaviour in order to maintain the reputation of the body of members. In the securities industry as a whole, there is a substantial body of statute law and in the case of licensed dealers in securities there is departmental supervision. The Bank of England has an over-all concern that the securities markets should operate soundly and effectively and in performing this function the Bank has the co-operation of those who operate in the markets. Thus the Bank has regular meetings with representatives of The Stock Exchange on matters of common interest. Self-regulation operates within this framework. The Stock Exchange is the prime example of self-regulation. It is a voluntary association of stockbrokers and jobbers which in no way depends on legislation but which has over many years exercised great authority over the securities market. Its existence and operations are recognized and accepted in the Companies Acts.

Under the provisions of the Fair Trading Act 1973 the Director-General of Fair Trading is required to encourage trade associations to formulate codes of practice for their members to protect the interests of consumers. A substantial number of such codes are in operation with beneficial results. The next few years will show whether this state encouragement of self-regulation will result in a permanent extension of the field of self-regulation or whether any shortcomings will be met by an extension of the substantial powers which the Director-General of Fair Trading already possesses rather than by a reform of the self-regulatory machinery.

The Take-over Code is unusual in that it spans several professions, some with their own self-regulatory systems. The link with the individual practitioner might be thought to be less strong than in a code devised and administered within a single profession: and how this has worked out in practice is one of the many interesting features of the history of the Code. The Code has also had to cope with fast-changing conditions and here again it might be thought that the number of interests involved would have been a disadvantage. The recently established Council for the Securities Industry, the formation of which has to some extent been influenced by the experience of the Take-over Panel, covers an even wider span. It too supervises the activities of a number of organizations and individuals who have voluntarily accepted its jurisdiction and is independent of the State.

Only the future will show how substantial a part self-regulation has to play in the scheme of things in the longer term. Self-regulation shows no signs of senility and indeed the creation of the Take-over Panel and the Council for the Securities Industry shows that self-regulation is a vigorous growth. Other promising developments are the improvements in their procedures introduced by the accountants and the steps being taken to secure a wider acceptance of self-regulation among licensed dealers in securities.

Where a self-regulatory body imposes restrictions in what it conceives to be the public interest it may find itself subject to examination under the restrictive practices legislation. Some bodies have secured exemption, others have not. There is here a potential danger to the self-regulatory system. It has also to be faced that the long-term influence of EEC will be in favour of state regulation. But these difficulties may be surmounted.

What seems to be clear is that, if State regulation takes over beyond a certain point, self-regulation tends to wither. Some element of state connection has its attractions as it may give a voluntary body more power and authority: but it has serious disadvantages. The US stock exchanges have powers delegated to them by the SEC but a good deal is lost in the conditions that are inevitably imposed when powers are given. Moreover, if things begin to go wrong, the remedy is usually sought in extending the powers of the official body rather than in trying to improve the voluntary bodies. This certainly happened in the United States in 1975 when the SEC increased its supervision over the stock exchanges and the National Association of Security Dealers. It is of interest that in its report on the accountancy profession dated 1 July 1978 the SEC said that the central issue was whether the profession should continue to be primarily and essentially self-disciplined and self-regulated or whether government should become directly involved in its regulation. In this case the SEC came down in favour of a continuance of voluntary self-regulation.

II

BEFORE THE FIRST ATTEMPT AT REGULATION

WHETHER mergers and take-overs should be encouraged or discouraged is a matter of public policy to be considered by the Government and ultimately by Parliament. What became the City Take-over Code arose out of problems in a narrower field—the methods by which take-over bids were effected. On this there was little statutory regulation, though the Companies Acts provided a mechanism for mergers between companies in the form of schemes of arrangement. The conditions which led to the widespread take-over bids of the fifties did not exist before the Second World War. The typical pre-war merger was an agreed amalgamation of companies in the same or a related line of business with a view to securing a greater share of the market or effecting economies. The key phrase was the 'rationalization of industry'. There might be an exchange of shares between the merging companies or a holding company might be formed in which the shareholders received shares in exchange for their existing shares. The essential point was that the scheme was agreed between the boards of the companies and it was unusual for a board to deal direct with the shareholders of another company.

After the war share prices did not immediately settle down to any coherent pattern. Industry was resuming its peace-time activities and trying to find its markets, but there were still many restrictions and controls, including the control of capital issues. Many fixed assets, especially property, remained at old values in balance sheets. This was the result sometimes of caution and sometimes of inertia: and few foresaw the escalation of property values, due to inflation and other causes, which was to occur in the fifties. This is illustrated by the small figure placed on development value by the owners of property in the returns they made under the Town and Country Planning Act 1947.[1] Further, there were several factors leading to restraint in the level of dividends; and this in turn depressed share prices because these prices were mainly related to the size of dividends. Company taxation during and after the war discouraged the distribution of profits. In general, higher tax was paid on distributed than on undistributed profits. Under the surtax legislation private companies had been required to distribute a substantial share of their profits, but in 1948 this requirement was eased in the interest of higher capital investment and of restricting private income and this 'umbrella' over restricted distributions continued until 1957. Dividend restraint was also extolled as a public duty and led to the depression of stock-exchange values. The result of all these factors was that, if the Financial Times share index in 1935 is taken as 100, it stood in 1952 at 105, representing a substantial fall in real value. An individual, with some hard work, could spot shares that were seriously undervalued in terms of asset values or the potentialities of the business. It was also true that, for a variety of reasons including wartime conditions, many businesses, including some old and honoured names, were not being efficiently managed and could yield better results in more competent, if sometimes more ruthless, hands.

In the fifties, before the issue in 1959 of 'Notes on Amalgamations of British Businesses' two phases can be distinguished. In the early fifties Mr Charles Clore (later Sir Charles Clore) and others made a number of take-over bids which were often strongly resisted by the boards of the companies concerned. These bids related primarily to the distributive trades. Towards the end of the fifties there was a spate of bids in which two (or more) bidders were contesting to take over a company. The board of a company might be resisting all comers or

---

[1] The Town and Country Planning Act 1947 proposed that £300,000,000, should be given to the owners of land for the loss of development value under the Act. In 1952 the eligible claims for compensation were estimated at £350,000,000 (Commons debates 26 Feb. 1952 col. 121). The Conservative Government of 1951–5 abandoned the scheme.

favouring one bidder. Industrial companies, as well as those engaged in distribution, were involved.

The Early Fifties

The first case of note was the successful take-over of J. Sears & Co. (True Form Boot Company) by Mr Clore. He had observed that the shops and other property owned by Sears were substantially undervalued in the balance sheet and that funds could be obtained by the sale of the properties to insurance companies and other financial institutions and leasing them back to the occupier. In January 1953 he made a bid through Investment Registry Ltd., at a price substantially higher than the market price. Sears shareholders who so wished could retain an interest in Sears through non-voting A shares. The directors of Sears opposed the bid: they recognized the need to take defensive action and they recommended an increased dividend and a bonus issue of shares and proposed to revalue the properties of the company. Sears shareholders, representing a substantial majority of the shares, accepted the Investment Registry offer. The new management sold and took back on lease the valuable shops and other property held by Sears. This gave more than £3,000,000 in cash. Haverton Holdings, owned by Mr Clore and his associates, was then sold to Sears for £3,500,000. The cash received by the sale and lease back of Sears's properties thus became more readily available for further take-over bids and other purposes.

In 1953 and 1954 there was intensive take-over activity, often involving contests between the bidder and the board of the company bid for. In the financial press of the time take-over bids were regarded as, on balance, a useful stimulus to efficiency. Some managements had become inefficient and slothful and were not using to best advantage the assets in their possession. The bidder, if successful, often produced a more efficient management. Even if unsuccessful, the bidder was regarded as a useful gadfly, stinging sleepy managements into action. There were, however, many critics. Labour Party spokesmen disliked the large tax-free profits made by successful bidders at a time when capital gains were not taxed. They also disliked the coach and four that was driven through a policy of dividend restraint during and after bid contests and argued that this impeded capital investment. Nevertheless, even Labour Party spokesmen admitted that some take-over bids had served a useful purpose, and they tended to ask for an inquiry rather than for immediate action against bids.

In these circumstances, it is perhaps not surprising that the action taken by the authorities did not go beyond a request by the Governor of the Bank of England in December 1953 to the members of the British Bankers' Association and the insurance companies 'to exercise very special care when dealing with special facilities for take-over transactions in cases where there appears to be a speculative element'. The request was brought to the notice of the London offices of overseas banks.[1] More than ten years were to pass before power was taken to refer an impending or completed merger to the Monopolies Commission for investigation of whether it was against the public interest.

In the conduct of bids there was from the start, on a number of points, a consensus of opinion about what was regarded as good practice, though that did not mean that all were likely to conform. Thus it was regarded as good practice to extend to all shareholders the terms offered to those first approached who might hold a controlling interest. This was done in 1953 in the take-over of Jackson the Tailor by Montague Burton and later in the same year in the take-over of the Fifty-Shilling Tailors by United Drapery Stores. Again, there was general agreement that directors should not study their own personal interests. The law indicated that the directors' duty was to the company (whatever that might mean in a specific case) rather than to the shareholders.

There was disquiet on a number of issues. One was the extended use of non-voting A shares. The bidders wished to have control of the companies they acquired and where they were offering paper, instead of cash or in addition to cash, they favoured non-voting shares. There was already some opposition

---

[1] In evidence before the Jenkins Committee (1960–2) the Accepting Houses Committee and the Issuing Houses Association expressed themselves strongly against any control of the financing of bids. 'We consider it is neither right nor practicable to attempt to introduce any measure of control over take-over bids by controlling the provision of finance for such operations.'

to non-voting shares. In November 1953 there was a lively correspondence in the columns of *The Times* on the merits of take-over bids. It was initiated by a letter from Lord Hacking objecting to the circulation of rumours of impending offers which led to fluctuations in the prices of the shares concerned. He also objected to the buying of shares by those who took elaborate precautions to cloak their identity by buying through a number of brokers in the name of many different nominees, and by withholding shares from registration and who then used the shares 'to coerce the directors'. He received some support, but other letters were more concerned to defend take-over bids as promoting industrial efficiency.

The Chairman of The Stock Exchange (Sir John Braithwaite) said in a speech in Bradford in November 1953: 'It is not a crime to make a take-over bid or to buy shares on The Stock Exchange with the object of acquiring control and it is not a crime to use the names of nominees for that purpose', but 'what has been regrettable about some recent cases has been the premature leakage of information' and 'what would be criminal would be the deliberate putting about of false rumours of take-over bids for personal profit. No case, happily, has so far been substantiated.'

In a Commons debate on 11 February 1954 Mr Hugh Gaitskell and Mr Roy Jenkins alleged that there had been what later became known as 'asset stripping' in textile companies which were taken over, though the Chancellor of the Exchequer (Mr R. A. Butler) said there was no evidence of 'widespread plundering or destruction of undertakings'.

At times criticism was concentrated on practices of the boards of companies bid for. In general, the financial press disliked directors who seemed to regard their own retention as inseparable from the interests of the company. In February 1953 the board of Stag Line were criticized when, in the face of a threatened bid, they described proposals for a bonus issue and capital distribution as 'necessary to ward off further attacks on the independence of the company'. *The Economist* of 21 February 1953 said that 'the Economist and those who think like it believe that industrial efficiency will best be secured if the whole economy is permeated by a restless search for the most profitable and productive form of risk investment'.

BEFORE THE FIRST ATTEMPT AT REGULATION

In some cases, the directors endeavoured to thwart a bidder by measures which had the effect of depriving shareholders of the power to take important decisions. This raised in an acute form the questions—who was ultimately in charge of a company and whose interests should be safeguarded? The *cause célèbre* was the successful attempt by the board of the Savoy Hotel Company in the autumn of 1953 to thwart a bid by Land Securities Investment Company of which Mr Harold Samuel was chairman. It was believed that Mr Samuel's aim was to get possession of the Berkeley Hotel, which was owned by the Savoy Hotel Company, and to use the site for offices. The Savoy Hotel directors transferred the Berkeley Hotel to a new company they set up called Worcester Buildings Co. (London) Ltd. Effective voting control of the new company was vested, not in the Savoy Hotel Company, but in the three trustees of the Savoy Hotel staff benevolent fund who included the chairman of the Savoy Hotel board. The new company leased back the Berkeley Hotel to the Savoy Hotel Company, with a condition that it could not be used otherwise than as a hotel without the new company's consent. Before these arrangements, the Savoy Hotel shareholders could have forced a change of policy in the use of the Berkeley Hotel site by removing or threatening to remove the Savoy Hotel directors. After the arrangements, the agreement of the new company's directors was required and they were not subject to the control of the Savoy Hotel shareholders. Faced with the prospect of an expensive battle to determine the legality of the scheme, Land Securities sold out to the Savoy Hotel directors, albeit at a high price.

Somewhat later, in 1956, the board of Scottish Motor Traction made an unsuccessful effort to thwart a bid by Sears Holdings (Mr Clore). The directors of Scottish Motor Traction agreed to buy a private company (Atholl Houses) for £850,000 and gave an option to another private company (Atholl Developments) to buy SMT properties for £1,400,000 on the understanding that they would be leased back. These transactions appeared to be intended to put cash and readily realizable property out of the reach of Sears Holdings and they were announced after a majority of the shareholders of SMT had accepted the offer by Sears Holdings. Faced with the prospect of litigation in the Scottish and English courts, the SMT board agreed with the Atholl companies for the cancellation of the transactions. Once again, the question of the responsibility of directors to shareholders had been raised, but not resolved.

The Later Fifties

As already indicated, the early fifties were marked by single bids, often opposed by the board of the company bid for. The later fifties was the period of two or more bidders engaged in contest for a company. This brought regulation nearer, because it was in some ways easier to lay down rules for rival bidders than to hold the scales evenly between bidder and biddee.

BRITISH ALUMINIUM

In the autumn of 1958 Tube Investments, in association with Reynolds Metals of the United States were buying British Aluminium shares with a view to making a bid for British Aluminium. Tube Investments were advised by Schroders and Helbert Wagg and Reynolds Metals by Warburgs. The board of British Aluminium needed funds to develop bauxite deposits in Australia and to build a new smelter in Canada. When they got wind of the intentions of Tube Investments, they hastened negotiations which were already in progress for a closer link between British Aluminium and the Aluminium Company of America (Alcoa). British Aluminium were advised by Hambros and Lazards. British Aluminium signed a contract with Alcoa on 14 November 1958 by which Alcoa was (subject to Treasury consent) to buy 4,500,000 authorized but unissued shares in British Aluminium for £13,500,000 (being £3 per £1 share). This would have given Alcoa a third of the British Aluminium ordinary capital. The details were not, however, published until 5 December.

On 24 November Tube Investments informed the board of British Aluminium that they intended to make an offer of one Tube Investment share and 78s. in cash for every two British Aluminium shares. The British Aluminium shares were to be vested in a company of which Tube Investments would own 51 per cent and Reynolds Metals 49 per cent. This offer was posted to British Aluminium shareholders on 15 December and the offer document revealed that Tube Investments and Reynolds

Metals already owned about 13 per cent of the British Aluminium ordinary capital. The board of British Aluminium advised their shareholders against the Tube Investments/ Reynolds Metals bid on the grounds that the offer was inadequate and would deprive shareholders of their direct interest in British Aluminium. They promised higher dividends. Later a group of fourteen City institutions, including five merchant banks, associated themselves with Hambros and Lazards in advising British Aluminium shareholders against the offer. This consortium offered British Aluminium shareholders 82s. for half of their shares, on the understanding that they kept the other half until the end of March 1959. The offer was not open to the Tube Investments/Reynolds group and the consortium reserved the right to limit acceptances to £7,000,000.

Reynolds Metals replied by heavy buying in the market, which increased the Tube Investments/Reynolds Metals shareholding in British Aluminium to 45 per cent. Some 3,000,000 shares were bought at a cost of £12,500,000. This buying kept the price above the 82s. per share offered by the consortium. On 4 January 1959 Tube Investments made an amended offer of one share in Tube Investments and 88s. in cash for two British Aluminium shares. By 9 January 1959, when the offer closed, Tube Investments announced that they had over 50 per cent of the British Aluminium shares and they declared their bid unconditional.

The contest raised a number of contentious points. When in May 1958 British Aluminium had secured the agreement of its shareholders to an increase in its authorized capital by £3,000,000, there had been no discussion of the matter at the annual general meeting and it had been generally assumed that the unissued shares would be used at some future date to raise funds from shareholders or from the public. The investment trusts and insurance companies, as shareholders, objected to unissued shares being used to give an outsider a strong stake in a company without consulting the shareholders. The British Aluminium board were slow in announcing the arrangement with Alcoa. It was arguable that the British Aluminium board had shown scant consideration for the interests of their shareholders when they plumped for a deal with Alcoa, rather than with Tube Investments and Reynolds Metals. The consortium also differentiated between shareholders by offering 82s. to shareholders except Tube Investments and Reynolds Metals, and reserved the right to limit their total acceptances. Memories of this contest were revived in September 1978 when Reynolds Metals disposed of its interest in British Aluminium, partly by the sale of about 8 per cent of the share capital to Tube Investments but mainly by a sale of shares to about 100 institutions in the UK.

SALT (SALTAIRE)

Illingworth Morris held 29 per cent of the 5s. ordinary shares of Salt (Saltaire). In the autumn of 1958, when the ordinary shares of Salt stood at 4s. $7\frac{1}{2}d.$, Illingworth Morris made an offer of 7s. per share for a further 4,000,000 shares (30 per cent). This would give Illingworth Morris control. The bid was open for only a short time and applications were to be treated on the basis of 'first come, first served'. The directors of Salt considered that the price was reasonable but urged that the offer should be open for all the outstanding shares. The offer was closed at 11.20 a.m. on 24 October 1958 when acceptances had been received in respect of 4,000,000 shares. Later the shares fell back to 4s. $7\frac{1}{2}d$. Because of poor trading no final dividend was declared in respect of 1958/9, in contrast with 6 per cent in 1957/8 and an interim dividend of 4 per cent by the former Salt board in respect of 1958/9. The 40 per cent of the shareholders whose shares had not been bought by Illingworth Morris had had a raw deal.

CHIVERS

In October 1958 the chairman of St Martin Preserving Company indicated to the chairman of Chivers that St Martin was prepared to make a bid. In January the Chivers board informed the chairman of St Martin that they would be embarrassed if they had to advise shareholders on a bid before Chiver's full accounts for 1958 were published. On 6 June, on the eve of the publication of the accounts, Schweppes made an offer for Chiver's ordinary shares worth 59s. 6d. compared with a pre-bid market price of 47s. 6d. This had the support of the Chivers directors; and the Chivers family interests, who controlled $47\frac{3}{4}$ per cent of the equity, indicated their acceptance of the

Schweppes offer. Indication of acceptance by other shareholders brought intended acceptances to about 50 per cent. St Martin tabled a counter-bid worth 71s. 3d. per share, but were unable to make headway against the block of shares committed to Schweppes. There was criticism of the Chivers directors for appearing to ignore the interests of the other Chivers shareholders by favouring the lower-priced offer.

WATNEY MANN

For two years Mr Clore made no bid for any public company and by the spring of 1959 Sears Holdings had £8,000,000 in cash. Sears Holdings then made a bid for the brewery company, Watney Mann, whose shares stood at 51s. 3d. The bid offered the ordinary shareholder 45s. in cash with a promise that when the shares were split into 5s. units, one in four would be returned to the acceptors of the offer. This made the bid equivalent to 60s. per Watney Mann share. The Watney Mann directors opposed the bid vigorously. The share price went up to 72s. 6d., then fell back to 67s. 6d., and then went up to 75s. and 77s. It was rumoured that at one point Mr Clore was selling shares in order to keep the price down.[1] Mr Clore seemed reluctant to increase his offer and eventually Sears Holdings withdrew their bid.

HARRODS

The take-over of Harrods by House of Fraser in 1959 illustrates the extent to which a take-over could result in one class of shareholders being unfairly treated. In this case it was the majority of the preference shareholders who suffered, although the preference shares carried voting rights and the total preference vote was equal to the rest of the voting rights. House of Fraser and Debenhams made offers which were roughly equal in value. The directors of Harrods, who were regarded as having put the facts and arguments fairly before their shareholders, recommended the ordinary and preference shareholders to accept the Debenham offer. United Drapery Stores put in a better bid. House of Fraser then upped its bid and eventually succeeded with 66s. 8d. in cash and $2\frac{1}{4}$ House of Fraser

---

[1] *The Economist*, 30 May 1959, p. 865.

shares for each Harrods ordinary share. As regards the preference shares, House of Fraser in its original announcement proposed 40s. in cash (market price before announcement 28s.) and the price of preference shares in the market rose to 45s. House of Fraser secured some preference shares at 45s. and decided to concentrate attention on the ordinary shares. The formal offer gave only 30s. for the preference shares.

LINTANG INVESTMENTS AND ELY BREWERY

The Jasper group of companies was set up in 1956/7 and engaged in taking over property companies. H. Jasper & Company in July 1959 secured 51 per cent of the ordinary share capital of Lintang Investments by a private deal at a price that was not revealed. They then made an offer of 24s. per 5s. share to the other shareholders conditional on 80 per cent acceptances. The offer went unconditional on 31 July; but the funds were not available to implement the purchase. A firm of solicitors which made the offer said that it was acting on behalf of H. Jasper & Company which in turn was acting as a merchant bank on behalf of Mr F. Grunwald as a private client. An offer for Ely Brewery by H. Jasper & Company on behalf of Mr Grunwald in August 1959 went unconditional but could not be completed because Mr Grunwald was not able to produce the necessary funds.

GENERAL

By the summer of 1959 *The Times* was commenting that in recent weeks there had been such a flow of take-over bids that, if the trend continued, bids would cease to be news. 'That the take-over bid has become respectable is a gain. The gain will be less if it is not understood that there are right ways and wrong ways of bidding'.[1] There was widespread unease about the methods used by some operators. In a number of cases, the shareholder did not seem to be getting a square deal, particularly the unsophisticated shareholder with a relatively small holding.

---

[1] *The Times*, 19 June 1959.

III

FIRST EFFORTS AT REGULATION

In June 1959 the Governor of the Bank of England (Mr C. F. Cobbold, later Lord Cobbold) asked the executive committee of the Issuing Houses Association in collaboration with the Accepting Houses Committee, the Association of Investment Trusts, the British Insurance Association, the Committee of London Clearing Bankers and the London Stock Exchange to consider what guidance could be given on the conduct of takeover bids. Others were also active in this field. The Institute of Directors set up a committee of seven under Sir Edwin Herbert (later Lord Tangley) and the Association of British Chambers of Commerce also set up a committee.

There were those who doubted the value of these exercises. On 4 July 1959 *The Economist* was saying:

> Industries and companies are constantly on the move. The take-over bid is but one of the mechanisms of change. To believe that a code of conduct can be drawn up to govern that mechanism assumes that the market is a club from which any undesirable outsider can be blackballed and where the established members can be left to doze peacefully in their armchairs.

Notes on Amalgamations of British Businesses

The Issuing Houses Association and their associates took only a few months to produce the code of conduct, which was published at the end of October 1959 under the title 'Notes on Amalgamations of British Businesses'.

The Notes opened with a short historical account of amalgamations and acquisitions and with an explanation of the factors since the 1939–45 war which had stimulated the process of amalgamation. The Notes said:

> The process is a natural one and, since it is generally based on the best utilisation of physical capacity, managerial experience and available labour, it has almost always proved to be in the national interest. Indeed, no industrial community could thrive without such a process and it is therefore important that it should continue and should not be artificially impeded.

The Notes distinguished between principles and procedure. The principles were quite short:

(i) There should be no interference with the free market in shares and securities of companies.

(ii) It is for a shareholder to decide for himself whether to sell or retain his shares.

(iii) To enable him to come to a considered decision, the shareholder should have in suitable form and at the right time, all relevant information, and it is the duty of the Board of his company to make every effort to ensure that such information is provided and to give him their advice.

(iv) Every effort should be made to avoid disturbance in the normal price level of shares until the relevant information has been made available.

On procedure, the Notes set out a number of suggestions. The board of the offeree company was normally the best channel of approach to shareholders. Therefore the offer should first be addressed to the board which was entitled to be informed of the identity of the offeror and of the evidence that he had the necessary resources for full acceptance of the offer. The board should be given sufficient time to assess the merits of the offer. Secrecy should be preserved in the preliminary talks. An announcement should be made if a speculative market was developing, but not before it seemed certain that an offer would be forthcoming. The offeree board was under an obligation to inform the shareholders of the offer as soon as reasonably possible and the information with which it should supply its shareholders was indicated. If the offer was wholly or partly in shares in the proposed combined company, the offeree shareholders should be given the fullest information about the future prospects of the combined company.

As a general rule, an offer should be for the whole of the share

FIRST EFFORTS AT REGULATION

capital of a company or the whole of the class of share concerned. Partial offers were only fruitful in very exceptional cases and then should be made to all shareholders on a *pro rata* basis. Adequate time (three weeks was suggested) should be given for shareholders to consider an offer. After an offer had been declared unconditional, a further period should be allowed for acceptances from latecomers. A board should be wary of refusing to put to its shareholders any serious and responsible offer. The well-being of the shareholders as a whole must prevail over that of the particular shareholders who were directors.

The Times (31 October 1959) welcomed the Notes. In a leader it said: 'The report strikes a fair balance between the bidder and the bid-for and it is concerned primarily to safeguard the interests of shareholders.' As sometimes happens, the City Editor was more cautious. Thomas Roberts (Westminster) had just made a partial bid for half of the shares of Roads Reconstruction and had indicated that they intended to purchase in the market enough shares to ensure that they had 51 per cent of the voting rights. The City Editor regarded it as unfortunate that the authors of the Notes had fought shy of defining the 'very exceptional circumstances' in which a partial bid became respectable.

The *Financial Times* (31 October 1959) thought that the Notes made reasonably firm recommendations on most of the main points at issue. It was, however, troubled about the dilemma that 'professional codes are flexible but unenforceable: whereas laws are enforceable but rigid'. The *Financial Times* rejected anything as 'cumbrous and unwieldy' as the US Securities and Exchange Commission, but it hoped for some small expert advisory body to keep the whole position under review.

The Economist (31 October 1959) said that the authors of the Notes did not deny businessmen the right to fight out an issue but had established Queensberry rules against low hitting and butting with the head.

In the light of subsequent events, later commentators were less flattering. One described the Notes as 'Given little publicity and heeded even less'.[1]

---

[1] Desmond Goch, *Certified Accountant*, vol. 66 (1974), p. 92.

Licensed Dealers (Conduct of Business) Rules

Meantime the Board of Trade was beginning to bestir itself. In the course of November 1959 it announced the intention to set up the Jenkins Committee on company law, with a specific instruction to examine the practice of take-over bids. There had been some criticism of the fact that licensed dealers, outside the stock exchanges, were only controlled in respect of offers to dispose of securities and not of offers to acquire securities, and it was urged that some regulation of take-over bids by licensed dealers was needed.

In the thirties a bout of share-pushing led to the passing of the Prevention of Fraud (Investments) Act 1939. This legislation was consolidated in the Prevention of Fraud (Investments) Act 1958. The effect of section 14 of the 1958 Act was that a take-over circular could be distributed only through an authorized channel or with the permission of the Board of Trade. In order to be an authorized channel, dealers who were not members of a stock exchange or of a recognized association of dealers or individually exempted had to obtain a licence from the Board of Trade and in conducting their business were subject to rules made by the Department.

In 1959 the Board of Trade began the lengthy process of adding to the rules they had made under the 1939 Act. In May 1960 a draft of the Licensed Dealers (Conduct of Business) Rules was circulated among interested parties for comments: and, after considering these comments, the Board of Trade laid the Rules before Parliament for approval. The Rules came into force in August 1960. The Act empowered the Board of Trade to regulate the conduct of licensed dealers. It did not operate directly on offerors or offerees. Thus, although the Third Schedule to the Rules is headed 'Requirements to be satisfied in relation to a recommendation by a board of directors of an offeree corporation recommending acceptance of an offer', the Rules were to the effect that a licensed dealer could distribute a recommendation made by the offeree directors only if its terms complied with the Third Schedule.

The Licensed Dealers Rules followed the legislation governing prospectuses for new issues in the sense that they set out minimum requirements to be met, had no provision for anyone to exercise a discretionary power and did not require licensed dealers to get any clearance for offers. The Rules related primarily to the content of the offer document. The complexity that follows from putting fairly simple provisions into precise legal form can be illustrated from the requirement that an offer document should give the price of the shares of the offeree company just before the offer. The Rules then have to deal with shares not recently dealt with, unlisted shares and overseas shares. What is essentially a simple provision occupies more than half of a page of close type.

In the Licensed Dealers Rules, a take-over offer means an offer to acquire securities which is made to more than one holder of securities and which is calculated to result in any person acquiring or becoming entitled to acquire control of that corporation; and 'control' means the exercise of majority voting power. Hence, strictly speaking. the provisions relating to take-over offers do not apply to partial bids that would not give control nor to bids for the remaining shares by a holder of shares who already has over 50 per cent of them (though such documents would be subject to the rules relating to investment circulars). Both The Stock Exchange Rules and the Code apply more widely to all offers.

In relation to take-over bids, the Rules required the terms of the offer to be submitted to the offeree company at least three days before the offer document was sent to the offeree shareholders. Any offer must not be conditional on the offeree shareholders approving any payment or other benefit to a director of the offeree company. If the offer related to less than the total amount in issue of any class of security, the offer should be open to acceptance by all holders and if too many acceptances were received the acceptances should be scaled down pro rata. An offer unless withdrawn should remain open for acceptance for at least twenty-one days. Where an offer was subject to conditions, such as the level of acceptances, the level had to be indicated and also the last date on which the offeror could declare the offer unconditional.

An offer document had to reveal the identity of the offeror. If the consideration included securities in the offeror company, financial information about these securities had to be provided. The offeror had to say how many securities he held in the offeree company and give details of any proposed compensation to offeree directors for loss of office and any other arrangements with them. The offeror had to give any material change in the prospects of the offeree company, known to him, since the last published balance sheet. Also any arrangments for the transfer to other persons of securities acquired by the offeror under the offer. Any recommendation by the offeree board to accept the offer issued by a licensed dealer, had to indicate the holdings in the offeree company by each director, whether he intended to accept the offer, whether he was receiving compensation from the offeror or had other arrangments with him and any interest by the director in a contract with the offeror.

The Board of Trade informed the Jenkins Committee that the Licensed Dealers Rules had been made because of the need to provide certain safeguards in regard to take-over bids and because the subject was more suitable for rules than for legislation. They contemplated amending the Rules as necessary to keep them up to date and they did not think it would be wise to 'freeze' the Rules by writing them into legislation. The Board of Trade regarded the Rules as proper for all concerned with take-over bids. They applied to licensed dealers because under the Act only licensed dealers were subject to regulation. The Jenkins Committee reported that, although the Rules statutorily applied to licensed dealers only, Stock Exchange brokers and other authorized dealers in securities also broadly complied with them when issuing circulars containing a take-over offer or a recommendation by the directors of an offeree company to accept such an offer. The Board of Trade could authorize others than licensed dealers to make bids and the Board of Trade required compliance with the Rules as a condition of authorization. When issued, the Rules were welcomed by the financial press. The Jenkins Committee reported that most witnesses had expressed the view, with which the committee agreed, that the Rules provided a most effective and useful guide to the proper conduct of take-over offers.

Jenkins Committee

The Jenkins Committee was appointed by the President of the Board of Trade on 10 December 1959 to examine the workings of the Companies Act 1948 and the Prevention of Fraud (Investments) Act 1958 and the Committee was specifically instructed to consider, in relation to take-over bids, what should be the duties of directors and the rights of shareholders. In their report, the Committee did not engage in any general discussion of the respective spheres of responsibility of directors and shareholders but examined certain specific issues. Thus they recommended that directors should not be able, without the approval of the shareholders, to dispose of the whole, or substantially the whole, of the assets of the company. Again, shareholders' approval should be required for the issuing of unissued shares within the authorized capital of the company.

On the subject of take-over bids, the Committee pointed out that, whereas anyone could issue a prospectus for a new issue subject to compliance with the provisions of the Companies Acts, offer documents in connection with take-over bids could be issued only by limited classes of persons, subject to a variety of rules. They considered that take-overs should be regulated in the same way as new issues. Anyone should be able to issue an offer document, subject to compliance with statutory rules. Accordingly, the Board of Trade should have power to make rules, by statutory instrument, in respect of all take-over offers and of all circulars containing a take-over offer or a recommendation by the directors of the offeree company to their shareholders. These rules would be based on the Licensed Dealers (Conduct of Business) Rules 1960; but would be amended in various respects. They would be kept up to date by the Board of Trade after discussion with a Consultative Committee on Company Law which was to be set up. Among the changes in the 1960 Rules proposed by the Jenkins Committee were the following:

1. A copy of every circular recommending acceptance of a take-over offer, with the enclosed documents, should be sent to the Registrar of Companies and the Registrar should be entitled to refuse to register any circular that did not comply with the Rules or seemed likely to create a false impression.
2. If the offeror varied the terms of his offer by increasing the price, an acceptor of the intitial offer should be entitled to receive the higher price.

3. A limit should be set on the period during which the offeror might keep his offer unconditional. The Committee suggested that if an offeror had not declared his offer unconditional within thirty five days of the issue of the offer document, an acceptor should be free to revoke his acceptance of the offer.
4. When an offer was declared unconditional, the offeror should be required to disclose the number and proportion of shares of each class he then had or controlled.

Revised Notes on Company Amalgamations and Mergers

By 1963 the position was that the 1959 Notes had been supplemented by the Board of Trade's Licensed Dealers (Conduct of Business) Rules 1960 which were legally binding only on licensed dealers but which the Department considered should be observed by all involved in take-over bids. There were also the specific recommendations made by the Jenkins Committee to which reference has already been made. The subject that led to the calling together again, under the aegis of the Issuing Houses Association, of the Working Party which had drawn up the Notes was the interaction between a bid and purchases of shares otherwise than through the bid. This was a matter which was to exercise the City greatly in the future. The Notes had given, as the first of the principles governing take-overs, that 'there should be no interference with the free market in shares and securities of companies'. Both the Notes and the Rules were concerned with the conduct of bids, regarded in isolation, and the only point at which they impinged on the market in shares was in stressing the need for secrecy in the preliminary discussion of a take-over bid, so that insider dealings or rumours would not lead to price movements. Two important cases at this time raised further problems.

ICI/COURTAULDS

In 1962 Imperial Chemical Industries launched a bid for the ordinary and preference shares of Courtaulds. The initial offer was worth nearly £200,000,000 and there were later revised offers. The bid was hotly contested by Courtaulds and in the end ICI failed to secure control. The defensive tactics taken by the board of Courtaulds included proposals for an increase in dividend, the payment of a tax-free capital distribution, the issue to shareholders of £40,000,000 of loan stock and the creation of a new subsidiary to contain most of Courtaulds' trade investments. On 28 February 1962 ICI said that they had decided to declare their offer for the ordinary stock of Courtaulds unconditional, irrespective of the percentage of acceptances received by the closing date (8 March 1962). By the end, after an extension of the closing date, ICI had acceptances for 37.4 per cent of the Courtaulds' ordinary stock, 44.6 per cent of 5 per cent preference and 59.8 per cent of 6 per cent preference stock. The offer for the preference stocks then lapsed, but ICI was left with 37.4 per cent of the ordinary stock. At a later date, this was exchanged for Courtaulds' 50 per cent shareholding in British Nylon Spinners.

The closing of offers at less than 50 per cent acceptance meant that a company could go some way towards control with an offer and then secure full control by subsequent purchases, possibly at a higher price than the offer. This was unfair to the shareholders who had accepted the offer. ICI had not acted in this way, and the problem had not therefore been raised in a form calling for early action. The City Working Party had to grasp this particular nettle in 1968.

RICHARD THOMAS AND BALDWIN/WHITEHEAD IRON AND STEEL

In January 1963 Stewart and Lloyds (steel-makers) made an offer for Whitehead Iron and Steel (steel-rollers) at 70s. per share. The shares had stood at 30s. in December 1962. Richard Thomas and Baldwin, a nationalized steel company, then announced that it would make a counter-bid and meantime it bought heavily in the market, particularly from some institutional shareholders to whom it undertook to make good any difference between the market price and the final bid price whatever that might be. Stewart and Lloyd meantime increased their bid to 85s. Richard Thomas and Baldwin secured 64 per cent of the shares by market purchases. The preferential treatment given to certain institutional shareholders was widely criticized and two of the larger institutions refused to accept it as unfair to the other shareholders. The point had not been dealt with explicitly in the 1959 Notes but was contrary to the general intention of the Notes. In the end Richard Thomas and Baldwin made an offer of 85s. 3d. to the remaining shareholders. *The Economist* of 9 February 1963 stigmatized the contest as the sharpest and most reckless of the City take-over battles.

PROVISIONS OF THE REVISED NOTES

The Working Party was convened in July 1963 and the Revised Notes were published on 31 October 1963. The Revised Notes were not simply a revision of the original Notes, but a rewriting of the subject in a more logical order. The Revised Notes were couched in general terms, no doubt because the authors 'are concerned as much with the spirit in which these transactions should be conducted as with the strict procedure to be followed'. A good deal of space was devoted to the reasons for various proposals.

The Board of Trade had indicated, when the Licensed Dealers (Conduct of Business) Rules were published, that they regarded the Rules as of general application. The authors of the Revised Notes referred to the Rules and described them as setting out minimum requirements. The Revised Notes did not attempt to reproduce the Rules and may be regarded as supplementing the Rules. Thus the Revised Notes did not repeat the requirements of the Notes that 'shareholders should be given adequate time (say, three weeks) for accepting it (the offer)'. The Licensed Dealers Rules had specified twenty-one days. The precision of the Rules would not have fitted easily into the general form of the Revised Notes.

A good deal of space was devoted to the circumstances in which a preliminary announcement of an impending bid should be made, so as to prevent speculative movements in the market—also the responsibilities of directors to play fair by their shareholders. On the specific issue raised by the Richard Thomas/Whitehead affair, the Revised Notes said:

... an offeror who has published such an intention (to make or revise an offer) and who subsequently acquires effective control by buying, in the market or otherwise, should without delay revise his existing offer or make a formal offer to all uncommitted shareholders at a fair price having regard to the prices paid in the market. Purchases of some of the shares of any particular class, whether made through the market or otherwise, should not be made with special conditions attached which are not available to all shareholders of that class.

FIRST EFFORTS AT REGULATION

The Revised Notes incorporated certain proposals made by the Jenkins Committee which did not require legislation:

(a) where an offeror increased the price for shares in a revised offer, an acceptor of the earlier offer should receive the higher price;

(b) where an offeror declared an offer unconditional he should indicate the number of shares he had acquired by that time, so that shareholders who had not accepted the offer could re-assess their position.

STOCK EXCHANGE'S GENERAL UNDERTAKING

The Stock Exchange exercised control over listed companies by the general undertaking which directors had to give as a condition of listing on The Stock Exchange. The earliest form of general undertaking appeared in the London Stock Exchange rule book in September 1930 and the text was revised from time to time. On 22 February 1943 a requirement was introduced that proofs of circulars addressed to shareholders should be submitted to the Share and Loan Department (now the Quotations Department) of the London Stock Exchange for prior approval. As time went on, this led to the submission of circulars addressed by directors to the shareholders of another company to whom they were sending a take-over offer.

In the autumn of 1959, following the issue of the Notes, the Share and Loan Department began to check that a circular stated that funds were available for full acceptance of the offer, stated that the offer was open for at least three weeks, indicated whether the directors of the offeree company had been consulted, specified any compensation for an outgoing director, and set out the intention of the offeror regarding continuance of the business and the future of employees. Although there was no control over offers made by issuing houses, bankers, solicitors and others, most issuing houses and merchant banks submitted the proofs of offer documents to the Share and Loan Department for comments. This tendency was strengthened when the 1959 Notes contained the following passage: 'It is desirable that documents concerning offers for securities which are quoted on a Stock Exchange be cleared with The Stock Exchange authorities before their issue. This should not normally involve any delay.'

IV
FIRST CITY CODE AND PANEL

NEARLY five years separate the issue of the Revised Notes from the issue of the first edition of the Code in its present form and the establishment of the Panel. This was a period of great activity in the field of acquisitions and mergers. Owing to mergers, there was, between 1961 and 1968, a substantial reduction in the number of industrial companies with net assets of £500,000 and over. There were between 600 and 1,000 acquisitions by quoted companies each year between 1960 and 1970 and the expenditure on acquisitions trebled in this period, owing mainly to some very large mergers in the later years.

In addition to take-overs of companies in the same line of business or of companies that were suppliers or customers, 'conglomerate' mergers began to attract attention. These were mergers between companies that did not produce similar products and were neither actual or potential suppliers of the others. The offeror might be a financial group, primarily interested in the financial results of acquisitions. Slater Walker got going in 1964.

The period also saw a greater resort to paper than to cash as the consideration for taking over the shares of offeree companies. Among larger acquiring companies, the cash element in the total consideration offered fell from 60 per cent in 1964 to 33 per cent in 1967 and fell further to 22 per cent in 1970. Many companies could not have produced the cash for a take-over and offered their own paper instead. The institution of Capital Gains Tax in 1965 also lessened the attractiveness of bids involving the payment of cash, since accepting shareholders would usually be liable to pay tax, whereas a share exchange was not an occasion imposing liability to tax. The form of Corporation Tax introduced at the same time (1965) made the issue of debentures and loan stock attractive to the offeror company. Under cash payments the shareholder of an offeree company had no further interest in the merged concerns. With paper, the shareholder had a right to be assured that the offeror was giving something which was at least as good as the shares he was surrendering.

A great deal of attention was concentrated on the merits of individual take-overs. The Monopolies and Mergers Act 1965 empowered the Board of Trade to refer to the Monopolies Commission a merger or take-over or a proposal for a merger or take-over where a monopoly was likely to result or where the value of the assets taken over exceeded £5,000,000. That brought within the ambit of government the merits of the larger take-over proposals. The Industrial Re-organisation Corporation was established in the same year with the implication that take-overs which were thought to produce a more efficient industrial structure were desirable in the public interest.

With a great deal of take-over activity, it was inevitable that attention should be concentrated again on the rules under which the game was conducted. The Board of Trade, in spite of statements that revision was contemplated, had not revised the Licensed Dealers (Conduct of Business) Rules 1960 and the question arose whether any new Code should be comprehensive and include the provisions that would have been included in any revised Board of Trade Rules. There was a general fall in share prices in 1965 and 1966. In 1967 the position changed. Share prices rose dramatically and take-overs warmed up. Dissatisfaction with their regulation led to a demand for closer supervision. The developing situation can be presented by a brief description of the main take-over battles after 1963.

SUITS/THOMSON/OUTRAM

The contest in 1964 between Sir Hugh Fraser (later Lord Fraser of Allander) and Lord Thomson for the control of the Glasgow publishing firm of Outram illustrated the extent to which the Revised Notes were failing to check what many regarded as undesirable practices. Lord Thomson made the opening cash bid. Sir Hugh Fraser, through Scottish and Universal Investments Limited ('Suits') made a higher bid in Suits shares, with a cash alternative. There were revised offers and counter-offers. Suits then engaged in an intensive but carefully concealed purchase of Outram shares on the market and at one point paid substantially more than the offer price for two large holdings of Outram shares. Suits also declared their offer unconditional before they had secured 50 per cent of the shares. Eventually Suits emerged with 88 per cent of the Outram shares. The Revised Notes had indicated, in somewhat qualified terms, that an offeror who acquired effective control by buying in the market or otherwise should make a formal offer to all uncommitted shareholders 'at a fair price', having regard to the prices paid in the market. The authors of the Revised Notes had assumed that a change in the law would be needed for a requirement to be imposed that the acquisition of significant shareholdings should be made public. Neither the Notes nor the Revised Notes had indicated a minimum level of acceptances before an offer could be made unconditional, but the Board of Trade Rules for licensed dealers, which the Revised Notes regarded as setting out 'minimum requirements', had said that the offer document should indicate the minimum number of acceptances on which the offer was conditional. The Outram case indicated the need for a more precise formulation of requirements.

In the years 1966 and 1967, as take-over activity revived, there were a number of cases that caused disquiet.

PHILIPS/THORN/PYE

In 1966 the Dutch electrical group, Philips, and Thorn Electrical Industries were both endeavouring to secure control of the radio manufacturing company, Pye. Philips won after announcing a revised offer of 12s. a share (against Thorn's 10s. 9d.). Philips said that they had also made substantial purchases in the market, including 19 per cent of Pye's ordinary shares bought on one day. Many of the shares had been bought from two firms of stockbrokers who had been warehousing the shares over a substantial period and whose exact relationship to Philips was not established.

GEC/TELEPHONE RENTALS

At the beginning of December 1966 the General Electric Company announced a bid for Telephone Rentals, a telephone equipment company which relied for expansion on retained profits and pursued a cautious dividend policy. The board of Telephone Rentals indicated opposition to the bid and refused to supply GEC with information on various points. The formal offer document was issued in January 1967 and the offer was raised later that month, but the board continued to indicate opposition, while endeavouring to placate their shareholders by promising a more progressive financial policy. GEC accepted defeat on 27 February 1967. Telephone Rentals had been under siege for about three months.

COURTAULDS/MACAINE/COOK & WATTS

In 1967 Courtaulds and a textile wholesaler, Macaine, were in competition to acquire another textile wholesaler—Cook & Watts. Cook & Watts, who favoured a merger with Courtaulds, bought a Courtaulds' subsidiary and gave Courtaulds in exchange 28 per cent of Cook & Watts' shares. Macaine, which was backed by a small merchant bank, increased its bid and Courtaulds then bought Cook & Watts' shares in the market at higher prices than the bid price. When Courtaulds secured control of Cook & Watts by these purchases it promptly ceased purchasing shares and made no general offer to shareholders. The share price then fell heavily, leaving shareholders without the higher prices that had been reached and leaving Macaine and its backer with a substantial loss on their purchases of shares.

COURTAULDS/MACAINE/WILKINSON & RIDDELL

Shortly afterwards Courtauls made a bid at 11s. 6d. per share for another textile wholesaler—Wilkinson & Riddell. This had the support of the offeree board. A rival bid was made on behalf of Macaine with the assistance of the same merchant bank as before. When bid and counter-bid had reached 15s. 3d., Courtaulds made their offer unconditional with 29 per cent acceptances. The contest was then transferred to the stock market, where the rival bidders took the price per share to 65s.

Eventually those acting for Macaine secured 51.8 per cent of the shares. The whole episode was closed a month later when Courtaulds made an agreed bid for Macaine.

ABERDARE/THORN/METAL INDUSTRIES

Also in 1967 there were rival bids for Metal Industries. In May, Aberdare Holdings made an opening bid worth about £10,000,000. The board of Metal Industries favoured a merger with Thorn Electrical Industries and advised rejection of Aberdare Holdings' offer, also of a raised offer by Aberdare Holdings worth £11,800,000. On 1 July Thorn made an offer worth £15,300,000. Meantime Aberdare Holdings had been increasing its holdings of Metal Industries shares, not by direct purchases but through Morgan Grenfell, and was able to announce that it had holdings or acceptances representing 53 per cent of the voting capital. Aberdare Holdings made a new offer of Aberdare shares, convertible unsecured loan stock and cash which was more valuable than the Thorn offer. The board of Metal Industries then gave nearly 5,000,000 authorized but unissued shares to Thorn Electrical in exchange for a subsidiary of Thorn engaged in the manufacture of gas appliances. The contract was conditional on Thorn gaining full control of Metal Industries. The condition made it a purely paper transaction, of no significance save to thwart the Aberdare Holdings' bid. By this device Aberdare Holdings' 53 per cent of Metal Industries became only 32 per cent. Thorn then made a revised and higher offer for the rest of the shares and Hambros Bank gave a cash alternative equal to the value of the share offer by underwriting the Thorn shares offered for Metal Industries shares. Both Aberdare and their advisers Morgan Grenfell agreed to accept the offer in respect of their large holding in Metal Industries. When the increase in share capital had been authorized by the shareholders of Metal Industries in 1960, the directors had said that they would not issue shares that affected the control of the company without consulting the shareholders. The directors also made the contract with Thorn after a majority of the shares had been pledged to Aberdare Holdings. Thorn gained control of Metal Industries but the case raised the whole question of how bids were to be effectively policed.

SHOWERINGS/INTERNATIONAL DISTILLERS AND VINTNERS

Towards the end of June 1967 Showerings announced a bid for IDV—four Showerings shares for seven IDV (putting a value of 17s. 7½d. on IDV), with a cash alternative of 16s. The IDV board who held one third of the IDV shares advised its shareholders to reject the bid and claimed that IDV would grow faster than Showerings in the next few years. Then a mystery buyer entered the field and towards the end of July Watney Mann said that they were the buyer and that they had picked up 15 per cent of the shares at 20s. 7½d., but had ceased buying. The share price fell to 18s. 3d. Watney Mann claimed to be neutral about the bid, but indicated that they were in negotiation with IDV for the sale to IDV of their wines and spirits business. Showerings increased their bid to the equivalent of 21s. towards the end of July and in the following month to 23s. with a cash alternative of 22s. 6d. IDV advised rejection of those revised offers. Watney Mann warned Showerings on 7 August not to interfere in the negotiation for the sale of Watney's wines and spirits business to IDV and said that they planned to conclude their current trading negotiations with the existing management. On 12 August Watney Mann said that they held 15 per cent of the IDV shares, but claimed that they had all been bought on three dates in July. On 19 August Watney Mann said that they were not interested in Showerings' offer. As the directors of IDV had between 35 and 40 per cent of the shares pledged to support them and Watney Mann held 16½ per cent, Showerings had no chance of success and withdraw the bid on 31 August. They refused to reveal what level of acceptance they had reached.

The Times drew attention to the unsatisfactory effect of the Watney Mann intervention on share prices. One insurance office was said to have sold to Watney Mann at 20s. 7½d., then bought on the market at 18s. 9d. and then assented to the Showerings' offer at 20s. 4½d. When the affair was over, *The Times* commented that institutions which had sold for cash to Watney Mann at 20s. 6d. might now be in the market to replace their holdings at the then current price of 18s. 6d. Dealings of this kind were not really open to the ordinary shareholder.

GEC/AEI

On 28 September 1967 The General Electric Company launched a bid for the ordinary shares of Associated Electrical Industries. GEC offered five GEC 'B' ordinary shares and £4 in cash for every eight ordinary shares of AEI. The offer valued each AEI share at about 50s. or 53s. and was worth £120,000,000 in all. The bid was hotly opposed by the board of AEI. The GEC board was advised by Hill Samuel and AEI by Barings.

The AEI board sold a 35 per cent interest in British Lighting Industries to Thorn Electrical Industries for £12,300,000. The AEI board also sold various properties for about £4,000,000, including their headquarters building to Land Securities for £2,800,000. The AEI board merged its telephone exchange business into a £30,000,000 company, to be jointly owned by AEI and General Telephone and Cables, the wholly-owned subsidiary of the US International Telephone and Telegraph Company. The deal was eventually made subject to the defeat of the GEC bid. ITT bought substantial numbers of AEI shares in an effort to preserve AEI's independence; but as there was then no requirement to disclose dealings, the exact amount was uncertain.

In September AEI had announced a substantial fall in profits for the first half of 1967. This indeed had sparked off the GEC bid. The AEI board now forecast recovery in the second half of 1967 which would produce profits for the year of £10,000,000 against £9,200,000 in 1966: and they forecast profits of £16,000,000 in 1968 and £20,000,000 in 1969. GEC made a strong attack on the AEI profit forecasts. After two revisions upwards of the GEC offer, GEC secured control of AEI.

Subsequently GEC reported that AEI had made a loss of £4,500,000 in 1967 instead of the £10,000,000 profit that had been forecast. The auditors of the two companies, in a joint statement, explained that the shortfall relating to 'matters substantially of fact' was £5,000,000 and that the balance of £9,500,000 related to 'matters substantially of judgment' (largely the provisions to be made in respect of losses on stocks and contracts). The controversy that ensued about the basis on

FIRST CITY CODE AND PANEL

which profits should be calculated was one of the reasons why the accountancy bodies set out to attempt to agree upon accounting standards.

These and other cases caused widespread unease and in the summer of 1967 the Chairman of The Stock Exchange approached the Governor of the Bank of England (Sir Leslie O'Brien, now Lord O'Brien of Lothbury) about a reconvening of the City Working Party that had drawn up the Notes and Revised Notes. As a result, towards the end of August 1967 the Issuing Houses Association reassembled the City Working Party. The Confederation of British Industry was represented for the first time. The meeting agreed a proposal which had been made by Sir Leslie O'Brien that a Panel, consisting of the chairmen of the bodies represented at the meeting, should be set up, under an independent chairman, to supervise the administration of a take-over code. It was also agreed that these bodies, after consulting their constituent members if necessary, should send to the secretariat of the Issuing Houses Association, within four weeks, any suggestions for strengthening the existing rules and for enlarging their scope.

On 20 September 1967 the Bank of England publicly announced the intention of the City organizations to set up a Panel which would come into operation when the revision of the Rules had been completed. Sir Humphrey Mynors, the chairman of the Finance Corporation for Industry and from 1954 to 1964 Deputy Governor of the Bank of England, was to be the chairman of the Panel. Its membership would be drawn from the bodies represented on the City Working Party (namely, the Issuing Houses Association, the Accepting Houses Committee, the Association of Investment Trusts, the British Insurance Association, the Committee of London Clearing Bankers, the Confederation of British Industry, the National Association of Pension Funds, and The Stock Exchange). A permanent secretariat would be provided by the Bank of England.

The drafting committee which drew up the new Rules (at the suggestion of The Stock Exchange, they were called a Code) consisted of Mr Michael Bucks of Rothschilds (chairman), Mr K. C. Barrington (now Sir Kenneth Barrington) of Morgan

Grenfell, Mr Peter Cannon of Minster Trust, and Mr R. A. Clark (now Sir Robert Clark) of Hill Samuel. Sir Humphrey Mynors attended the meetings and took part in the discussions. The first meeting of the drafting committee was held on 16 October 1967. The committee had before it the suggestions made by associations and practitioners in response to the invitation by the Issuing Houses Association. The committee met again on 20 October and thereafter a draft Code was prepared which was considered by the executive committee of the Issuing Houses Association and finally put before a meeting of all the associations on 5 January 1968.

A few amendments were discussed and agreed and a revised draft was circulated on 8 February 1968. The Code was finally published on 27 March 1968. The drafting committee did a remarkable piece of work in getting a draft of the Code into shape in a few weeks in the autumn of 1967.

The Revised Notes had proved to be couched in too general terms and to be imprecise on a number of points. At the same time, the drafting committee had been concerned lest any Code became too detailed and too specific, so that practitioners would feel that the wording mattered and not the intention. Revenue legislation was felt to be a dreadful warning of the dangers of too much detail. At the same time the Board of Trade's Licensed Dealers Rules had not been revised, notwithstanding an intention on various occasions to undertake a revision: and a reproduction of some of their provisions in a revised form was felt to be necessary. The CBI and others felt that there should be one document embodying all the rules governing take-overs.

The Notes and Revised Notes had distinguished between principles and procedure. In the Code there were ten General Principles and thirty-five Rules, setting out in detail how the principles were to be applied in the conduct of take-over bids. The Code covered not only the dealings of offeror and offeree boards with the offeree shareholders, including the handling of profit forecasts, but also market tactics during a bid. Of the ten General Principles, seven were new, namely:

(i) that the Code inevitably imposed limitations on what the board of an offeror or offeree company could do in support

of what it recognized as the best interests of its shareholders;
(ii) that after the board of an offeree company knew of a bona fide offer, it must not do anything to frustrate the offer without the approval in general meeting of its shareholders;
(iii) the board of an offeree company, faced with an offer, should consider whether to seek competent outside advice;
(iv) anything done to oppress a minority (in the general and not only in the legal sense of the words) was wholly unacceptable;
(v) an offeror should treat similarly all shareholders of the same class of the offeree company;
(vi) during a take-over bid or when one was in contemplation, no information should be given to some shareholders which was not made available to all shareholders;
(vii) take-over documents should be treated with the same standard of care as if they were a prospectus under the Companies Acts.

The main substantive provision introduced in the Code was that a bid for equity shares could be declared unconditional, only if the offeror, with shares he already controlled, had over 50 per cent of the voting power. With the agreement of the accountancy bodies, a requirement was introduced that the calculations and bases for any profit forecast had to be examined and reported upon by the auditors or consultant accountants. The forecasts and the assumptions on which they rested had also to be reported on by the company's merchant bank or other financial advisers. These reports had to be made in writing to the directors and also supplied to the Panel. The reports did not, however, have to be published. When a revaluation of assets was given in connection with an offer, the board was to have the support of the opinion of independent professional experts and the basis of valuation was to be clearly stated. Purchases in the market of shares of the offeror or offeree company by the offeror or offeree or their associates had to be disclosed immediately. Approval by the shareholders was required for any issue of shares or acquisition or disposal of assets by the board of an offeree company during the currency of a bid or when the board had reason to believe that a bid was imminent.

Various recommendations made in a rather tentative way in the Revised Notes became requirements in the Rules. Thus an offeror had first to notify a bid to the board of the offeree company, the principal's identity must be disclosed and the board of the offeree company must immediately issue a press notice and inform its shareholders of a firm offer. Many of the Licensed Dealers Rules, with revisions, were incorporated in the Code. Some of the detail about the contents of offer documents, prescribed in the Rules, was not reproduced. While the Code followed the Rules in requiring a pro rata offer to all shareholders of the class concerned, the Code described partial bids as generally speaking undesirable, though giving some flexibility by allowing the Panel in 'very exceptional circumstances' to authorize a deal with a significant minority without a similar offer to the other shareholders.

The Code continued the work of giving effect to the Jenkins Committee recommendations where they did not require legislation. If an offer had not been declared unconditional within twenty-one days of the first closing date of an initial offer (the Jenkins Committee suggested thirty-five days from the posting of the offer document) a shareholder could withdraw his acceptance. An offeror must announce where he stood about acceptances at the end of the period for acceptance. An offer document offering cash as a consideration had to contain confirmation from the offeror's merchant bank or other adviser that the necessary funds were available.

The Code and the appointment of the Panel were well received. The *Accountant* (vol. CL.VIII, p. 126) had said on 29 July 1967 that 'it is one thing for the City institutions to draw up a revised list of rules. It is quite another matter to ensure that the rules are enforced.' Now, after expressing some doubts, the *Accountant* (vol. CL.VIII, p. 438) said 'Nevertheless, one may have a high degree of confidence in the preventive effect of the Panel's very existence and the moral suasion it can bring to bear in borderline cases.' It added that the real strength of the Code would be found to lie in the proposal for consultation at any time before a formal offer was made.

The newly constituted Panel, under the chairmanship of Sir

Humphrey Mynors, became operative on 27 March 1968. *The Times* reported Mr Michael Bucks, chairman of the committee that produced the Code, as saying 'This is our last chance before legislation'—a sentiment with which we shall meet on later occasions. The Panel held its first meeting on 25 March 1968. At first it met fortnightly and later its frequency of meetings depended on the state of business. The Panel, as constituted in March 1968, met for the last time on 18 March 1969. When the Code was being drafted, there was some discussion how the Panel should operate. It was agreed that the Panel should offer to give advice at all stages, but there was a division of opinion whether the Panel should intervene actively in take-over operations where things seemed to be going wrong or should wait and sit in judgement afterwards. One of the Panel's first decisions, which determined the manner in which the Panel operated from that time onwards, was that it would intervene, where necessary, on its own initiative in the course of a bid and would not simply sit in judgement after the event. Whatever may have been the arguments advanced for the Panel to act after the event in a quasi-judicial capacity, experience has shown that the decision that the Panel should adopt an active and not a passive role was the right one.

Those involved in take-over transactions were urged to consult the Panel at an early stage on any points of difficulty. Mr W. P. Cooke of the Bank of England, as Secretary of the Panel, assisted by Mr P. R. Frazer and later by Mr C. E. Condren, both also of the Bank of England, were available for day-to-day consultation, as was the Chairman. As already indicated, the members of the Panel were the chairmen of the bodies represented on the City Working Party which was responsible for the Code and they had each another representative of their association to act as a substitute. This made it possible to summon a meeting of the Panel to deal with a particular problem at less than twenty-four hours' notice. In practice very much the larger part of the day-to-day work was conducted without formal meetings. If a Panel view was required before a decision was given, members were consulted by telephone. In all these arrangements, it was recognized that the Panel must not be a clog on the conduct of business and that, if intervention by the Panel was to be effective, it must be speedy.

In the ordinary case, where one party approached the Panel or the Panel approached one party, neither side would wish any publicity. This undoubtedly facilitated consultation; but it had the inevitable but unavoidable disadvantage that the great mass of the Panel's work remained unknown and unappreciated by the public at large. Sometimes a party to a take-over bid might wish to say that they had consulted the Panel and so secured Panel cover for the action they were taking. The Panel took the line that its communications with parties were in general confidential and it expected its consent to be obtained before its name was used in offer documents. The basic materials for the Panel's day-to-day operations were formal offer documents and related papers. The Panel did not encourage the submission to them of advance copies of documents which were in a recognized form and not likely to give rise to difficulties. From the outset a large number of companies and their advisers submitted draft documents to the Panel in advance if there was some unusual feature which they wished to clear.

It might have been thought that the failure to require all documents to be submitted in advance would have proved a disadvantage, since any correction had then to be by further circular or announcement. In practice little difficulty has been experienced over the years. Contributory factors have been the care with which documents are prepared by merchant banks and lawyers, and the need in most cases to submit offer documents in draft to The Stock Exchange for vetting by the Quotations Department. In the first year of the Panel's operation, the Panel's ruling or advice was followed in all cases where the Panel was consulted in advance on a particular course of action. The few occasions when the Panel felt it necessary to object to action being taken by the parties in a bid situation were all cases where prior clearance had not been sought in specific terms.

The Panel was set up at a time of unprecedented bid activity. By the end of 1968 the newspapers were full of headings like 'The Take-over Year', 'Take-over Fever', and 'Take-over Bonanza'. In the course of the twelve months to the end of March 1969 the Panel handled some 575 cases, of which 420 were take-over operations completed before the end of March 1969. Because the Code was new, the Panel were involved in a very high proportion of cases. Of the 420 completed cases, over 70 per cent required action from the Panel, on the initiative either of the Panel or of the parties concerned. In about 25 per cent of the bids technical points arose on documentation and in 50 per cent there were procedural points such as timing, market deals and bid tactics.

A considerable proportion of the work was handled by the Chairman, the Secretary and his assistants, but over the year the Panel considered over 200 specific issues at its formal meetings. Two-thirds of these arose out of about 80 bids; the remainder related to general matters of interpretation or questions concerning future possible bids. The Panel in its first annual report[1] set out some of the problems of interpretation with which it was faced.

In the 1968 issue of the Code, the only bid that was mandatory was where directors whose shareholdings effectively controlled a company transferred control to a buyer by selling their shares. In such a case the directors were expected to satisfy themselves that the buyer would extend a comparable offer to the remaining shareholders. There was an exemption 'in very exceptional circumstances' and anyone claiming that such circumstances existed was expected to consult the Panel in advance of any agreement to transfer shares. The Panel had to deal with a number of these cases, including ones in which the investment was described as a trade investment designed to secure an association between the two companies.

The manner in which the Panel operated meant that much of its work would be conducted in private. There were, however, a few cases in which the Panel felt obliged to make its views known publicly. As already indicated, they were all cases in which the Panel had not been consulted beforehand about the action that came under review.

DUFAY BITUMASTIC/INTERNATIONAL PAINTS

On 4 April 1968 Rodo Investment Trust announced that an offer would be made on behalf of Dufay Bitumastic Ltd. to acquire the issued share capital of International Paints (Holdings) Ltd. The offer document, dated 6 May, forecast that, in

---

[1] The Panel came into operation on 27 March 1968. Its first report and all subsequent reports are for the period 1 April to 31 March in the following year.

the absence of unforeseen circumstances, the profits before tax of Dufay Bitumastic for the full year to 30 September 1968 would be of the order of £500,000 against a figure of £327,123 for the previous year. Profit figures were not available for any part of the then current year, but the board of Dufay Bitumastic accepted responsibility for all statements of fact and opinion in the offer document. The Chief Accountant of the Paints Division of Dufay Bitumastic resigned from that post and informed the Panel that he was not satisfied with the profits forecast in so far as it was based on optimistic views about the profits of the Paints Division. For the information of interested parties, the Panel published an account of its discussions with the former Chief Accountant and with the Chairman of Dufay Bitumastic, with their conflicting views of the probable profits for 1967/8. The Panel added that 'the Panel express no opinion on the likely outcome of the current year in relation to the published forecast of the total profits nor is it their function to examine the detailed figures of particular companies'. It was, however, widely accepted that the publication of the disagreements about the profit forecast had dealt a serious blow to the likely success of the Dufay Bitumastic offer.

The Dufay Bitumastic offer had been revised upwards and extended in time and was due to close on 19 June. On 29 May Courtaulds, who were advised by Hill Samuel, had announced that they were interested in having talks with International Paints with a view to making an offer to acquire the company. No further announcement was made until 18 June, when International Paints announced that Courtaulds had informed them that, in the event of the Dufay offer not being proceeded with, they would make an offer for International Paints, as to three-quarters in Courtaulds' ordinary shares and as to one quarter in unsecured loan stock, but without indicating precise terms. This announcement, made the day before the Dufay Bitumastic offer was to expire, left the shareholders of International Paints to make a choice between two alternative offers without the facts necessary for an informed judgement of their relative merits. The Panel drew attention to this unsatisfactory feature in a public statement and went on: 'Rule 14 [now Rule 15] does not refer in terms to such a situation: but the spirit underlying it should be observed whatever the actual situation may be. The Panel therefore consider than an announcement of the type issued on 18th June should have contained fuller details of the offer, in the interests of those to whom it might shortly be made.' The difficulty with which the Panel was faced in securing acceptance of its authority was, however, illustrated by the rejection of its views by Hill Samuel in a public statement on 25 September 1968, and by the attack on the Panel by the chairman of Courtaulds in a visit to the Bank of England and in a press conference on 26 September. He claimed that the Panel should have consulted Courtaulds before issuing the statement and he said that an SEC on the American model was needed. It is true that Sir Frank Kearton (as he then was) also strongly criticized The Stock Exchange, other City institutions, and the accountancy profession. In the event, the Dufay Bitumastic offer failed and an offer by Courtaulds succeeded.

IMPERIAL TOBACCO/AMERICAN TOBACCO/GALLAHER

Imperial Tobacco held 36 per cent and American Tobacco 13 per cent of the share capital of Gallaher, the second largest manufacturer of cigarettes in the UK. In May 1968 Imperial Tobacco, through Morgan Grenfell, offered their Gallaher shares for sale at 20*s*. a share. The issue was only partly successful and the underwriters were left with more than one-third of the stock on their hands. American Tobacco bought none. On 26 June 1968 Philip Morris of the United States, advised by Warburgs, offered 25*s*. a share for half of Gallaher's ordinary capital. The Chairman of Gallaher said to his shareholders that the offer was quite unacceptable, notwithstanding the recent lack of success of the Imperial Tobacco sale at 20*s*.

On 16 July American Tobacco, advised by Morgan Grenfell, counter-bid 35*s*. a share for half of Gallaher's ordinary capital. At the same time the stockbrokers, Cazenoves, acting under instructions from Morgan Grenfell, purchased with great speed 12,000,000 Gallaher shares from selected institutions, some of whom, as underwriters, held shares as a result of the Imperial Tobacco offer for sale. The price paid was just under 35*s*. per share. These institutions were paid 35*s*. for all their shares, whereas other shareholders were being offered 35*s*. for half of their shares. The market price was then about 25*s*.

On 18 July 1968 the Panel issued a statement that at a

meeting on 16 July they had concluded that the dealings on that day constituted a breach of General Principle 7 [now 9] of the Code which stated that 'after a bid is reasonably in contemplation there shall not be made to a shareholder of an offeree company an offer which is more favourable than a general offer to be made thereafter to the other shareholders of the same class'. Morgan Grenfell and Cazenoves said that they could not agree with the conclusions of the Panel since they were both firmly of the view that, so far as they were concerned, they had complied with the Code in every respect. Their argument was that Rule 29 [now 31] said that all parties to a take-over were free to deal at arm's length in the market and that General Principle 7 did not explicitly deal with purchases in the market in a partial bid.

The case raised in stark form the question whether the Panel's decisions were to be treated as authoritative, particularly in areas not explicitly covered by the Rules, where the spirit of the General Principles had to be invoked. The Panel was widely regarded as having flinched when on 25 July they issued a statement which—while reiterating that there had been a breach of General Principle 7 and referring the matter to The Stock Exchange and Issuing Houses Association—seemed to accept Morgan Grenfell's and Cazenoves' justification of their action. The statement did, however, report that the Chairmen of Morgan Grenfell and of Cazenoves had said that they had not intended to flout the authority of the Panel and that Morgan Grenfell and Cazenoves had given an undertaking to observe the Code and wished to make it clear that they would always comply with a definite ruling of the Panel and would never knowingly put themselves in breach of the Code.

Neither The Stock Exchange Council nor the Issuing Houses Association found it easy to take effective action in the case. The Stock Exchange, in a statement published on 13 August, agreed with the Panel that there had been a breach of General Principle 7, but accepted Cazenoves' explanation that the competitive bid situation had been confused and the application of the Code unclear and that Cazenoves had acted in good faith. The Issuing Houses Association were still at that point of time unable to reach a conclusion on the matter.

On 15 August the Governor of the Bank of England (Sir

FIRST CITY CODE AND PANEL

Leslie O'Brien) sent a long letter to the Chairman of the Issuing Houses Association in which he deplored the extent to which published rulings by the Panel had been questioned and their general authority not always acknowledged. In the Governor's view it was in no one's interest that this state of affairs should continue, and he invited the Issuing Houses Association to consider how the Panel might be strengthened and made more effective for the future. The alternative was some form of statutory control which would not necessarily be more effective and would be more onerous and time-wasting for all concerned. On 23 August 1968 the Executive Committee of the Issuing Houses Association issued a statement saying that it had not passed judgement on the events of 16 July, but saying that the rulings of the Panel should be 'received with respect' by those held to be in breach of the Code. It referred with great concern to the attitude towards the Panel that appeared to have been adopted by Morgan Grenfell, following upon the Panel's ruling. There followed a reply from the Chairman of Morgan Grenfell that they had not intended to show any lack of respect for the authority of the Panel and would always observe the Code.

PERGAMON/NEWS LIMITED/NEWS OF THE WORLD

On 16 October 1968 Pergamon Press (Mr Robert Maxwell), advised by Hill Samuel and Flemings, made an offer worth £26,750,000 for the voting shares of the News of the World. Of these shares 30 per cent were held by Sir William Carr, Chairman of the News of the World, and 26 per cent by Professor Derek Jackson. Mr Maxwell was assured of Professor Jackson's support. The News of the World board, advised by Hambros, rejected the bid and Pergamon Press made a revised bid on 21 October worth £34,000,000 or 50s. per share. Hambros then began buying shares in the market on its own account and between 16 and 22 October acquired 11.8 per cent of the News of the World voting shares.

On 22 October Morgan Grenfell, acting for News Ltd. of Australia (Mr Rupert Murdoch), informed the Panel that an agreement had been reached between News Ltd. and News of the World and secured the Panel's agreement that Morgan Grenfell, subject to disclosure, could purchase shares in the market. The Panel pointed out to Morgan Grenfell and Hambros that, if the board of News of the World and their associates secured over 50 per cent of the voting shares, they would be able to deny the minority an opportunity to decide on the Pergamon offer. It would be necessary to show that the interests of shareholders generally were not being prejudiced. By 24 October Morgan Grenfell, on behalf of News Ltd., had bought $3\frac{1}{2}$ per cent of the voting shares. Sir William Carr and Mr Murdoch then announced that, in addition to the 45 per cent voting shares that they held, they had promises of support from a further 7 per cent. They announced that they would propose to the News of the World shareholders that Mr Murdoch should transfer certain important but unspecified assets to the News of the World and in return would give Mr Murdoch's Australian company 40 per cent of an expanded News of the World voting capital.

The position on the morning of 24 October was that there had been the announcement of a revised offer of 50s. by Pergamon but no formal offer document: and there was uncertainty when details of the proposed arrangement between News of the World and News Ltd. would be available. On the same morning (24 October), the Panel obtained the agreement of Pergamon Press and the News of the World not to purchase further News of the World shares. To ensure that Mr Murdoch and his associates did not purchase any, The Stock Exchange agreed to a temporary suspension of the News of the World quotation, pending the issue of proposals by both parties.

The Panel was criticized on the score that it had moved too slowly. By 24 October News Ltd., News of the World and associates had more than 51 per cent of the voting shares. A number of shareholders had promised firm support for the board of News of the World against the Pergamon offer. The scheme being worked out by News of the World and News Ltd. required the authorization of additional capital by the News of the World shareholders. The Panel got the agreement of the merchant bankers concerned that none of the parties or their associates would vote at the EGM in respect of the shares they had acquired during the bid situation. In fact, the EGM voted overwhelmingly in favour of the link with News Ltd.

On merits, the actions of the Panel did not prejudice what the

News of the World shareholders plainly wanted to do. It was, however, widely felt that, although the Panel found that there had been no breach of the Code, the arrangement adumbrated between News of the World and News Ltd. contravened the spirit of General Principle 3 [now 4] and that, if share dealings were to be stopped, this should have happened before 24 October. The Code was new and had to be interpreted on its application to the infinite variety of individual cases. The Code had also to be enforced, after a long period when the Notes and Revised Notes had on occasion been flouted. Even at this late stage, after the City had accepted the need for a code of conduct and a body to put it into effect, there were those who still basically rejected the idea of their activities being controlled in this way. Not for the last time, the reputation of the City Code and its administrators suffered from the fact that the Panel's best work was in guidance given privately. The whole essay in self-regulation tended to be judged from a few well-publicized cases where difficulties had arisen.

There were questions in the House of Commons and speeches in the Mansion House. The Labour Government had no wish to embark on a statutory scheme of control if self-regulation could be made to work: but there were different nuances in the manner in which this was expressed. On 6 November 1968 the President of the Board of Trade (Mr Anthony Crosland) said that, if the voluntary system could be made to work, it had obvious advantages for everyone, but that, if a reshaped system proved inadequate, he would not hesitate to take statutory powers. (Commons Debates, Written Answers, 6 November 1968 col. 89). At the Lord Mayor's banquet on 11 November the Prime Minister (Mr Wilson, now Sir Harold Wilson) said that the Government would vastly prefer that the City itself should provide the discipline—including self-discipline—that was required. 'The Government has no desire to introduce legislation to force on the City the much tougher and more wide-ranging interference which free enterprise America has devised in the form of the Securities and Exchange Commission, or indeed in any other form, for this job is far better done by the City.' He added, however, that the job was not yet being done effectively, that there was a demand for action by the Government, and if it became necessary they would act. On 11 December 1968 the Minister of State, Board of Trade (Mr Edmund Dell), reiterated that in the judgement of the Government it would be much better if a voluntary system of control could be made to work and it was to that end that they were currently working (Commons Debates: 11 December 1968: col. 396).

Although the Prime Minister's speech was regarded as less menacing than what the President of the Board of Trade had said, there was a general realization—which the Governor had already voiced in his letter of 15 August 1968—that, if the self-regulatory scheme could not be made to command greater authority, then some form of statutory control would become unavoidable. The Stock Exchange Council in their report for 1968/9 summed up the work of the original Panel as follows:

> The Panel has been the subject of some press criticism but the very large number of situations successfully and expeditiously dealt with by the Panel has too frequently been overlooked. Moreover it would certainly be most unusual if in such a contentious area of operations exceptional difficulties were not experienced in the formative years when the parties concerned in a bid situation had not yet become acclimatised to the working of the new City Code.

V

REVISION OF CODE AND REORGANIZATION OF PANEL

It is worth while to set out in full the letter which Sir Leslie O'Brien sent to the Chairman of the Issuing Houses Association on 15 August 1968 because it sets the scene for the developments that followed.

As you are aware, I have been in close touch with you, with the Chairman of the Stock Exchange and with Sir Humphrey Mynors, the Chairman of the Panel on Take-overs and Mergers, throughout recent events. I think it may be timely for me to review the general position as I now see it. I confess I find it a disappointing one.

A great deal of work was put into the preparation of the new Code on Take-overs and Mergers and, when it was published, it was widely accepted as providing a well-thought-out set of rules to guide the conduct of those concerned with such matters. It could not, of course, have been expected to be an infallible guide. In recent months the Code has been severely tested in practice and some deficiencies have been revealed. I know that revisions of the relevant sections of the Code are under urgent consideration and no doubt they will be published as soon as possible. Further revisions in the light of experience may be expected to follow at reasonable intervals. I am sure that constant attention will be given to removing uncertainty and ambiguity in the wording of the Code. But it is not and cannot be a legal document. It is a memorandum of guidance and its usefulness depends on those who use it understanding and subscribing to the objectives which inspired its preparation.

The purpose of the Panel is to give authoritative rulings on the interpretation of the Code and, so far as possible, to secure that these rulings are respected. I have kept closely in touch with the work of the Panel since its inception in March last. Throughout this period it has been extremely active in giving advice on the interpretation of the Code to many issuing houses, firms and others concerned with take-overs and mergers. Most of this work has received no publicity, but I believe it has nevertheless been most useful and helpful. In a few instances, after due deliberation, the Panel has felt obliged to state publicly that a breach of the Code has in its opinion occurred. In my view, these rulings were in each case entirely justified and I do not see that the Panel had any option but to make them public and to do so with the minimum of delay. The result, however, has been less than satisfactory. Much resentment has been aroused. The Panel's rulings have been questioned and even their general authority has not always been acknowledged. It is in no one's interest that this state of affairs should continue.

I know that the Panel are considering their methods and procedures. I shall be grateful if your Committee will consider how the Panel might be strengthened and made more effective for the future. Both Sir Humphrey Mynors and I will welcome any suggestions which you may have. I hope these will not exclude proposals for effective sanctions against wilful infringements of the Code.

I realize that a take-over battle will from time to time be only too well described as such. In these circumstances the urge to take quick and successful action is great. But action in breach of the Code is not justifiable in any circumstances. It harms the reputation of those who are guilty of it and is prejudicial to the good name of the City in general. I ask that you remind your members that the Code and the Panel are a voluntarily established mechanism which can only work if those who have adopted it to regulate their own conduct give it their full and consistent support. They should be guided by the spirit of the Code's intentions as much as by legalistic interpretations of its wording. They should consult the Panel whenever in doubt and abide by its rulings.

Despite recent difficulties, I do not accept that it is time, as some suggest, to write off the Code and the Panel as a failure; indeed, in my view, they have for the most part been a success so far. This experiment is still in its infancy. Longer experience of it is needed before any firm conclusions can sensibly be reached. If all are willing to learn the lessons to be drawn from the initial difficulties its future should be assured. If, however, the present arrangements prove inadequate, no doubt some form of statutory control will be considered. There is no certainty that such a control would be more effective, but there can be no doubt that it would be more onerous and time-wasting for all concerned.

I am writing a similar letter to the Chairman of the Stock Exchange and I am sending a copy to Sir Humphrey Mynors. Also, in view of

REVISION OF CODE AND REORGANIZATION OF PANEL 53

the wide-spread interest in this subject, I am making this letter available to the Press.

In addition to being responsible for the proposal to set up the Panel, Lord O'Brien showed a firm guiding hand in the difficult early days of the Code, and, as indicated in the Governor's letter, the revision of the Code was already under discussion. In June 1968 the Panel, after three months' experience, put a number of problems of interpretation to the Chairman of the Issuing Houses Association with a view to amendment of the Code. The Panel realized, however, that revision could not take place too frequently since this might weaken the authority of the Code. More important was the question of 'sanctions'—the means by which compliance with the Code could be enforced. Sir Humphrey Mynors and his Panel had realized that a better marshalling of sanctions was one key to a solution of their difficulties: and some preliminary work had been done.

The City Working Party gathered together in September 1968 and continued working through the autumn. On sanctions, there were discussions with the Board of Trade about a statutory basis but it was soon agreed that there were great difficulties about giving statutory powers to a voluntary body. There were also discussions of a scheme of monetary penalties, accepted by those who adhered to the Code, which would be imposed by the Panel on those who infringed the provisions of the Code. This also was felt to present insuperable difficulties. Various suggestions were examined but rejected because they might penalize innocent parties. These included a proposal that dealings during a take-over transaction should be made subject to a special form of settlement, so that transactions could be cancelled if anything went wrong. It was also felt that the suspension of the listing of a company, as a penalty, was fraught with difficulties. One draconian proposal was that the removal of offending directors from all public companies could be secured by providing that the Stock Exchange would withdraw listing from any company whose board contained a member of the offending company's board.

In the end it was agreed that the threat of public censure by the Panel would be a deterrent in many cases, that the associations should agree to expel a member for a serious breach and that the question of denying a practitioner the right to practise in the field of take-over bids should be explored.

The question of stiffer penalties inevitably raised the question of possible conflicts between the duties of directors and others under the law and under the Code. The draft of a revised Code was shown to Sir Milner Holland, QC, and he was asked to advise whether the Code appeared to involve any obvious legal difficulties or manifest inconsistencies. Sir Milner Holland saw no fundamental conflict between the Code and the law. Although he could envisage cases where difficulties might arise, he did not consider that in general the Code purported to impose on any person a duty to act in a manner which would be a breach of a duty which the law imposed on him. Even in the cases where he foresaw possible difficulties, he did not see how the Code could be reframed to deal with them and he did not consider that the possibility of such cases arising ought to lead to the abandonment of the Code in the form it took, especially as the Code usually authorized the Panel to allow for special cases. Sir Milner Holland suggested some amendments in detail.

Reorganization of the Panel

On 25 February 1969 the Bank of England announced a reorganization of the Panel, which took effect on 1 May 1969. Lord Shawcross became Chairman of the Panel in place of Sir Humphrey Mynors, who agreed to serve as Deputy Chairman for a term of twelve months. The Chairman of the Association of Unit Trust Managers joined the Panel. The staff of the Panel was strengthened and its work reorganized. Mr Cooke and Mr Condren remained for some time to facilitate the change to the new arrangements. Mr Ian Fraser, a director of S. G. Warburgs, became full-time Director General of the Panel. He was assisted by Mr W. S. Wareham, then head of the Quotations Department of The Stock Exchange, who was seconded by The Stock Exchange to become Deputy Director General. Mr A. R. Beevor, seconded from Ashurst Morris Crisp & Co., became Secretary. Mr P. R. Frazer, seconded from the Bank of England, was an Assistant Secretary. He had been with the Panel from the outset. Mr P. B. Mitford-Slade, seconded from

Cazenove & Co., also became an Assistant Secretary. The Panel, whose offices had been in Bank of England premises at New Change, moved in September 1970 to the twentieth floor of The Stock Exchange Building, alongside the Quotations Department of The Stock Exchange.

Revised Code

The revised Code, issued on 28 April 1969, incorporated changes based on the experience of the previous twelve months.

There was a new General Principle:

It is considered to be impracticable to devise rules in such detail as to cover all the various circumstances which arise in take-over or merger transactions. Accordingly, persons engaged in such transactions should be aware that the spirit as well as the precise wording of these general principles and of the ensuing rules must be observed.

In the Rules it was made clear in Rule 9 [now G.P. 11] that the good faith that the directors controlling a company must show in rejecting an offer or preferring a lower offer was 'good faith in the interests of shareholders as a whole'. An addition was made to Rule 12 [now 10] (offer document to be issued as soon as practicable after the announcement of the offer) that if an offeror who had announced an offer did not proceed with the offer within a reasonable time he must be prepared to justify the circumstances to the Panel. Purchases and sales of shares in the offeror or offeree company during the bid period by associates for investment clients had to be reported to The Stock Exchange and the Panel but not necessarily to the Press.

Rule 15 [now 16] was strengthened. This was the most important feature of the revision. The responsibility of directors for the accuracy of profit forecasts was stressed. As regards the reports by accountants, the main accountancy bodies, fearful that the association of some well-known accountancy name with a forecast would give it an air of certainty which forecasting could never enjoy, had recommended in July 1968 that accountants should not allow their names to be associated with the profit forecasts in published documents. This, however, proved to be unsatisfactory. It was widely felt that shareholders should see the reports and know who was giving them. As part of the process of strengthening the Code, the accountancy bodies agreed in 1969 that the report of the accountants on the calculations and bases of a forecast should not only be given to the directors but also communicated to the shareholders. The same arrangement was extended to the report of a merchant bank or other adviser. The consent of accountants and advisers to publication had to be secured before publication.

The Rules relating to partial bids were tightened up. If the offeror was aiming at less than 50 per cent of the voting rights, then the prior consent of the Panel must be obtained to the offer and the bid could be declared unconditional only if acceptances were received for the number of shares bid for (Rule 26, now 27). In a partial bid, the offeror and associates could not deal for their own account in shares of the offeree company during the bid period nor (if 50 per cent voting rights would not be secured) for twelve months thereafter (Rule 29, now in 27).

At various points, the consent of the Panel for the waiving of a Rule in exceptional cases was inserted—in respect of the failure to proceed with a formal offer within a reasonable period (Rule 12), failure to offer the weighted average price of market purchases in the bid period (Rule 31) and arrangements likely to change the situation of a company during a bid period which were not the result of formal contracts but of some obligation or other special circumstances (Rule 34, now 38).

Sanctions

The most important change was not, however, in the text of the Code but in the promulgation of the sanctions that could be applied in the event of a breach of the Code. This was the subject of a Policy Statement by the Panel dated 28 April 1969. If there was a breach of the Code, the Panel would have recourse to private or to public censure or, in a more flagrant case, to further action designed to deprive the offender temporarily or permanently of his ability to practise in the field of take-overs or mergers.

The Stock Exchange had agreed to amend their Rules to provide that the findings of the Panel would be accepted by the Council of The Stock Exchange as proof that the Code had been broken. It would be for The Stock Exchange to consider what

REVISION OF CODE AND REORGANIZATION OF PANEL

disciplinary action was taken. The Stock Exchange's disciplinary powers include the power to censure, suspend, or expel a member. The Executive Committee of the Issuing Houses Association had agreed to take the necessary steps to accept the jurisdiction of the Panel and to empower the Committee to suspend or expel a member, though this would not in law prevent the issuing house concerned from continuing in business. The Accepting Houses Committee, the Association of Investment Trust Companies, the British Insurance Association, the Committee of London Clearing Bankers, the National Association of Pension Funds, and the Association of Unit Trust Managers had expressed their support for the Code and agreed to take appropriate steps to engage the support of their membership. The Association of Stock and Share Dealers and associations representing various overseas dealers operating in this country had agreed to take action similar to that of The Stock Exchange.

The Board of Trade had assured the Panel that they would consider disciplinary action in any case involving a licensed or exempted dealer where public reprobation did not seem to be an adequate sanction. The Board also agreed that when they authorized someone, other than an authorized dealer, to make a take-over bid they would draw attention to the requirements of the City Code and send a copy of the Code. In the event of a take-over involving exchange control consent, the Panel had arranged to keep in close consultation with the Bank of England during the currency of the offer, so that the Bank could satisfy itself that the conditions under which consent was given were being properly observed.

In view of the more severe penalties that were envisaged for serious breaches of the Code, an Appeal Committee was constituted under the chairmanship of Lord Pearce, a former Lord of Appeal, to which a person likely to be adversely affected by a decision of the Panel could appeal.

VI

PANEL ESTABLISHES ITSELF

THE new edition of the City Code on Take-overs and Mergers (the 'Blue Book') came into effect on 1 May 1969, and at the same time the day-to-day administration of the Panel's business was taken over, on a full-time basis, by the newly appointed director general and deputy director general reporting directly to Lord Shawcross, the chairman. Until then the Panel had largely administered the Code directly. Now the full Panel became for the most part a supervisory body. The Panel held quarterly meetings to hear progress reports and to consider general questions of policy in the interpretation of the Code. There was a right to appeal to the full Panel against any ruling of the Director General. The Panel held *ad hoc* meetings to hear these appeals, also to consider disciplinary cases where the question of a reprimand or other penalty was involved: and the Panel also considered any question which raised difficult issues that were best handled from the outset by the Panel itself.

The new Panel was more fortunate than the original Panel in so far as it had an initial period of about two years before take-over activity reached a fresh intensity. There was, however, plenty to do, since the reduction was rather in the size of the companies merging than in their number. There was also a feeling in some quarters—which subsequent events did not altogether support—that asset stripping was probably over because the Companies Act, 1967, required directors to state the value of assets if they differed materially from book values.[1] It was thought that most mergers henceforth would be for the

---

[1] See, for example, W. G. Medlam, 'The Accountant's Role in Take-over Bids', *Accountancy* (Nov. 1968), pp. 818–32.

purpose of integration into an industrial or trading group.

Lord Shawcross, in his first Annual Report, for the year from 1 April 1969 to 31 March 1970, said:

As the Code is constantly improved by amendment and clarification so is the Panel steadily acquiring more experience in its administration. At the same time, I hope and believe, companies and their advisers are able to place ever greater confidence in the system of self-regulation represented by the Code and the Panel, and are taking increasing advantage of the possibility of the earliest consultation (to facilitate which the officers of the Panel and myself try to be available in the most informal way, even on our home telephones!). To justify this confidence the Panel has to apply the rules of the Code in a manner which is easily intelligible, is manifestly fair and is, as far as ever-changing circumstances permit, consistent. I am firmly of the opinion that we are moving towards this ideal and that in a few years' time self-regulation in the take-over bid field will be taken for granted even by those who today are its sternest critics.

Again, in his foreword to the 1970/1 Report, the Chairman reported:

The Panel has been rather less 'in the news' during the past year: a welcome circumstance, not, as I think, solely attributable to the fact that few major problems have had to be dealt with, but also resulting from a general acceptance of the Panel's activity as part of the normal machinery of the City. Certainly the co-operation of the City community, sometimes in cases with significant financial implications, has continued to be very high. In the same sense it may be observed that the cynicism, which sometimes arose on the question whether a voluntary system such as the Panel operates would work, is now less often heard and a number of foreign countries, including Japan, Sweden and France, have sent representatives of Government or of Stock Exchanges to study just how the system does operate. Indeed, the Basle Stock Exchange has proposed that arrangements broadly similar to our own should be adopted officially for all Swiss Stock Exchanges and in Germany a voluntary code of conduct has been introduced to deal with 'insider' transactions.

PRACTICE NOTES

Because of the extent to which the work of the Panel executive consisted of giving advice in private to a party to a take-over bid, its interpretation of the Code could not become generally known. In its Report for 1968/9 the Panel said that it had considered the possibility of issuing 'practice notes' from time to time, setting out interpretations of the Code of fairly general validity but had deferred action because of the need to gain experience and of the then impending revision of the Code. In 1969/70 three Practice Notes were issued dealing with

(1) private companies and unquoted public companies;
(2) directors' emoluments and particulars of service contracts; and
(3) publication of information.

In 1970/1, Practice Notes were issued on

(1) profit forecasts and asset valuations; and
(2) disclosure of dealings.

These Practice Notes were intended to serve as a guide to the Panel's current interpretations of the relevant sections of the Code. They were prepared by the Panel executive in consultation with the members of the full Panel, but they did not in any way override the Code nor did they purport to carry the same degree of authority as the Code itself. Broadly speaking, they could be divided between those explaining how the Panel executive operated the rules of an administrative character and those interpreting general principles and rules that imposed restrictions. It was realized from the start that the Panel must not trespass, particularly in the latter type of note, on the province of the City Working Party.

LEASCO/PERGAMON PRESS

The April 1969 revision of the Code had provided that an offeror who announced his intention to make a bid, but did not proceed with the offer, would be expected to justify his action to the Panel. This was put to the test by the withdrawal on 21 August 1969 of the United States company, Leasco, from its announced offer for Pergamon Press, of which Mr Robert Maxwell and his family held about 31 per cent of the equity. On the same day, the Panel requested each company to make an early public statement, asked The Stock Exchange to consider suspending dealings in Pergamon shares pending a clarification of the situation (which The Stock Exchange did), and invited Leasco and its advisers to justify the withdrawal in the presence of Mr Maxwell.

The hearing before the Panel lasted two and a half days and

Mr Maxwell during the hearings spoke for about nineteen hours in all. The parties made an effort to reach agreement between themselves but this failed. The Panel's statement, dated 27 August, accepted Leasco's explanation for its withdrawal from the proposed offer, though the Panel reiterated its view of the seriousness of a withdrawal from an announced offer because of the false market which might have been created. The Panel directed that Leasco should not make any further purchases of Pergamon shares. As a result of its inquiries, the Panel was doubtful whether the Pergamon shareholders had been given adequate information about the affairs of their company, particularly about International Learning Systems Corporation, a company which Pergamon owned jointly with the British Printing Corporation. The statement said:

It must be made clear that the Panel possesses no general supervisory powers to ensure that directors of public companies make full disclosure to their shareholders of all relevant matters. This is indeed a most important duty of directors and that it should have been continuously discharged becomes a matter of especial importance as soon as any question arises of an offer for shares. It is for this reason that under its constitution the City Panel's interest in the matter of disclosure is attracted whenever a question arises of a prospective offer, as well as during the course of negotiations about an offer or in the aftermath of an offer which has been made. It may be suggested that the Panel is only concerned with disclosure in the offer document (if indeed one materialises) or in any reply made by the offeree company, but the Panel considers this too narrow a view. When the intention to make an offer is publicly announced share prices are likely to be significantly affected and directors of companies should realize that in order that shareholders may protect their interests in the interim and be able to form a reasonable assessment of the value of their holdings in the event of an offer being made, or on the contrary of an expected offer not materialising, they should be kept continuously informed about the affairs of their company. It is not only in offer documents or replies that full disclosure is called for, although it is only in the context of an offer situation that the Panel can draw attention to any inadequacy of disclosure. Observance to the full of this obligation to disclose is essential if public confidence in the securities market is to be maintained.

The Panel expressed disquiet about apparent non-disclosure on a number of points and called the attention of the Board of

Trade to these matters with a view to the Board considering whether an inquiry should be held.

The Panel's statement showed that the Panel was not inclined to take a narrow view of its responsibilities and this has remained its attitude.

Mr Maxwell lodged an appeal against the part of the Panel's findings relating to non-disclosure to Pergamon shareholders. He argued that the Panel was not entitled to extend the scope of its jurisdiction to these wider issues. He did not, however, object to the publication of the Panel's statement and it was, therefore, published immediately, and the findings of the Appeal Committee published later.

Mr Maxwell's appeal failed before the Appeal Committee. On the question of the Panel's jurisdiction, the Committee said:

> The first point is the contention that the Panel strayed beyond its proper sphere. The Panel's statement shows that it was well aware of the fact that its task was to deal with the take-over situation and that a possible view was that it was only concerned with the disclosure in the offer document or in any reply made by the offeree company. But it rejected that view as being too narrow. One of the main objects of the Panel is to secure fair treatment for the investing public. This object can be seen plainly to run through the City Code. In particular paragraph 3 of the General Principles says 'Shareholders shall have in their possession sufficient evidence, facts and opinions upon which an adequate judgement and decision can be reached, and shall have sufficient time to make an assessment and decision. No relevant information shall be withheld from them'. And paragraph 5 says that 'It must be the object of all parties to a take-over or merger transaction to use every endeavour to prevent the creation of a false market in the shares of an offeror or offeree company'.
>
> Mr. Pearson, a director of Robert Fleming & Co. Ltd., in giving his evidence before us said 'I would certainly have expected that the Panel would have enquired into the background information because it seems to me that in the situation which developed it would only have been half an enquiry if it had dealt with disclosure at one particular moment of time ... Therefore I certainly expected the Panel would enquire into all relevant published documents.' We agree with that view of the matter.
>
> Information given at the time of a bid cannot be wholly divorced from pre-bid information which the shareholder has been given or ought to have been given. The full Panel made a careful investigation as to the take-over situation. But this was inevitably limited by an

inability to conduct a long and detailed enquiry into the accounts of inter-related companies. The Panel was composed of eleven persons of standing and experience in the City of London. Their collective knowledge and judgement were very weighty. In their investigation they found a situation which in their opinion called for an enquiry by the Board of Trade in the interests of everybody concerned. The problem which they consciously faced was whether they should take a narrow view, suppress that opinion as not being their business, and, as it were, 'pass by on the other side'. They considered that their duty to the public did not allow them to take that course. They, therefore, expressed the opinion they had formed. In the particular circumstances of every case it must be a question of fact and degree whether such an expression of opinion is justifiable. In this the importance of the suggested non-disclosure and its relevance to the existing and future situation of the company would be factors to be considered. That question of fact and degree must be decided in the light of fairness and commonsense. That decision in this case was made by men whose knowledge of the City made them particularly suitable to form such a judgement. We think that the course taken by the full Panel was reasonable in the circumstances and we see no reason to differ from it.

On 9 September 1969 the Board of Trade appointed Mr R. O. C. Stable, QC, and Sir Ronald Leach to act as inspectors to investigate the affairs of Pergamon Press and also of International Learning Systems Corporation. In paragraph 311 of their report of 2 June 1971 the Inspectors said:

The far lengthier inquiry which we have been able to make into the affairs of International Learning Systems Corporation and Pergamon and into what the shareholders of Pergamon were told about the affairs of International Learning Systems Corporation than the Panel was able to make wholly vindicates the misgivings of its members and justifies its suggestion for further enquiry.

The Pergamon case came at a crucial point in the history of the essay in self-regulation represented by the City Code. If the Panel had failed, the subsequent course of events might have been very different. The Press realized the significance of the event and praised the Panel for its firm handling of the case. One later commentator,[1] after noting that the circumstances placed the Panel in a near-impossible situation, went on:

[1] Michael Blanden, 'City Regulations on Mergers and Take-overs', Chapter XI, *Readings in Mergers and Take-overs* (1972).

Yet, for all that, the Panel came out of the situation with its own reputation enormously enhanced. Whatever the outcome, it had left no doubts in anybody's mind that it had the will and power to make its authority felt, the strength to stand no nonsense from the personalities involved, the ability to give quick decisions and at the same time to perservere with a course of action, even if it meant working half the night, and the complete support of the authorities, including the Board of Trade.

BOVIS/TRAFALGAR HOUSE/CEMENTATION

The other notable case in 1969/70 illustrated the change that was coming over the City scene. At the beginning of 1970 Bovis Holdings (advised by Samuel Montagu) and Trafalgar House Investments (advised by Kleinwort Benson) were engaged in competitive bids for The Cementation Company. Both were offering shares and loan stock. As at 16 March 1970 Trafalgar's offer for Cementation was worth about 19s. 6d. and that of Bovis about 21s. 1d. Nevertheless, Cementation confirmed that it was recommending shareholders to accept the Trafalgar offer. This kept the market price below 21s. and on 18 March Samuel Montagu, acting on behalf of Bovis, announced that, by purchases in the market, they had accumulated 25.9 per cent of the Cementation ordinary shares at prices of which the maximum was just over 20s. Shortly afterwards Trafalgar raised their paper bid in shares and loan stock to about 22s. On 20 March Bovis announced that it was not increasing its offer and in effect was withdrawing from the contest; and Kleinwort Benson announced almost simultaneously that they had agreed to buy the Samuel Montagu holding of 3,634,500 ordinary shares of Cementation at 20s. 9d. per share. At that time the Cementation shares stood at around 19s. 6d. in the market and the value of the Trafalgar paper in their offer was 21s. 10d.

The Panel held that under General Principle 8—'all shareholders of the same class of an offeree company shall be treated similarly by an offeror company'—Trafalgar were obliged to offer a cash alternative at 20s. 9d. per Cementation share to shareholders to match the terms on which the Samuel Montagu holding had been acquired. The Panel held that Rule 31 (which enabled Trafalgar and associates to buy for cash in the market, subject only to increasing the value of the offer if any shares were purchased at a higher price than the value of the offer) related to acquiring shares in the market from a number of separate shareholders and not to the acquisition of a control block of shares from a specific shareholder. The liberty to make purchases for cash in the market existed only where any shareholder so minded could, during the currency of the cash purchases, take advantage of the facility. This was not the case with Cementation, since only Samuel Montagu had its shares bought for cash at a price above the market price. At the time of the purchase the paper bid was valued at 1s. 1d. a share more than the cash price and the Panel was not prepared to regard the cash transaction as 'similar' to the paper bid within the meaning of General Principle 8. Paper bids which were not underwritten for cash were by their nature much subject to market fluctuations. Kleinwort Benson had agreed to abide by the decision of the Panel and they provided a cash alternative of 20s. 9d. for each uncommitted Cementation share (including those already assented to the offer) at their own expense.

DEVELOPMENTS IN 1971 AND 1972

The Panel had established its position and the Chairman could claim in the foreword to the 1970/1 report that there was general acceptance of the Panel's activity as part of the normal machinery of the City. There were of course voices asking how long it would all last. In the early part of 1971, some fears were publicly expressed that the system of self-regulation might not survive in the long run—mainly owing to doubts whether voluntary service of the necessary calibre would continue to be available to man the City's regulatory bodies.[1]

About this time there was some exploration whether the authority of the Panel could be made more effective if it was given a statutory right to call for documents, to summon witnesses and to take evidence on oath. The subject received an airing at a Press conference held on 24 May 1971 on the publication of the 1970/1 report of the Panel. The conclusion eventually reached was that the difficulties in seeking legal powers were too great and that legal powers might be hedged about with restrictions which would make it difficult for the Panel to operate effectively and with speed.

[1] See, for example, *The Times's* leader of 27 January 1971, following an Institute of Directors/*Financial Times* conference on the role of the non-executive director.

Meantime there was a steady stream of take-over bids. The year 1972 saw a large number of substantial bids—Watney Mann for International Distillers and Vintners (bid worth £156,000,000), Grand Metropolitan Hotels for the enlarged Watney Mann (£390,000,000), Imperial Tobacco for Courage (£285,000,000), Bowater for Ralli International (£97,000,000), Cavenham for Allied Suppliers (£83,000,000), British American Tobacco for International Stores (£67,000,000), Consolidated Gold Fields for Amey (£59,000,000) and so on. The Department of Industry put the total expenditure on acquisitions and mergers of industrial and commercial companies in 1972 at £2,532,000,000, as compared with £911,000,000 in 1971, £1,304,000,000 in 1973, £508,000,000, in 1974 and £291,000,000 in 1975.

BIDS AND MARKET PURCHASES

The main theme in discussions regarding the Code in 1971 and 1972 was the repercussion of purchases of shares in the stock market on a bid. This is not surprising in view of the fact that in the United States the offeror is not allowed to buy shares during the currency of the bid.

The original Notes had said, as their first principle, that 'there should be no interference with the free market in shares and securities of companies'. There was a strong feeling, then and later, that the operation of The Stock Exchange should, so far as was practicable, be left untrammelled. This stemmed from a belief that the stock market was the best available mechanism for determining the value of a company and of its shares and indeed also of relative values. In the material submitted in the preparation of the 1968 Code the National Association of Pension Funds considered that it would be wrong to prevent purchases in the market while a bid was outstanding 'because the market is always the right place for sale and purchases to be made, even during the currency of an offer, and also the market is the only place where true values can be determined'. The strength of this feeling came out very clearly when the Monopolies Commission in its report on the bid of the Rank Organization for De La Rue (Commons Paper 298 of 1969, paragraph 82) said that the Commission was a better judge of the relative efficiency of the two companies than the stock market. This attracted a good deal of comment hostile to the Commission's view and illustrated the wide belief in the virtues of a free market.

Events were, however, upsetting the grounds on which it had been considered that a completely free market and take-over bids could run in parallel without difficulty. There were two broad respects in which market purchases were impinging on take-over practice as it had developed in the sixties.

The first arose out of the development of the paper bid. In 1964 cash formed more than half the total consideration in take-over bids. By 1970 the cash proportion had fallen to 23 per cent. The introduction of capital gains tax in 1965 made paper more attractive than cash, since no tax was then immediately payable and the introduction of corporation tax made debentures and loan stock attractive to the offeror company. Rising share prices made an offeror with a high price/earnings ratio more ready to offer his shares in consideration for offeree shares. The value of the offeror's paper became important and that was determined by market prices.

The Monopolies Commission in its report in June 1969 on the proposed Unilever/Allied Breweries and Rank/De La Rue mergers pointed out that, if a company's shares had a high price/earnings ratio, it was well placed to offer its own shares, on terms favourable to itself, as consideration for a take-over bid. It could then, after a successful bid, often show an increased earning per share (thus possibly justifying a still higher share price) although there had been over-all no increase (or even some decrease) in profits or efficiency. This was a point that had been developed in several United States studies of merger activity.[1]

The Commission wished the offeror's shareholders to be given certain information when the consideration was more than a given percentage (which they did not specify) of the value of the issued capital of the offeror. This obviously related to paper offers. Further, if the share price of the offeree company was rising, the requirement than an offeror who had obtained control by market purchases should offer the remaining share holders the *average* price he had paid was felt to offer

[1] See for example, E. R. Aranow and H. A. Einhorn, *Tender Offers for Corporate Control* (1973), pp. 2–4.

too low a price as compared with the current price of the shares. An offeror could make an offer in securities of doubtful value, then buy in the market for cash, then offer the same securities to the value of the average price of his cash purchases, but no one had any certainty that the securities would retain their value.

In late 1970 and early 1971 the Director-General (Mr Ian Fraser) became troubled about cases in which a company—which might be a shell company or a small company operating in a field wholly different from that contemplated for the merged company—made a paper bid for a company bigger than itself. The bidder then went into the market and bought sufficient shares to gain control. The remaining shareholders had then only two courses open to them, neither of which might be satisfactory—to accept paper that might not hold its value or to find themselves in a minority position that might prove very uncomfortable.

The second broad respect in which market purchases were having an unsettling effect was more fundamental and related to the manner in which the control of a company was secured. Since 1968 the Panel had gradually consolidated the position that those who acquired a significant block of shares selectively, i.e. from directors or from large shareholders who controlled a company, must make an offer on the same terms to the remaining shareholders. Rule 10 provided that directors who effectively controlled a company should not transfer control unless the buyer undertook to extend a comparable offer to the remaining shareholders. Rule 26, although dealing mainly with partial bids, stated that only in very exceptional circumstances could the Panel relieve someone who had made a deal with a significant minority from an obligation to make a similar offer to the other shareholders. 30 per cent of the voting rights in the hands of directors or controlling shareholders was considered to give effective control.

This interpretation of Rules 10 and 26 had hitherto been consistent with freedom in the market. The conventional wisdom was that it took a long time to buy control through market purchases—perhaps up to two years in a large company with widely distributed shareholdings—and that a shareholder would thus have ample opportunity to realize what was happening and to decide whether to sell in the market. The case often cited was Pilkington's acquisition of Triplex over a period of several years. As late as September 1970 the Panel Executive informed a firm of stockbrokers that the Code envisaged that a purchase of control through the market was unobjectionable, because purchases in the market did not quickly lead to a change of control and shareholders had adequate warning of what was afoot. In line with the view that it was enough to warn the shareholders of efforts at control through purchase of shares, the Jenkins Committee had recommended, and the Companies Act 1967 had provided, that the beneficial ownership of 10 per cent or more of the shares of a company should be reported to the company and entered in a register. There had also to be registration of a director's transactions in the shares of his company.

However, market purchases became an important weapon in the arsenal of a bidder and the more closely bids were regulated, the more attractive were purchases outside the bid. Moreover as the small private investors came to hold fewer shares and share registers began to show more and more large holdings by insurance companies, pensions funds, unit trusts, and trading companies, the idea that the acquisition of control by market purchases was a slow business ceased to be generally true. Substantial holdings could often be acquired quickly by an approach to financial institutions holding large blocks of shares.

By the end of 1970 and beginning of 1971, it was being noted that an offeror could obtain control by market purchases long before a formal offer was made to shareholders generally. The acquisition in 1971 of Dorland by Barclay Securities and of Regis Property by British Land were cases in point. It is against this general background that one must examine the action taken by the City Working Party and the Panel in the booming take-over activity of 1971 and 1972.

WAREHOUSING

At a quarterly meeting of the Take-over Panel held on 9 June 1970 the Director General (Mr Ian Fraser) reported that the executive was concerned because some of the younger generation of financiers were, to use an American expression, 'warehousing' before a bid. There had been recent instances where a number of apparently independent parties accumulated within a short period blocks of shares in a potential offeree company in circumstances where no individual holding was large enough to call for disclosure under the Companies Act 1967 but where the total holding acquired by these parties, who were acting 'in concert', represented a critical factor in the mounting of an offer. Those concerned might accumulate holdings in a number of companies and it would be a matter for discussion who should make the bid in any particular case. The Panel asked the City Working Party whether amendments should be made to the Code with a view to ensuring that the purchases of these critical holdings by persons acting in concert, effected within six months before the date of the offer, had to be disclosed and so come under the scrutiny of the Panel and of public opinion.

In September 1970 the City Working Party amended Rule 8 to provide that, where an offer is announced, not only must any existing holding by the offeror in the offeree company be disclosed but also the holding in the offeree company of any company owned or controlled by anyone acting in concert with the offeror in relation to the offer. Rule 16 [now 17] was amended to provide that similar information should be provided in the offer document. The amendments of Rule 8 and Rule 16 are an illustration of the ability of self-regulatory machinery to take action quickly and at an early stage of a development. A government department would almost certainly have felt obliged to wait for more positive evidence of abuse before it could move in the matter.

ADEPTON/WILLIAMS HUDSON

In the course of 1970 there was some concern about cases[1] in which a potential offeror built up a sizeable stake in a company, made a paper offer (often in loan stock) which might not be very attractive to the offeree shareholders and then made large purchases in the market which gave him control, or a large measure of control, of the company. These market purchases might be mainly from large investors who were anxious to sell rather than be landed with the paper: and they might be spaced out to prevent the average price paid rising too high. If the average price was above the value of the paper offer, a revised

---

[1] Notably Sterling Guarantee Trust's bid for Gamages in the autumn of 1970 and British Land's bid for Regis Property in the early months of 1971.

offer would have to be made, but this could still be in paper and the fear might be that the paper would not maintain its value in the longer term. The remaining offeree shareholders (many probably small shareholders) then had the choice of accepting the paper offer or of remaining as minority shareholders in the taken-over company. Experience suggested that most shareholders would feel obliged to take the paper, however little they liked it, rather than be locked in the taken-over company. The general view was that this technique gave the offeror a means of acquiring a company very cheaply and could be unfair to offeree shareholders who were induced or coerced, by the obtaining of control through market purchases, into accepting paper about which they had doubts regarding its long-term value and indeed its true existing value.

The general issue came to a head in the offer made in March 1971, by Adepton for the ordinary shares of Williams Hudson. Adepton was a listed company with interests in property and finance. A majority of the Adepton shares were owned by Argo Caribbean Group Ltd., a private investment company resident in the Bahamas and controlled by the trustees of a settlement by Mr David Rowland. Adepton had an authorized share capital of £2,000,000 of which £972,000 had been issued. At the end of 1970, the net assets of the company were estimated to be worth £2,205,000 against a book value of £1,012,000. The directors forecast profits (before tax) of £80,000 for the fifteen months to 31 March 1971. In connection with a current acquisition of a controlling interest in Consolidated Signal Company, Adepton was due to issue convertible unsecured loan stock 1990/5 at $8\frac{1}{2}$ per cent to a maximum amount of £1,184,665. At the beginning of March 1971 Adepton had also incurred a guarantee liability of £1,200,000.

Williams Hudson was a much larger company, being a listed holding company with subsidiaries engaged in sea and land transportation. It had an issued capital of £3,054,000 and Adepton estimated its net tangible assets to be worth £8,814,000. Profits before tax for the year ended 31 March 1970 had been £824,000: less was expected for 1971 but £1,000,000 was forecast for 1972. In 1970 and the early months of 1971, Argo acquired by market purchases 14.46 per cent of Williams Hudson's share capital. On 5 March 1971 Adepton announced an offer of 80p nominal of 9¼ per cent convertible unsecured loan stock 1990/5 for every Williams Hudson ordinary share. If the loan stock was valued at par, this offer was worth 80p per share, compared with an average price over the previous three months of 73.2p. The offer document was issued on 6 March. After the announcement of the offer Adepton bought heavily in the market. The price of Williams Hudson shares rose from 80p on 4 March to 90p on 12 March. By 15 March Adepton held in all 41 per cent of the Williams Hudson shares in issue and then stopped buying.

Williams Hudson appealed to the Panel on a number of points and in particular asked the Panel to rule, on the basis of General Principles 1, 3, and 8, that the Adepton offer should be underwritten for cash. The Panel considered that many shareholders had not in practice an opportunity to sell their shares during the few days that Adepton stood in the market. Knowledgeable shareholders, close to the market, had an advantage over the small shareholder, particularly if the latter did not have speedy access to a stockbroker. The Panel did not consider that any of this was contrary to the then existing Code.

Between two sessions of the Panel Adepton produced a revised offer under which for every six Hudson ordinary shares they offered five Adepton ordinary shares and £2.40 of 8½ per cent convertible loan stock, 1990/5, being a further tranche of the loan stock issued to the Consolidated Signal shareholders. The Panel did not consider that it was possible to place a firm figure on the value of the securities that were being offered, which made it difficult to apply Rule 31 [now 32]. This required an increase in an offer if shares were purchased at prices above the value of the offer. The Panel insisted on a cash alternative which was eventually settled at 87½p per share. The Panel said that those who make offers in paper and follow their offer with massive purchases in the market would do well to assure themselves, in the light of all the circumstances relating to the two companies and their consolidation, that the paper would have a market value capable of reasonable estimation. More important for the future were the Panel's general observations. The Panel said:

'It may be that our constituent bodies will wish to consider whether the Rules of the Code should be altered to secure a greater degree of equity as between all shareholders. The aim would be to consider how the Code could best be amended to impose suitable and practical limitations on the existing freedom of an offeror for paper to conduct a market raid on the shares of the offeree in the opening stages of his bid. We believe that it should be possible to reconcile the principle of a free market with the principle that the offeree shareholders should all be treated similarly and should have reasonable time and sufficient information to form a judgment on the offer'.

The Panel's statement on the Adepton/Williams Hudson case was dated 2 April 1971. On 8 September 1971 the City Working Party promulgated Rule 29A [now 33]. Under this Rule, if the offeror or anyone acting in concert acquired 15 per cent of the shares to which the offer referred, during the offer period or within one year before its commencement, then, except with the specific approval of the Panel, the offer must be in cash or accompanied by a cash alternative at not less that the highest cash price (excluding stamp duty and commission) paid for the shares acquired in the offer period and one year beforehand. The Panel could also apply the Rule when there were exceptional circumstances and where the application of the Rule seemed to be needed to give effect to General Principle 8 (all shareholders to be treated alike). By amendment of Rule 16, any purchases in the year before the offer had to be disclosed in the offer document. The new Rule 29A made much more difficult the aggressive reverse bid—i.e. where a small company with a high gearing attempted to acquire a much larger company. The statement issued at the time by the City Working Party indicated that the need for the new rule had been strongly pressed by institutional investors.

An article in *The Times* of 15 September 1971 commented:

There are times when the City seems to stick to traditional concepts and principles when they are no longer in concert with the facts of life. It is the real measure of the success of the Take-over Panel that it can both treat some of those concepts with disdain and persuade those who operate under its aegis to do the same. And in that respect there has been no more significant City decision in the past two or three years than this month's new rule of the Take-over Code . . . It sounds innocent enough but it finally puts paid to a hoary concept which has disrupted every attempt in the past twelve years to inject equity into the conduct of take-over bids. The concept was enshrined in the first of the four sets of rules of conduct for bids and has been transmitted ever since in the immortal phrase that it is undesirable 'to fetter the market'.

Of course if you have an open securities market it is self-evidently undesirable to impose unnecessary restrictions on the freedom to deal in securities. But the history of regulation in London has been a history of the attempt to reconcile that laudable aim with the equally laudable aim that all shareholders in a company are entitled to be treated alike.

OZALID/NORCROS/CONSOLIDATED SIGNAL/VENESTA

In October 1971 Ozalid Company announced their intention to make an offer for the issued share capital of Venesta International. The offer was to be partly in shares and partly in convertible unsecured loan stock and was valued at 42p. The Venesta shares had been as high as 78p but had fallen to 18p at one point in 1971. On the Ozalid offer, they rose above 50p. In November Norcros announced a rival bid, also in shares and unsecured loan stock, which valued the Venesta share at 52p; it had the support of the Venesta board.

Meantime Consolidated Signal Company, on 2 November, had privately purchased a block of 1,000,000 Venesta shares at 55p. Further purchases were made at prices ranging up to 57p and on 17 December Consolidated's brokers announced that Consolidated had just over 50 per cent of the Venesta shares and had acquired 'legal control' of Venesta. The Panel examined a number of allegations made against Venesta, principally in relation to the possible frustration of the announced offers, which could contravene Rule 33 [now Rule 37], but did not find them proved. The Panel pointed out that the then existing Rules did not impose any obligation on an individual who had acquired control by a series of purchases in the market to endeavour to obtain the remaining shares. If, however, the object of the purchaser was to frustrate a bid, the then Rule 33 came into play. The Panel thought that the City Working Party should consider the difficulty of elucidating and establishing the true motive in many of these cases.

In the meantime we think it right to say that the Panel consider that in the case where a third party intervenes in a bid situation for an offeree company, in which prior to the announcement of the offer he had no interest, the Rule would justify the executive requiring such third party, once he had secured 10 per cent of the issued shares of the offeree company, to satisfy them affirmatively that he was buying for investment purposes only and would stop short of control. In an appropriate case, the Panel executive might well permit further purchases to be made only up to a limited total or at a price not exceeding the value of the offer. In such a case, therefore, the intervener might have to consider the alternative of making a general offer.

The Panel's statement was dated 6 January 1972. On 18 January 1972 the City Working Party promulgated a new Rule—29B—to deal with the situation. In a statement issued with the text of the new Rule, the City Working Party said that since the Take-over Code was first instituted there had been an underlying principle that the purchase of effective control or even legal control of a company through the normal operations of the stock market did not constitute a take-over or merger transaction which would bring into operation the provisions of the Code. This view was based on the assumption that as a matter of practice it would be impossible to acquire control of a company through market purchases except over a very extended period of time, during which shareholders would be aware of what was happening and could take their own decisions regarding their personal investments.

This view was no longer tenable against the background of the increased awareness of investors of the implications of bid situations and the fact that it had proved possible for effective control of companies to be acquired through marker purchases in a matter of days. This problem had been considered by the City Working Party in relation to the revision of the Code, which was then in hand, and it had been decided to adopt a new Rule which would bring within the control of the Panel any purchases which involved the acquisition of 40 per cent or more of the voting rights attributable to the equity share capital of a company.

The City Working Party said that to ensure that everyone was aware of the situation, the new Rule was not being held back to be incorporated in the revised rules, but was being brought into effect at once. Rule 29B provided that any person who acquired, whether by a series of purchases over a period of time or not, shares which (together with shares purchased by other persons acting in concert with such person) carried 40 per cent of the voting rights attributable to the equity share capital of a company must (except in a case specifically approved by the Panel) extend within a reasonable period of time an unconditional offer to the holders of the remaining equity share capital of the offeree company. This offer should, in respect of each class of equity share capital, be in cash or be accompanied by a cash alternative at not less than the highest cash price (excluding stamp duty and commission) paid by such person(s) for shares of that class within the preceding year. The Rule did not apply in a case where a person already held shares carrying 40 per cent or more of such voting rights on 18 January 1972.

Once again, the City Working Party had shown how quickly and decisively it was prepared to move, on need being shown. The Working Party had held strongly to the view that the purchase of control through the market did not represent a take-over transaction. Faced, however, with the fact that control could now be acquired in the market in a matter of days, the Working Party did not hesitate to make a fundamental change in its previous thinking.

SHUT-OUT BIDS

While these cases, involving the purchase of large blocks of shares, were under examination, the Panel was also grappling with the problem of a prior commitment to accept an offer in respect of a large and perhaps decisive block of shares. A bid in which the offeror had obtained the prior agreement of directors or shareholders holding a controlling interest to accept the bid before the bid was launched became known as a 'shut-out bid'. The name was probably derived from the analogy (not very close) of the bridge player who makes a bid so unexpectedly high that he effectively silences his opponents. If the offeror had bought a controlling interest beforehand, Rule 10 of the 1969 Code would normally operate to require him to make a general offer to all the shareholders, but he would of course have acquired control irrespective of the offer. There was no Rule in 1970 or 1971 that dealt specifically with an irrevocable commitment in respect of a controlling block of shares to accept a forthcoming bid. Some potential offerors were reluctant to make an offer, if there was going to be a struggle between rival bidders; and this might mean that, without the certainty of success, no offer would be made. But obviously the practice of prior commitment could be detrimental to shareholders, if it resulted from collusive actions between two boards of directors who, for whatever reason, were determined to ensure that no rival offer, though perhaps better, could be made.

Three cases[1] had to be considered by the Panel in 1971, on appeal from rulings by the Panel executive. Shut-out bids were not then expressly governed by any Rule and the Panel had to consider the cases in the light of General Principle 3 (shareholders to have sufficient information to reach a decision), General Principle 7 (control to be exercised in good faith), General Principle 11 (directors to consider the shareholders' interests taken as a whole) and Rule 9 (directors should act in the interests of shareholders taken as a whole, but shareholders in companies effectively controlled by directors to remember that the attitude of the board is decisive). The legal right of a shareholder to sell his shares to whom he chose had, in the case of directors holding controlling interests, to be reconciled with the duty of directors to act in the interests of the whole body of shareholders. While the Code expressly said that the Panel could not be expected to pronounce on the merits or demerits of any individual offer, it was difficult in these cases to avoid some appraisal of merit especially if the offeror was offering shares in his company as all or part of the consideration.

In one case the Panel pointed out that the reconciliation of General Principle 11 and Rule 9 [now in General Principle 11] could cause difficulties in cases where directors held a majority of the shares. 'While it is clear that the paramount duty of directors is to consider the interests of the general body of shareholders, and, in the advice they give or decisions they take, not to prefer their own interests or those of any special group or section, it is also the case that the control of companies lies with a majority of the shareholders rather than with a minority' (Coral statement of 18 June 1971). The Panel decided that the test must be whether in their view the directors had acted in good faith (i.e. whether they had observed General Principle 7 and Rule 9).

[1] The companies bid for and the dates of the Panel statements were J. Coral (18 June 1971), Blaskey Wallpapers (29 September 1971), and W. Wood and Son (3 December 1971).

In October 1971 the Panel suggested that the City Working Party, in revising the Code, should consider the position of shut-out bids. Meantime, the Panel issued Practice Note 7 which *inter alia*, indicated:

(a) Where more than one party has made an approach to a board and seems to be contemplating a bid, no shut-out bid should be accepted without all parties being made aware that a potential competitive situation exists and being given an opportunity to make a statement to the shareholders of the offeree company before the shut-out is given.

(b) The Panel executive should be consulted before any shut-out bid is accepted.

As illustrating the prevalence of shut-out bids, there were seventy between October 1971 and June 1972.

1972 REVISION OF THE CODE

The City Working Party, in issuing a revised Code in February 1972 had the advantage of the Panel's experience in handling nearly 1,200 take-over transactions since April 1969. The fact that in this period of nearly three years only sixteen cases had required reference to the full Panel for adjudication spoke well of the smooth working and co-operation between the Panel executive and those who were professionally engaged in take-overs and mergers.

Rule 33 incorporated Rule 29A which had been made in September 1971 in consequence of the Adepton case. Rule 35 incorporated Rule 29B and placed an obligation on those who acquired shares carrying 40 per cent of the voting rights to extend an offer to the rest of the shareholders. In the light of experience, important amendments were made to deal with directors and their associates who had controlling interests in companies and who were negotiating a transfer of shares to a potential offeror. The purchaser from a limited number of sellers of a significant holding that conferred effective control had to extend the offer to the remaining shareholders (Rule 34). Originally the responsibility had been placed on the controlling offeree directors who sold their shares to obtain an undertaking from the purchaser of their shares to make a general offer to the remaining shareholders. Now the obligation was placed specifically on the purchaser of the shares to make a general offer (Rule 34). Directors who contemplated rejecting an offer or preferring a lower offer were recommended to take competent outside advice (Rule 9).

There was a Rule dealing with shut-out bids (Rule 11). Directors and persons acting in concert with them who contemplated entering into an irrevocable commitment to accept an offer in respect of shares that gave effective control were required to secure the prior consent of the Panel. The intention was to ensure that the directors had taken into account all relevant considerations. (A few months later the Panel, at a quarterly meeting, agreed that it should be a prerequisite of Panel consent to a shut-out that the directors had received competent outside advice.) Controlling shareholders who were not directors, or acting in concert with directors, were not subject to the Rule. The 1971/2 annual report said that the Panel executive would normally give consent where it was reasonably established that no competitive offeror had made approaches in the recent past or where the company concerned was facing a crisis of survival. There was no requirement for a company to advertise its availability before a shut-out was concluded.

Where an offeror bought shares during a bid period at a higher price than that contained in his offer, he had to increase his offer to the highest price paid for the shares so bought (Rule 32). The previous Rule, which depended on a calculation of the weighted average price of shares bought above the offer price had proved increasingly difficult to work in practice. It was also thought to have worked unfairly in some cases where the average price could be well below the value of later paper bids, particularly in contested bids.

A previous Rule had provided that an associate of the offeror or offeree should satisfy the Panel that dealings by him, in the market or otherwise, were not frustrating a bid and acting contrary to the interests of shareholders. The Rule was now restricted to associates with a commercial interest in the outcome of the offer (Rule 37). It was considered that shareholders and their associates were entitled to buy shares in an offer situation with the intention of building up holdings that would result in the offer failing. On the other hand, the value of shares to a buyer with a commercial interest might bear no relation to the value of the same shares for an ordinary investor.

One change did not attract notice, though it had been the subject of much discussion since the days of the Notes and Revised Notes. Rule 30 forbad those who were 'privy to the preliminary take-over discussions' from dealing in the shares of the offeree company before the publication of the offer. The offeror was now relieved of this restriction on dealing in the offeree shares. The arguments for allowing the offeror to deal were that a company was entitled to draw benefit from the fact that it put a higher value on a security than the rest of the market and that no question of a misuse of confidential information for personal advantage arose. To have insisted that an offeror should disclose his intention or not buy would have suggested that the securities market operated on the basis of complete disclosure of all relevant facts on both sides. It could not be said that this degree of 'market egalitarianism' was expected. There was also the practical problem that in some cases it was difficult to determine when an offeror had formed an intention to offer. This relaxation was confined to the offeror company itself and did not extend to directors, employees, or anyone connected with the offeror.

The 1972 changes in the Code raised in some minds the question whether the rules had been tilted against offerors and whether in consequence there might be fewer bids and in particular fewer large bids. The reasoning was that a large company endeavouring to acquire another large company would normally have only a limited amount of cash at its disposal and would want to offer paper. It would not have cash to finance all or most of the transaction. Yet, if it acquired 15 per cent or more of the shares of the offeree company in the market, it would have to make a cash bid for the oustanding shares or at least offer a cash alternative. Again if it had 40 per cent or more of the voting rights, it had to make a cash offer for the remainder. The failure of Commercial Union in its bid (worth £120,000,000) for Metropolitan Estates and Property Corporation and of Allied Breweries in its bid (worth £131,000,000) for Trust Houses Forte seemed to confirm the difficulties of the larger bidder. The failure of United Drapery Stores in May 1972 to acquire Debenhams seemed to tell the same story. However, in June 1972 Grand Metropolitan Hotels succeeded in gaining control of Watney Mann in a bid worth £435,000,000 and showed that the day of the large bid was not over.

VII

RECESSION AND AFTERWARDS

In the uneasy climate of the early 1970s any 'scandal' inevitably led to a questioning of the adequacy of the supervisory organization. The affairs of Lonrho—'the unpleasant and unacceptable face of capitalism'[1]—and of Sir Denys Lowson led to renewed speculation about the need for an American-style Securities and Exchange Commission. The real or imagined defects of the existing arrangements were paraded in great detail, and as often on these occasions the assumption, against all experience, was that new institutions would operate with dazzling efficiency. There was also a tendency to propose that a form of SEC should be inserted into the existing arrangements and to assume that the existing machinery could then go on functioning as before.[2] This has never been self-evident.

Lord Shawcross took up the cudgels on behalf of a system of voluntary self-regulation in his foreword to the Panel's report for 1972/3.

Without being in any way complacent, I am, for my own part, convinced that the system of voluntary self regulation which the City and industry established under the aegis of the Governor of the Bank of England remains more appropriate to the circumstances of this country than would be any statutory counterpart here of the Securities and Exchange Commission as it operates in the United States. It is true that occasionally some contrary opinion is expressed by publicists but our own study of the work of the S.E.C and our not infrequent conversations with those who conduct [business] in the different climate of the United States leave us in no doubt that the

[1] Used by Mr Edward Heath in a Commons debate on 15 May 1973.
[2] See, for example, Mr Victor Sandelson's long article in the *Sunday Times* of 29 April 1973 and the rejoinder on the following Sunday.

introduction of a statutory system here would in fact be a retrograde measure. We believe this to be the general conclusion of informed opinion.

In a statutory system those concerned are entitled to exercise their ingenuity in so ordering their affairs as to avoid the application of prohibitory or inconvenient rules. If a particular course of conduct is not expressly forbidden it is permissible: there is no grey area. With the City Code broadening down from precedent to precedent and obligatory in the spirit as well as in the letter, immediate steps can be taken to stop abuses as soon as they are discovered, and the fear of possible action undoubtedly prevents many abuses arising. This flexibility, the advisory function, the great expedition of its work and the authority behind it, are not, I believe, capable of reproduction in a statutory system.

The year 1973 proved to be particularly difficult. There were doubts about the merits of a number of take-over bids. Although the Panel did not concern itself with merits, some of the doubts and anxieties inevitably rubbed off on the Panel. There were allegations that companies were failing to observe the spirit of the Code and were twisting the rules to their tactical advantage. In a number of cases, the offeror, who was offering his own shares as consideration in the bid, used associates to buy them in the market in order to keep up or drive up the value of the paper being offered. The Code provided that such transactions by associates had to be publicly disclosed, but it did not go beyond that. This was a cause of disquiet, although *The Times*, in a leader of 14 May 1973, admitted that there seemed no obvious way of dealing with the matter.

Mr J. H. G. McMahon's failure in the summer of 1973 to make a bid for the printing and publishing firm of Maclehose in Glasgow, after he had acquired 35 per cent of the equity by selective purchases, illustrated the difficulty which the Panel had in dealing with parties that were not in the main stream of City activities. The case was complicated by legal proceedings instituted by Mr McMahon against the Maclehose board and against the Panel. Prophets of doom were hard at work and the *Guardian* of 22 August 1973 reported that 'some merchant banks thought that these legal moves could lead to an early demise of the panel in its present form'. The legal proceedings delayed action by the Panel and in the end Maclehose was taken over by another company.

In the spring of 1973 The Stock Exchange tightened up its requirements about what an offer document should tell shareholders regarding the offeror's future intentions. The offeror had to explain his policy for 'the continuance of the business of the offeree company', also 'any major changes intended to be introduced in the business, including redeployment of the fixed assets of the offeree and the setting out of the commercial justification of the proposed offer'. The offer document had also to state the offeror's plans 'for the continued employment of the existing employees of the offeree company, setting out the extent of any steps to be taken towards ceasing such employment'. This was also the time when the Panel and The Stock Exchange recommended that insider dealings should be made a criminal offence (see Chapter XIII below). The year 1973 was also marked by the passage of the Fair Trading Act (see Chapter XI below).

Recession

Although there had been some changes in general economic conditions since the inception of the Code, there had been no serious recession until the end of 1973. The broad assumption underlying most provisions of the Code was that an offeror would want to proceed with his offer and many of the provisions of the Code were designed to temper his ardour where he was pursuing his aim, or the offeree was trying to thwart him, in ways that were thought to be undesirable. Once an offer document had been issued, contractual obligations could arise between the offeror and offeree shareholders. The sensitive points were the withdrawal of an offer that had been announced but not yet formally proceeded with, or a failure to proceed with an offer rendered mandatory by the purchase of shares. The 1972 Code provided that the Panel had to be consulted before an announced offer was publicly withdrawn (Rule 8). No withdrawal from a mandatory bid was contemplated.

The recession at the end of 1973 came quite suddenly. A leader in *The Times* of 7 December 1973 said that the then existing world economic crisis had not been foreseen and that its future course could not be predicted in any reliable way. In this country a dispute about miners' wages led to a ban on overtime by the NUM, a three day week for industry and the declaration of a state of emergency. The Conservative Chancellor of the Exchequer (Mr Anthony Barber, now Lord Barber) announced on 17 December 1973 that the Government proposed to impose new and more onerous taxation upon property developers; and this and other factors had an adverse effect on the shares of property companies. The property boom collapsed. Towards the end of 1973, or in January 1974, several companies which had announced bids, or were under an obligation to make bids because of large acquisitions of shares, approached the Panel executive for agreement that they might withdraw from their offer because of the change in economic conditions. The executive refused to agree and, where there was an appeal to the Panel, the Panel upheld the executive's ruling.

ST MARTINS PROPERTY CORPORATION/HAY'S WHARF

The most important case, because of the amounts involved and the complexity of the issues, concerned St Martins' bid for Hay's Wharf. There had for a considerable time been discussions between the management of St Martins and that of Hay's Wharf about a possible merger. In November 1973 St Martins which already held 2 per cent of the Hay's Wharf ordinary shares acquired a further 32 per cent from Lockfold, a finance company: and this created an obligation under Rule 34 to make an offer for the remaining shares. St Martins had enough authorized but unissued shares to provide the shares that were part of the consideration for the 32 per cent shares it had acquired, but St Martins shareholders' approval would be required to authorize the capital needed for a general offer, part of which would be in St Martins shares. On 28 December Warburgs, on behalf of St Martins, said that, in the light of the general situation and the Chancellor's statement of 17 December, the directors of St Martins could no longer recommend their shareholders to approve the increase in share capital required to implement the offer. The Panel, after a lengthy hearing, decided that the company had an obligation to make an offer for the outstanding Hay's Wharf shares on the same terms as those afforded to the holders of the 32 per cent.

An extraordinary general meeting of the St Martins shareholders was held on 25 March and voted against the increase in capital and also against the bid for Hay's Wharf. A poll was not resorted to. The Panel then issued a long statement, dated 5 April 1974, in which it accepted that the shareholders were free to vote as they chose, but that the effect of their action was to put the company in breach of Rule 34. The Panel outlined the sanctions it could apply, including a recommendation to the Council of The Stock Exchange to suspend the listing of St Martins shares. This, however, would impose hardship not only on the shareholders who had chosen to disregard the Panel's ruling but also on those who had supported it. The Panel therefore decided to give instructions to the directors with which they could comply without further recourse to shareholders, in the following terms:

1. St Martins shall not exercise the voting rights attached to its present holding until it has made a general offer to all shareholders in accordance with the requirements of Rule 34 on the same terms as those obtained by Lockfold.
2. St Martins shall not acquire any further shares carrying voting rights or any other securities convertible into shares carrying voting rights until it has made such a general offer. This prohibition will not apply to the acquisition of shares or convertible securities under bonus or rights issues but such shares (and the shares derived from conversion of any convertible securities) will be treated, for the purposes of this Ruling, as if they formed part of the present holding.
3. St Martins shall not dispose of any part of its present holding (or any further shares derived from such holding under bonus or rights issues) until it has made such a general offer. St Martins will however be entitled to accept a general offer made by an unconnected third party, but only with the consent of the Panel if that offer is not recommended by the Hay's Wharf board. This paragraph shall not prohibit St Martins from disposing of new shares, nil paid, arising from any rights issue.

When the Kuwait Investment Office acquired St Martins in September 1974 they accepted the restrictions which the Panel had imposed in respect of the Hay's Wharf shares. The restrictions were removed in May 1977. They had been imposed as a measure of protection for the shareholders of Hay's Wharf and by May 1977 the board of Hay's Wharf was no longer asking for their retention. The surrounding circumstances had also changed, with a current bid and possible further bids.

GENERAL STATEMENT

On 15 January 1974 the Panel issued a statement of which the main provisions were as follows:

Changes in circumstances

The City Panel will of course give careful consideration to the facts of each particular case which may come before it. In general, however, the Panel considers that a change in economic or industrial conditions, or even in legislative policy, which may suggest that a proposed acquisition will not be as advantageous for the offeror company as was hoped when the intention to offer was first announced, is one of the hazards which has to be accepted in a take-over situation. Even in more normal conditions than now exist, markets are volatile and it must be expected that they will sometimes over a period show wide fluctuations, which may for a time put a different complexion on the economics of a particular offer. On the other hand, falls in market levels or depressions in the general economy are usually followed after a time by recovery. Similarly legislative policy depends upon the exigencies of the time. The City Panel consider that a change in economic, industrial or political circumstances would not normally justify the withdrawal of an announced offer. To justify unilateral withdrawal the Panel would normally require some circumstance of an entirely exceptional nature and amounting to something of the kind which would frustrate a legal contract. It must be remembered that the terms and timing of an announcement of intention to offer and of the posting of offer documents are, subject to the Code, entirely in the hands of the offeror. It is therefore right that an offeror should accept the risk of a change of circumstances in the intervening period. Once an offer is announced, the market in the shares of the offeree company is likely to be, at least to some extent, supported by the price at which the offer has been fixed. It follows that withdrawal would contribute to the market having been a false one.

The Panel has been asked about the position of directors of a company who, having announced an intention to make an offer, become convinced, before a legally enforceable obligation to offer has arisen, that circumstances have changed so as to make the proposal no longer economically advantageous to their company. Directors are of course trustees for their company in the exercise of their powers. They must always act in good faith; they ought to consider the long term interests of the company and to have regard not only to immediate financial considerations but to the company's public reputation. Thus they should not neglect consideration of the public interest, the regulations of The Stock Exchange (which attach great importance to compliance with the City Code) and the City Code itself, adhered to as it is by the Confederation of British Industry. Consideration of such factors as these have been described as constituting enlightened self-interest on the part of the company concerned, which is expected to behave as a 'good citizen'. It is not for the Panel, nor even for lawyers, to indicate to directors how they should act in the best interests of their company; this is a matter on which each director must satisfy his own conscience after having regard to all relevant considerations. The Panel can only say that for their part they expect companies to accept the Code as binding upon them; it is well established that the courts will not interfere with directors' exercise of discretionary powers unless it is proved that they have acted from some improper motive or arbitrarily and capriciously. Compliance with the requirements of the City Code voluntarily adopted by the City institutions and by industry in order to promote orderly markets and secure fair treatment for shareholders would certainly not be so considered. The general position is indicated in General Principle 2 of the Code and directors must give due weight to this and the other requirements of the Code.

The general acceptance of the Code, as administered by the Panel, has in more than one case in the past led to the acceptance of some economic disadvantage in the short term. To be offset against this disadvantage is the long term benefit to investors and the financial and industrial community as a whole and to the company in question—as part of that community—which the Code seeks to achieve.

COMBINED ENGLISH STORES/DAVID GREIG

At all times the Panel emphasized that each case must be examined in relation to the particular facts of the case. On 3 January 1974 the boards of Combined English Stores and David Greig announced an agreed bid which placed a value of 175p in each Greig share. On 28 January the two boards indicated that they would seek Panel approval for new terms which placed a value of 136p on a Greig share.

In agreeing to the revised offer, the Panel had regard to the facts that the board of Combined English Stores entered into the bid on an understanding about the level of recent profits which proved to be wrong and for which some responsibility must rest with the Greig board, also that there were no substantial purchases of shares at the original offer price from directors or substantial holders of shares. The Panel was satisfied that the case did not turn on a change in economic circumstances but on a mistake in the preparation of figures for a past period. The Panel, however, took the occasion to say again:

> The withdrawal of a public offer, once announced, is a matter of serious concern since such offers affect market values. This is particularly so when the offer is being withdrawn or revised on the ground that the offer was too high, since a false market will have been created. Thus shares in the offeree company may have been bought at a price above the previous market price in the belief that the offer would be proceeded with, and existing shareholders may have refrained from selling for the same reason.

BOOTS/HOUSE OF FRASER

The boards of Boots and House of Fraser announced on 6 November 1973 that they had completed negotiations for a merger of the two businesses. Details of the offer to be made by Boots for the ordinary shares of the House of Fraser were published on 8 November. On 27 November the proposed merger was referred to the Monopolies and Mergers Commission. On 30 November the two parties confirmed that they would go ahead with the merger if the Monopolies and Mergers Commission did not object to it. This was not a mandatory bid. On 1 March 1974, the Panel met to consider an application by the board of Boots to be allowed to withdraw the offer. The board of Boots said that they would be unable to recommend their shareholders to increase the share capital of Boots for the purpose of the merger, because of the radical change in trading conditions since November which, in their view, was likely to affect House of Fraser more adversely than Boots. They, therefore, wanted to withdraw the offer. Boots estimate of the likely fall in the profitability of the House of Fraser was disputed by the board of the House of Fraser. The Panel refused to allow the offer to be withdrawn and decided to issue a further general statement. In the event, the Monopolies and Mergers Commission found against the merger and this was accepted by the Government.

FURTHER GENERAL STATEMENT

On 13 March 1974 the Panel issued a further general statement. After rehearsing the main points made in the statement of 15 January 1974 the Panel indicated the need for all conditions to which an offer was subject to be clearly set out.

Conditions should not be included which were dependent on subjective judgements by directors or the fulfilment of which were in the hands of directors, since such conditions created unnecessary uncertainty. In regard to the need for approval by the shareholders of the offeror company, the statement went on:

Shareholders' Approval—There remains the question of the position of directors and shareholders where a resolution of the shareholders of the offeror company is required, e.g., for an increase in authorised capital or under the Regulations of The Stock Exchange.

A refusal by offeror shareholders to pass any necessary resolution should not be equated with a withdrawal by directors of an offer. The condition of shareholders' approval would have been specified at the outset.

The Panel does not take the view that directors are obliged by the Code to recommend shareholders to vote in favour of such a resolution in all circumstances. Equally, the directors are not free to ignore what they have done in the name of the company. The failure to proceed with an announced offer, even an offer subject to conditions, is a serious matter and the directors must bear this in mind in their recommendation to shareholders. The Panel will not criticise a board that has weighed up, and is seen to have weighed up, all factors in its recommendation. The shareholders are free to take their decision in the light of all the circumstances.

The position is different where a company has already incurred under the Code a mandatory obligation to make an offer because of large purchases of shares. Most of these cases involve a cash offer and it is exceptional for the consent of shareholders to be required. Obviously, directors should not incur an obligation to make an unconditional offer under the Code unless they are in a position to honour the obligation. In the highly exceptional case where the approval of shareholders is required, directors have to give their advice to shareholders in the knowledge that a refusal by shareholder to pass the necessary resolution will give rise to a breach of the Code and will result in some penalty or sanction, depending on the circumstances, being imposed on the company in breach.

Announcements of offers—In view of the above the Panel stresses the serious responsibility that lies on directors at the time of making an announcement of an offer.

OFFER PRICE UNDER RULE 33

Rule 33 required an offeror who had purchased 15 per cent or more of the offeree's voting shares in the twelve months before the offer to make the offer in cash, or with a cash alternative, at the highest price paid for the shares. Inevitably in the changed economic situation there were requests that the Panel should exercise a power given under the Rule and waive the requirement to offer the highest price. The Panel, in considering these applications, had regard to the size and timing of purchases during the twelve months. It was less likely to make a concession if the purchase was from an insider. It also considered whether the lower price suggested was acceptable to the offeree board.

DISPOSAL OF HOLDINGS

The worsening economic situation forced some companies to realize shareholdings. In some cases these might have been built up before the acquisition of 30 per cent of the voting shares involved an obligation to make a bid for the remaining shares. Sometimes those concerned argued that they could get a better price for the shares if they sold them as one holding to one purchaser, but the Panel was not prepared to waive the requirement that any purchaser who bought 30 per cent or more had to make a bid.

CREST/CORPORATE/ASHBOURNE INVESTMENTS

The same period saw the start of the Panel's longest case—Ashbourne Investments—which is described in Appendix A. On 6 December 1973 Crest International Securities and Corporate Guarantee Trust and their associates announced that they then held 43 per cent of the ordinary share capital of Ashbourne and that, in accordance with the Code, they would make an unconditional cash offer for the balance of the ordinary capital. The financial backing intended for the offer vanished in the collapse of the property boom and by July 1974 the failure of the consortium to issue an offer document was engaging the attention of the full Panel.

Mandatory Bids

The 1972 Code placed an obligation to make a general offer to all shareholders in two different sets of circumstances:
    (1) the purchase from directors or a limited number of sellers

of significant holdings which conferred effective control (Rule 34), and
(2) the acquisition of shares which resulted in holding 40 per cent of the voting rights (Rule 35).

The Panel executive usually treated a purchase of about 30 per cent of the shares from directors or holders of blocks of shares as conferring effective control. In the ordinary way directors with holdings totalling 30 per cent or more, would in fact be in control of the company and the purchaser of their shares stepped into their shoes. This was usually an easier way to secure control than by market purchases from various shareholders, when entrenched directors might have to be tackled as a separate and later operation: and a higher figure than 30 per cent (namely 40 per cent) was justified in respect of miscellaneous purchases. There was therefore a good reason for the two different standards.

There was, however, no agreement what percentage of voting rights gave effective control and in individual cases much depended on the distribution of the remaining shares. A block of 35 per cent would obviously not give control, if there was another block of 40 per cent. Counterwise a block of 20 per cent could give control of a company, if the remaining shares were widely spread in small holdings.

Statute law did not give much help on this issue. There was an inference in section 193(1)(c) of the Companies Act 1948 that one-third of the voting power gave control. Section 8(7) of the Monopolies and Mergers Act 1965 regarded anyone holding one quarter or more of the voting shares of a newspaper as having a controlling interest. Section 7 of the Insurance Companies Act 1974 regarded one third or more of the voting power as giving control of an insurance company. The Fair Trading Act 1973 in dealing with mergers, regarded a person as having control of a company in a variety of circumstances described in words but not in percentages. In practice the Panel, and more particularly the Panel executive, found difficulty in administering the two different standards of Rule 34 ('effective control') and Rule 35 (40 per cent), especially when regard had to be paid to acquisitions by persons acting in concert.

WEYBURN ENGINEERING

In 1972 two individuals built up from a limited number of sellers a holding of 29.75 per cent of the ordinary share capital of Weyburn Engineering Company. They then endeavoured to change the composition of the board in their favour at an extraordinary general meeting, but were defeated. In March 1973 they announced that they now held 39.3 per cent of the ordinary capital and intended to make a bid for the rest at $167\frac{1}{2}$p. Was this a mandatory bid, in which case it was made unconditionally, or an ordinary bid, in which case the offerors had to secure acceptances, which with their own holdings exceeded 50 per cent? The Weyburn board argued for the latter, in view of the unsuccessful effort to exercise control and change the composition of the board. The Panel executive ruled that, as the holding had been built up from selective purchases and now exceeded 30 per cent, this was a mandatory bid under Rule 34 and was unconditional. When the offer closed the offerors had secured in all 44.8 per cent of the ordinary share capital. The offerors then, by purchases and promises from supporters, built up their holding to over 50 per cent. One purchase of 42,000 shares at $180\frac{1}{2}$p was from a single seller who had bought the shares during the offer period. The Weyburn board claimed that, in the particular circumstances of Weyburn, effective control had not passed to the offerors until they had over 50 per cent of the shares and that the latest purchase should spark off a fresh general offer at $180\frac{1}{2}$p.

The Panel found against the Weyburn board. The Panel executive had ruled that effective control had been obtained at 39.3 per cent and that Rule 34 then came into operation. The board had accepted this. Once Rule 34 had been brought into operation and the offer period had expired, Rule 34 could not be invoked again. As in the case of a general offer under Rule 21 or Rule 35, once the offer period had expired, market purchases, whether selective or not, were permissible, and the effect of the Rule had been spent. Although in the present case the purchase of the 42,000 shares on 5 July was a selective one on a 'put through' from a single seller and certainly placed the fact of control beyond doubt, there was nothing in the Rules or practice of the Code to prevent it and the Panel suspected that in any event the purchase would not have been critical to the reality of effective control. Whether it would have been more equitable if the Weyburn shareholders had all been offered the higher price paid for that block of shares was another matter. There was a limit beyond which the Panel, in interpreting the express rules of the Code, could not go in the search for what might appear to be the most equitable solution.

The case highlighted the ambiguities and inconsistencies which arose in operation of the rules relating to the build-up of holdings by selective purchases and by market purchases. The case illustrated the anomaly that under Rule 21 (which dealt with an ordinary general offer) the offer might not be made unconditional until acceptances of over 50 per cent of the equity had been received, whereas under Rules 34 and 35, dealing with acquisitions made in the absence of a general offer, the assumption was that effective control arose with a lower holding than 50 per cent and the offer which those Rules required to be made had to be unconditional.

MARC GREGORY LTD/GREENCOAT PROPERTIES

In November 1972 Marc Gregory had secured, mainly from two shareholders, just under 30 per cent of the issued share capital of Greencoat. Being under 30 per cent, Marc Gregory had not incurred an obligation under Rule 34 to make a general offer to the remaining Greencoat shareholders. Later Marc Gregory made a number of fairly small purchases in the market which brought its total holdings to $32\frac{1}{2}$ per cent. This was not then regarded as requiring a general offer, on the ground that the latest acquisitions had not been made by selective purchases. One had, in effect, moved from Rule 34 to Rule 35 where the acquisition of 40 per cent by market purchases required a general offer. The argument was that the latest purchases had been made in the market, that the market should not be fettered, and that these acquisitions might have been made from any shareholder. Nevertheless, there was a feeling that it was somewhat artificial to allow a purchaser of shares to bring himself within an ace of securing 30 per cent by selective purchases and then to be able to reach the control point by purchases in the market. In the event, someone whom the Panel regarded as acting in concert with Marc Gregory, bought

1½ per cent of the issued share capital from one shareholder and the Panel ruled in July 1973 that this placed an obligation on Marc Gregory under Rule 34 to make an offer to the remaining shareholders. Rule 34, unlike Rule 35, did not specifically refer to persons acting in concert with the principal purchaser, but the Panel had treated persons acting in concert as bringing Rule 34 into operation and had so indicated in its report for 1972/3. At the end of its statement on the Greencoat case, dated 24 July 1973, the Panel said: 'This case and others have brought to attention some ambiguities and inconsistencies in the Rules, notably in the treatment of the building-up of holdings by selected purchases and by market purchases. Accordingly, the Panel will invite the City Working Party to examine the points raised by such cases.'

The matter was also convassed in the Press, including two articles in *The Times* of 16 and 17 July 1973 by Mr John Gillum of Samuel Montagu.

CST INVESTMENTS/GRENDON TRUST

From July to September 1973 Mr Christopher Selmes and his associates, Mr G. H. Camamile and Mr D. A. Taglight, together with companies controlled by them, bought and warehoused sustantial numbers of shares in Grendon, the holding in each case being less that 10 per cent of the issued capital. On 27 September, the Selmes Group announced publicly that it had acquired 40.6 per cent of the equity of Grendon and would make an unconditional offer for the remainder of the shares at the highest price the Group had paid. The offer was made by a new company, CST, controlled by Mr Selmes and his associates. At the time these transactions were criticized on the ground that, although not against the letter of the City Code, the warehousing was against the spirit of the Code (e.g. in an article in the *Sunday Telegraph* of 28 October 1973). Other aspects of these transactions were investigated by the Panel and subsequently by inspectors appointed under the Companies Acts.

DETAILS OF 1974 CODE AMENDMENTS

The upshot of these various happenings was an amendment of the Code in June 1974. Old Rules 34 and 35 were combined and replaced by one set of requirements (a new Rule 34). A general offer had to be made when a person (together with persons acting in concert with him)

(a) acquired shares which resulted in his having 30 per cent or more of the voting rights of a company or
(b) already holding between 30 per cent and 50 per cent of the voting rights, increased his percentage by more than 1 per cent in any period of twelve months.

The general offer was no longer to be unconditional but was to be conditional on the offeror receiving acceptances which, together with shares already owned, resulted in the offeror holding shares carrying more than 50 per cent of the voting rights. (The only other condition allowed related to a possible reference to the Monopolies and Mergers Commission.) It followed that any acquisition of shares which might give rise to an obligation to make a general offer could not be made if the implementation of the offer would depend upon the approval of offeror shareholders or upon any other consents or arrangements, such as exchange control consent or the completion of underwriting arrangements. Rule 11, which required directors transferring effective control to secure from the purchasers an agreement to make a general offer, was worded to correspond with Rule 34 and referred to directors transferring 30 per cent or more of the voting rights.

The principal effect of these changes was, first, to eliminate the problems arising under the old rules from the distinction between purchases from selected sellers and general market purchases, and secondly to establish 30 per cent of the voting rights of a company as effective control for Code purposes in virtually all circumstances. The new requirement that such an offer should be conditional on the receipt of a minimum level of acceptances was introduced because the requirement under the old rules that the offer should be unconditional operated against the interests of the majority of shareholders in some circumstances—particularly in cases where there was, or might have been, competition from another bidder. There had been superficial attractions in insisting that a mandatory bid should be unconditional, but a bidder with an unattractive offer could edge forward towards greater control by acquiring more than 30 per cent under price terms favourable to himself and then making an offer that might attract only a further 5 or 10 per cent of the shares.

In regard to the acquisition of shares, and for some other purposes, the Code included 'persons acting in concert' with the main party. The definition of persons acting in concert has proved to be a matter of great difficulty. The 1974 revision specified various categories of relationship where there was to be a presumption (which, however, was rebuttable) that action taken by any one member of the group (either a company or an individual) was motivated by a common group interest.

In its 1972/3 Report the Panel had indicated the importance it attached to the requirement of Rule 15 that an offeror must state its intentions with regard to the future of the offeree company. In the 1974 amendments Rule 15 was extended and amplified and required a statement by the offeror in the offer document as to:

(i) its intentions regarding the continuance of the business of the offeree company;
(ii) its intentions regarding any major changes to be introduced in the business, including any redeployment of the fixed assets of the offence;
(iii) the long-term commercial justification for the proposed offer;
(iv) its intentions with regard to the continued employment of the employees of the offeree company.

This was in line with Stock Exchange requirements (see page 84).

One of the objects of the Code was to prevent an offeree company from being under seige for a prolonged period. A new Rule (35) provided that, where a bid had been unsuccessful, the unsuccessful offeror must not acquire shares in the offeree company, during the twelve months following his offer, which would require him to make a mandatory bid under Rule 34. The long debate on bids which the offeror did not want to proceed with because of the change in the economic situation had its repercussions in a clarification and tightening up of the relevant rule—'An announced offer cannot be withdrawn without the consent of the Panel, which will be granted only in exceptional circumstances.' (Rule 9 now 10.) A number of procedural amendments were made in the light of experience.

VIII

FURTHER REVISION

TAKE-OVER activities remained quiet in 1974. General business uncertainty made firms unwilling to embark on acquisitions. Until an up-turn in 1976/7, activity remained low, though there were a number of large bids. Large bids do not necessarily involve more work for the Panel than small bids. A large bid is likely to be arranged by a major merchant bank that knows the rules and has every intention of abiding by them. The paper bid continued to be a feature of many large bids, though usually in the form of equity shares and not of loan stock. The long-term trend of interest rates was too uncertain for most offerors to want to issue loan stock at the then current rates. For bids as a whole, the feature of the period between 1974 and revision of the Code in 1976 was the decline of the paper bid and the revival of cash bids. With equities at a low level, offerors were reluctant to issue further ordinary shares where they had the ability to pay in cash. Nor did cash necessarily have any disadvantage for an offeree shareholder who at the time might be seeing a loss on his investment. Inquiries into allegations of insider dealings took up a great deal of the time of the Panel executive. In work more strictly concerned with the interpretation of the Code, mandatory bids under Rule 34 (as revised in 1974) continued to present problems, particularly in regard to persons acting in concert.

MANDATORY BIDS

The fact that the percentage holding that triggered off a mandatory bid had been brought down to 30 per cent for all classes of case meant that the holdings of persons who might be regarded as acting in concert became more important. There was also some widening of the responsibility of persons acting in concert. In the case of market purchases, the old Rule 35 had restricted the obligation to make a bid to those who had acquired shares in the offeree company by the time the mandatory obligation was triggered off and did not extend to those who bought or agreed to buy after that event. The 1974 provision was not as restricted. These changes affected directors, company pension funds and financial advisers, also subsidiary companies with their officers and advisers. There were a great many cases on which to rule: and in so far as each case tended to have features special to itself it is difficult to give a summary of this field of activity. In all cases the fundamental test was whether persons were actively co-operating, through the acquisition by any of them of shares in a company, to obtain control of the company. With that had to be taken the rigid provision that 'control' meant a holding, or aggregate holding, of shares carrying 30 per cent of the voting rights of a company. As regards persons presumed to be acting in concert, notably directors presumed to be acting in concert with their company, anyone in these categories who dealt in the shares of the offeror or the offeree when an offer might be imminent or during the offer period was regarded as acting in concert and would have difficulty in establishing the contrary.

In the ordinary case, the leader among those acting in concert was obvious and it was possible to look to him to arrange the bid. The Panel was mainly concerned to ensure that a bid was made by someone and it might in fact be made by a company specially set up for the purpose. Difficulties, however, arose if a bid was not forthcoming reasonably soon. It was arguable that the formal obligation rested on the person in concert who made the last acquisition of shares that brought the aggregate holding to 30 per cent. The Panel, however, moved to the position that the obligation rested with the principal member or members of the group acting in concert: and that in the last resort each was severally liable to make the full offer.

SHUT-OUTS

Reference has already been made to shut-outs in connection with the 1972 revision of the Code. Opinion had then hardened against shut-outs. There were, however, always two schools of thought on shut-outs. One considered that controlling directors were entitled to sell their shares to whom they liked or to refuse to sell their shares, provided that they acted in good faith and did not seek any special personal advantage. It should be assumed that they were concerned to obtain the best deal and that this would also be the best deal for the shareholders. If directors had regard to the long-term interests of their shareholders and the interests of the employees and of creditors, the offer with the highest price was not necessarily the best offer. Moreover, if the Code insisted on what might seem to be a public auction of the company, a potential offeror willing to offer good terms might find this prospect unattractive and go away: and then all concerned would be losers. The other school of thought was fearful of cases (admittedly not numerous) in which the interest of the controlling directors did not coincide with the interests of the remaining shareholders. For example, directors might be attracted to a bid at a lower price because they were reasonably well assured of places on the board of the amalgamated concern. Or there might be personal animosity towards an alternative offeror, or they might be influenced by considerations other than the best interests of their company and of the remaining shareholders.

There were peripheral problems. In deciding whether the offeree has secured effective control, did one include shares (possibly qualifying shares) which directors retained when they were proposing to give a shut-out on the remainder of their holdings? Are options on shares and first refusals to be treated as irrevocable commitments? What is the position of an offeree company in the hands of a liquidator?

Gradually, attitudes changed. There were a surprising number of cases where the Panel's consent to a shut-out was sought—150 between October 1971 and March 1973. The Panel's Annual Report for 1972/3 set out in detail factors that had to be considered in these cases and in some quarters this was regarded as indicating a more favourable attitude to shut-outs (*Guardian* 24 May 1973). British Match in their bid for Wilkinson Sword in the summer of 1973 announced that they already held irrevocable undertakings to accept the offer from directors and other shareholders of Wilkinson representing

54.5 per cent of the voting ordinary shares and 22 per cent of the non-voting shares. In adjudicating on shut-outs, it was difficult for the Panel not to get involved in the merits of bids or potential bids.

In the end City opinion came to the view that the disadvantages of regulating shut-outs were greater than the advantages. It was considered that the directors could be expected to endeavour to get the highest possible price for their shares (General Principle II gave some general guidance to directors), and deals with directors with favourable conditions attached were regulated by Rule 36. The restrictions on shut-out bids could frighten away companies that were not prepared to engage in an auction or a fight, but who nevertheless might be prepared to make the best offer. It was also difficult to find out whether there were better offers about, without the Panel seeming to put the company up for sale to all and sundry. One was moving towards the removal of references to shut-outs which took place in the 1976 revision of the Code.

HOW LONG DO RESTRICTIONS LAST?

As the years passed, the question increasingly arose whether restrictions which were imposed under the authority of the Code were of indefinite duration. Most of the text books on take-overs and mergers refer in critical terms to a remark attributed to the director of a merchant bank in 1967 that 'to suggest that an intention seven years ago is binding is to do the English language an injustice'. The reference was to an undertaking which directors of a company had given to their shareholders in 1960, when an increase in share capital was authorized, that they would not, without the agreement of shareholders, issue any further share capital if the result would be materially to affect the control of the company or the nature of its business. Yet in 1967 the directors had done just that. So far, the Panel has been reluctant to relieve parties from obligations under the Code unless circumstances change radically as in the case of Hay's Wharf already referred to.

In 1970 Mr Clive Raphael was allowed to acquire a controlling interest in Land and General Developments Limited from the then Chairman without being required to make a bid for the remaining shares. It was argued that the then Chairman was ill, Mr Raphael could not afford to go further, and the alternative was probably the liquidation of the company. The Panel Executive imposed the condition that Mr Raphael would in due course enfranchise the large number of non-voting 'A' shares. Mr Raphael was killed in an air crash in 1971. There was a dispute about his will. About the end of 1974 the Panel was grappling with the undertaking to enfranchise the 'A' shares. This was eventually achieved in 1975 after a great deal of discussion and further meetings of the Panel.

If it is obvious that there is no prospect at all of fulfilling a Code obligation, the Panel has to accept the fact and rely on censures or penalties on the defaulting parties. In general, however, the Panel has had to take a stiff line on Code obligations, since the authority of the Code would be greatly impaired if the impression was created that the Panel could be worn down and would accept in the end a failure to carry out a Code obligation.

OVERSEAS OFFEREE COMPANIES

The status of the offeree company determined whether the Code applied. The Code was regarded as applying to any offeree company listed on The Stock Exchange, of which a substantial number of shareholders (say 10 per cent to 15 per cent of the whole) were, or seemed to be, in this country.

Scottish Australian. Scottish Australian was an Australian registered company with a substantial number of UK shareholders and a listing on The Stock Exchange. Two Australian companies bid for it in 1974 and one bought on the market above its bid price and did not raise its bid. This was permissible in Australia. The Stock Exchange, at the instance of the Panel, suspended the listing of Scottish Australian—the only course open to it as the bidder was not listed here. The ground was that, if overseas companies wished to deal in this country, they must observe our rules. Some disquiet was felt about the action taken, which of course, had no effect on transactions in Australia.

Union Corporation. In August 1974 Gold Fields of South Africa (Hill Samuel) made an offer for the shares of Union Corporation (Hambros) and posted their offer document on 26 September. On 30 September General Mining (Morgan Grenfell) announced their intention of making a rival bid for half of the shares of Union Corporation. All three companies were registered in South Africa, with listings in London. Union Corporation, which had a substantial number of shareholders in the UK, opposed both bids. The Panel refused to give its consent to the proposed partial bid by General Mining and maintained this refusal against a later variant of the offer. The Panel made no difficulty about Gold Fields of South Africa keeping open their offer for four months after the posting of the offer, since this was required by South African law. The laws of the country concerned overrode the Code. General Mining and others who were opposed to the Gold Fields' bid then made purchases which placed the success of the Gold Fields' offer in jeopardy. General Mining and associates ended up with 29.9 per cent of the capital of Union Corporation.

In December 1974 Gold Fields improved its offer and the board of Union Corporation advised its shareholders to accept. The Panel had to rule on the exact time when Gold Fields had to declare whether their offer had become unconditional or had lapsed. It was considered that it would be consistent with South African law to adhere to the Code on this. The Gold Fields offer failed to achieve the necessary level of acceptances and lapsed at the end of January 1975.

London Tin. On 29 May 1975 it was announced by the board of directors of Pernas Securities Sendirian Berhad and Haw Par Brothers International Limited that arrangements had been finalized under which Haw Par would purchase from Pernas the entire issued share capital of its wholly-owned subsidiary, Tradewinds (Malaysia) Sendirian Berhad. The directors of Haw Par had agreed to issue new shares in Haw Par in exchange for the share capital of Tradewinds representing approximately 39.7 per cent of the enlarged capital of Haw Par. The principal assets of Tradewinds included some 20.36 per cent of the issued ordinary share capital of London Tin, an English company. Haw Par already held some 29.98 per cent of London tin.

On 3 June 1975 the Panel ruled that Pernas and Haw Par were acting in concert when shares in London Tin were purchased by Tradewinds. Accordingly, both companies had a joint and several obligation under Rule 34 of the City Code to make or procure a bid for the ordinary shares in London Tin not already owned by them at $197\frac{3}{16}$p per share. This was the highest price paid for shares they acquired during the previous year. Haw Par then went through serious financial and managerial changes and the Panel by April 1976 accepted that, while the bid obligation on Haw Par remained, there was little likelihood of their being able to meet the obligation in the immediate future. Pernas put forward a compromise proposal which the Panel, in the exceptional circumstances of the case, agreed to accept as a discharge of the obligation of both companies to the London Tin shareholders. As London Tin was an English company, the Panel's jurisdiction was clear.

General. There had been unease for some time about exercising jurisdiction over overseas companies. Companies listed or even registered in the UK sometimes had very large overseas shareholdings—as happened with tea and rubber companies. There had been complaints about the conduct of three separate bids for a major Canadian newsprint supplier listed on The Stock Exchange. One bidder had offered to buy up to 50 per cent of the equity by standing in the market in Toronto and Montreal for three or four days; but this did not give the UK shareholders time to consider whether to sell. The Panel took no action, as the procedures accorded with Canadian law and practice. The Panel at a quarterly meeting on 14 January 1975 agreed that UK shareholders in an overseas offeree would have to look to local law for their protection.

On the occasion of a general revision of the Code in April 1976 the Panel, with the agreement of the City Working Party, incorporated in paragraph 7 of Practice Note 1 a statement that any offer for a company that was not resident for Exchange Control purposes in the United Kingdom (including the Channel Islands and the Isle of Man) does not normally come within the Code, even though the company is listed on The Stock Exchange.

Sime Darby. Subsequently, on 1 December 1976 the Panel considered an application by Sime Darby that the Panel should exercise jurisdiction over a proposal by or on behalf of Pernas Securities Sendirian Berhad, which is a subsidiary of the National Corporation of Malaysia, to change the composition of the Sime Darby board. Sime Darby was a company registered in England and listed on The Stock Exchange in London, and on those of Kuala Lumpur, Singapore, and Hong Kong. It was not resident in the UK for tax or exchange control purposes and most of the shareholders were not UK residents. Kleinwort Benson, on behalf of Sime Darby, submitted that the proposed change in the composition of the board would result in Malaysian interests obtaining control of Sime Darby and, furthermore, that this would automatically carry control of three major subsidiary companies of Sime Darby which had shares listed in London, Consolidated Plantations Limited, Assam Frontier Tea Company, and Sime Darby London Limited.

The Panel had no evidence that any rule of the Code had been broken and in particular was not satisfied that a 'concert party' existed in circumstances which would give rise to the obligation to make an offer to all shareholders. Accordingly, without defining the circumstances in which jurisdiction would be exercised, it did not propose to assume jurisdiction.

Irish Republic. The Stock Exchange now covers the Irish Republic, as well as the United Kingdom. Accordingly an offer for a company in the Irish Republic listed on The Stock Exchange is subject to the Code. No insurmountable difficulties have arisen so far, but in this field the Panel, like Agag, treads delicately.

FINANCIAL ADVISERS

The Code refers to financial advisers but does not define their responsibilities *vis-à-vis* offeror or offeree. The extent of the involvement of a merchant bank or other adviser in a take-over varies from case to case. Accordingly in cases that come before it, the Panel has to apply what good practice and ethics seem to require, consistently with the spirit of the Code.

In 1974 the Panel adjudicated on a fairly simple issue. A financial adviser had advised offeree shareholders to accept an offer and had said that he proposed to accept it in respect of his own holding. He then sold his own shares in the market without informing the offeree board or offeree shareholders. The Panel found this to be unacceptable conduct.

In connection with the Ashbourne case, the Panel had to consider the position of a merchant bank that had advised the offeror and had arranged a form of underwriting of which it took a part itself. No offer was in fact made. The merchant bank had had to satisfy itself that the necessary finance was available to the offeror to implement the offer. Did the bank thereby become an insurer or guarantor that the offer would be made? The Panel thought not, provided that the bank had exercised a high degree of care and expertise at all stages. The Panel did not consider that the underwriter of a mandatory offer, by reason of his underwriting alone, could be regarded as acting in concert with the offeror and the same was true of a banker who lent money for the acquisition of shares.

In its report for 1976/7 the Panel referred to the problem of a financial adviser's duty if he has reason to doubt the accuracy or completeness of information being given to the Panel.

When a financial adviser finds himself in such a difficult position and is faced with a situation where he thinks the Panel is being misled, the Panel considers that his over-riding duty is to the Panel. If, despite his advice, he believes that his client intends to pursue a course of conduct misleading to the Panel, he may ultimately decide to resign. If he does resign, the Panel considers that he then has no obligation to inform them of his misgivings about the former client's conduct.

The CBI, as the member of the Panel most closely representative of the corporate clients of financial advisers, has confirmed that it supports the need for full disclosure and accepts that the financial adviser should not be expected to shield a client who was endeavouring to mislead the Panel during an investigation.

It will be observed that the passage deals with a current intention to deceive. Where a client had already deceived the Panel and this came to the notice of a financial adviser, the obligation to be completely frank with the Panel was clear.

In the statement issued on 19 July 1978, in connection with a bid by Mooloya Investments for Customagic Manufacturing Company, the Panel said that doubts felt by a financial adviser whether a proposed transaction was permissible under the Code should have been communicated to the Panel Executive when discussing another related transaction.

CODE REVISION (1976)

The revised Code issued in April 1976 was the first thorough revision since 1972. As in previous revisions, the City Working

Party did not hesitate to re-arrange the material, where this made for greater clarity, though the numbers of the General Principles and Rules were preserved so far as possible. A preliminary section, dealing with the procedure of the Panel and the Appeal Committee, was drawn in part from the Annual Report for 1969/70 and in part from the introduction to the previous edition of the Code.

Two new General Principles were added. One (General Principle 13) underlined the great importance that the Panel attached to Rule 34 and to the obligation to make a bid which attached to the acquirer of control of a company. The other (General Principle 14) stressed the need for careful consideration before announcing a bid: and the need for the offeror and his financial advisers to have every reason to believe that he would be able to implement the offer. There had been little change in the General Principles since 1968. These additions were based on the experience of recent years.

Perhaps the most important change made in the revision was in relation to the obligation to make a mandatory bid under Rule 34. The situation which the 1974 Code envisaged was one in which a company or an individual took the lead in acquiring shares in another company and on whom the obligation to make a bid could be placed. But the situation was not always so clear-cut. If there was not clearly a leader, did an obligation to make a bid lie on the person who had acquired a final parcel of shares that triggered off the obligation and what about persons acting in concert? The new Rule 34 still envisaged a person who was a leader but it went on to say 'In addition to such person each of the principal members of the group of persons acting in concert may, according to the circumstances of the case, have an obligation to extend an offer.'

The definition of persons acting in concert was improved and made more explicit at various points. Where a person had not less than 30 per cent and not more than 50 per cent of voting rights, the 1974 Code required a bid if that person acquired more than a further 1 per cent in any period of twelve months. This had proved rather vexatious, for example where there was a forced sale following a death and the market in the shares was very narrow. The percentage was accordingly increased to 2 per cent.

In previous editions, the board of the offeree company had been required to seek independent advice in an offer only if the offer was not completely at arm's length. This advice was now required for every offer (Rule 4). Partial bids were no longer comprehensively labelled as undesirable. The Panel's consent was still required before a partial bid was made, but where an offeror was aiming at holding more than 50 per cent of the voting rights the recommendation of the board of the offeree company was no longer a prerequisite to consent. Offers aiming at between 30 per cent and 50 per cent of the voting rights would be granted consent 'only in exceptional circumstances'. The requirement that a shut-out should be cleared with the Panel was abolished.

RECENT PROBLEMS

Offeree Shareholders. The Code imposes many obligations on boards of directors and for the most part it deals separately with directors and shareholders. Thus an offeror (i.e. normally a board of directors) must not make an acquisition of shares which would lead to an obligation under Rule 34 to make a mandatory bid, if the implementation of the offer would be dependent on the later agreement of the offeror's shareholders. An exception is Rule 38 which frees a board from certain restrictions on steps designed to thwart a bid, if the board has secured the agreement of its shareholders in general meeting. It accords with this general approach that the requirements of Rule 34 to make a mandatory bid when a certain percentage of shares has been acquired cannot ordinarily be waived by a meeting of the offeree shareholders. Every offeree shareholder has the protection of the Rule. There is the additional reason that the acquisition of shares is a matter between the acquirer and the holders of the shares. It is not company business. It is difficult to see how it could be brought before the general body of shareholders or what form the discussion could take.

There are, however, circumstances in which Rule 34 can operate too drastically and possibly against the interest of offeree shareholders. A company may wish to issue shares in return for the acquisition of an asset or for a cash injection and the result may be that the seller of the asset or the provider of funds may find himself with more than 30 per cent of the voting rights and a Rule 34 obligation to make a general offer for the remaining shares. The transaction is company business; and the Panel is prepared to waive the Rule 34 obligation if, at the shareholders' meeting to approve the issue of capital, a majority of shareholders not involved in the transaction vote in favour of the issue. The exclusion of interested parties from voting is strictly enforced, and latterly it has been usual to insist on a poll of members.

The question has recently arisen to what extent a shareholders' meeting can 'whitewash' a Rule 34 obligation, particularly where there was both a purchase of shares and the acquisition of shares in return for an asset. The matter came to a head at the end of 1977 when a US company, Allegheny Ludlum Industries, bought from Swedish Match a 29 per cent stake in Wilkinson Match and agreed that Wilkinson Match should buy an Allegheny subsidiary in return for shares which would bring Allegheny's total holding in Wilkinson Match above 50 per cent. The terms were subsequently modified and brought Allegheny's holding below 50 per cent. In accordance with the practice in one or two previous cases, the Panel executive treated the two transactions as separate and the issue of shares for the Allegheny subsidiary was approved by an independent vote at a meeting of Wilkinson Sword shareholders. In a review of general policy the Panel later decided that a purchase of shares giving the purchaser just less than 30 per cent of the voting rights, followed (in agreement with the board of the company) by the issue of shares to the purchaser in exchange for assets or cash would have to be looked at as a whole and would give rise to a Rule 34 obligation unless the Panel was satisfied that there were no negotiations or understandings with the directors of the company, relating to the asset injection and the issue of the new shares, before the most recent share purchase.

Formula Bids. In the course of the last few years there have been cases in which offers for investment trusts were based on the value of the underlying assets at the time when the offer became unconditional. The Panel accepted that offers for investment trusts could be expressed in this way, but a substantial number of points arose on the interpretation of the rules:

and the promulgation of these interpretations in the course of 1978 illustrated once again the flexibility of the Code in its application to a developing situation.

In formula bids for investment trusts, the offer is a cash payment equal to x per cent of the 'net asset value' per share on the date on which the offer becomes unconditional. The trusts regard this concept of 'net asset value' as the value of the trust as a going concern—investments are taken at mid-market values, prior charge borrowings deducted at market rather than nominal values, and no deductions made for contingent liabilities on capital gains. Offerors for investment trusts have tended (though not always) to calculate net assets at the lower 'break-up' valuation, which calculated prior charges at their nominal value and deducted capital gains tax on unrealized gains. As break-up value is normally less than going-concern value, an offer is likely to be a higher percentage of the former than of the latter. There were variants on break-up value, depending on how preference capital was treated and whether deduction was made for the cost of terminating existing management arrangements. The Panel decided that the offeror could use any basis so long as the details were fully and clearly spelt out to the offeree shareholders.

It was also necessary to decide how to determine the value of the offer for the purpose of Rule 32. This was taken to be the value of the formula bid on the day on which purchases for cash were being made. The application of Rule 32 to formula bids was thus identical to that in the case of a share exchange offer, where purchases of offeree shares at above the ruling value of the share exchange offer required an equivalent improvement in the offer terms.

Arising out of the bid by the National Coal Board Pension Funds for British Investment Trust, the Panel decided on 10 November 1977 that Rules 33 and 34, if brought into operation, would require a cash offer. The effect would be that when the offer was declared unconditional as to acceptances, shareholders would receive the higher of the formula price ruling that day and of the highest cash price paid in respect of share purchases to which Rules 33 and 34 applied. The Panel decided that, if offerors reserved the right to lapse the offer in the event of movements in the securities market exceeding certain specified limits, a similar right to withdraw must be given to accepting shareholders. It was also decided that the formula should not operate after the offer was declared unconditional as to acceptances, since the contrary decision would have meant different prices for different shareholders.

Shut-Offs. Rule 23 provides that, after an offer has become unconditional, the offer should remain open for acceptance for at least a further fourteen days. This enables those who have opposed a bid but who have no wish to remain as a minority shareholder, to accept a bid after it has been successful. In this form, the rule could have remained simple and fairly straightforward. It was, however, felt that an offeror should be able to deny the offeree shareholders the extra fourteen days if he had given sufficient notice of his intention to shut-off the offer at the expiry date. The rule therefore provided that the offeror could shut-off the offer if he had given to the offeree shareholders at least fourteen days notice in writing. The rule had to be applied to quite complex situations owing to the ingenuity of merchant banks in devising offer arrangements. Thus, in the year from 1 April 1977 to 31 March 1978, the Panel Executive dealt with 214 offers divided as follows in respect of the considerations offered:

Shares only	21
Cash only	118
Loan stock only	1
Mixture of above	16
Shares with cash alternative	26
Cash with share alternative	13
Mixture with cash alternative	14
Mixture with share alternative	1
Cash or loan stock	2
Mixture or shares with cash alternative	1
Cash with mixture alternative	1
	214

Cash alternatives had to be divided between those provided by the offeror and those provided by underwriters. There was also the problem of competing bids. A shareholder who had accepted the first offer might not receive his shares back in time to accept a higher second offer, unless the second offeror was required to keep his offer open for a further period of fourteen days or longer. Some of the issues were discussed in a Panel hearing on 27 May 1977 about the BTR offer for Silentbloc in which the Panel ruled that a cash underwritten alternative came within Rule 23 and that it had to be extended for fourteen days after the offer went unconditional because adequate notice of shut-off had not been given. The existing practice is set out in some detail in Practice Note 9, as revised in December 1978.

Abolition of Exchange Control. The abolition of exchange control in October 1979 has presented the authors of the Code with a problem of definition, since the distinction between home and overseas companies was expressed in terms of exchange control. More importantly it has ended one way of regulating the activities of overseas bidders for shares in UK companies, namely the need to secure exchange control permission.

Substantial Share Purchases. Linked with the abolition of exchange control has been disquiet about the build up of substantial holdings in UK companies. When the Companies Act 1976 required the acquisition of a holding, totalling 5 per cent of the voting shares, to be reported to the company, it was not thought to be practicable to introduce into the legislation the concept of persons acting in concert, though this was pressed for by The Stock Exchange and the Panel. There have been recent cases of overseas holdings falling just short of 5 per cent, where the owners of the holdings were closely related and where delay in registration has left their identity unknown.

Then again there has been discussion about the fairness to other shareholders of purchases (often by overseas companies) of shares in UK companies at a high price which were for substantial amounts but not sufficient to give rise to a Rule 34 obligation to make a bid. The cases have varied in respect to the speed of the transactions and the extent to which purchases were made in the market or from selected institutional shareholders. The most spectacular was the acquisition of 11 per cent of the share capital of Consolidated Gold Fields, at a price substantially higher than the market price and at a cost of £101 million, in a few minutes on 12 February 1980. Some would propose to reduce below 30 per cent the level of acquisitions at which a Rule 34 bid has to be made; but this re-definition of what constitutes control is open to a number of objections. Others would require that everyone acquiring more than *x* per cent of the share capital of a company at a price substantially higher than the market price make the offer available to all shareholders, either in the market or by the more elaborate device of a formal partial offer. Others see difficulty in any attempt to fetter purchases of this kind.

Profit forecasts. These continue to be a problem. The range from estimating the profits for a year that has already passed to guessing profits for a year that has not yet begun. In respect of bids between 1 May 1969 and 30 September 1971, the Panel executive compared profit forecasts, where given by offerors or offerees, with actual turn-outs. The details were given in the Annual Reports for 1970/1 and 1971/2. The total number of forecasts was 418, and of 80 cases where profits were either under-estimated or over-estimated by more than 10 per cent of the forecast, only in five cases was there failure to give an acceptable explanation of the error. It was decided that there was a reasonably high standard of forecasting and that companies should not be required to justify their forecasts as a matter of routine. Since October 1971 the Panel executive has kept an eye on forecasts, carried out random checks (about one in four) and investigated complaints.

In 1977 and 1978 there were some forecasts that failed by a substantial margin, notably by the directors of Dunford and Elliott in connection with a bid by Lonrho, and by the directors of Crane Fruehauf when opposing a bid by the Fruehauf Corporation. There is no obligation on companies to make profit forecasts in connection with take-over bids; but Rule 15 of the Code provides that shareholders should be put in possession of all the facts necessary for the formation of an informed judgement as to the merits or demerits of an offer. The Panel has therefore encouraged boards to inform their shareholders about current prospects. Boards must not be reckless or irresponsible in their statements but at the same time the Panel tries not to be so restrictive that boards are afraid to make forecasts.

The failure of a profits forecast is not prima-facie evidence of negligence since there is usually a substantial element of uncertainty how events will turn out. Moreover there are sometimes difficulties in deciding how badly a forecast has worked out. The offeree company may have merged into an enlarged group and have lost its separate identity. Accounting dates may have been changed and management policies and accountancy principles may be different. The Panel has to endeavour to judge what the results would have been if the bid had not succeeded and the offeree board had been reporting to its shareholders the results as an independent company.

Advertisements. The General Principles and the Rules emphasize the need for facts to be put fully and fairly before shareholders. In the heat of a contested bid, the participants may publish advertisements or express views in the Press or on the air which are regarded as unfair or unbalanced. In a case in 1979 in which many of the offeree shares were in the hands of small shareholders, advertisements of an emotive character were published by the offeror and by the offeree board. The Panel decided in 1979 that the wording and format of advertisements should be cleared with the Panel executive. This seemed to be the only way to prevent the damage which would be done by a misleading advertisement, though it places a difficult task on the executive. The alternative would be to limit closely what could be said in paid advertisements. Directors and company advisers were told to be careful what they said to journalists during the currency of a bid. As regards television and radio, the Panel is opposed to confrontations between parties when things may be said which confuse the issues facing shareholders. None of this makes the Panel particularly popular with the media when the issues arise in individual cases.

CODE REVISION (1980)

These and other matters, some of a technical character, are under consideration in connection with the code revision which is now in train. Broadly speaking, both operators and those representing company and shareholder interests appear to be reasonably satisfied with the Code in its present form. It seems likely therefore that the current revision will cover less ground than the 1976 revision and will not be undertaking any fundamental changes.

IX

THE FUTURE OF THE CODE

Council for the Securities Industry

THE framework within which the Take-over Code operates was changed by the setting up of the Council for the Securities Industry by the Governor of the Bank of England in March 1978.

In recent years there had been various discussions whether the securities industry, or a wider City group including the commodities markets, needed new machinery for supervision and regulation. The example of the Securities and Exchange Commission in the United States was frequently referred to, and the Commission was sometimes endowed with qualities of ruthless and all-pervasive efficiency which knowledgeable admirers would not necessarily claim for it. The subject was kept alive by the troubles of Lonrho, of Sir Denys Lowson's companies and of the businesses (London and Counties Securities, Slater Walker, etc.) involved in the collapse of secondary banks in 1974.

The Bank of England and The Stock Exchange already performed some general functions in this field. The Bank had long supervised the banking system and money markets and it exercised a general supervision over the securities and other markets. It was responsible for the steps that led to the establishment of the City Capital Markets Committee, the Take-over Code and the Panel and of other committees dealing with special aspects of the securities market. Since the 1930s The Stock Exchange has widened its field, beyond its own members, to regulate the conduct of companies listed on the Exchange.

The various steps taken by the Government in recent years in regard to the regulation of the securities industry are described in detail in Chapter XI. Here it is necessary only to mention the developments in the field of self-regulation.

In the course of 1977 Mr Gordon Richardson, the Governor of the Bank, had discussions on the general surveillance of the securities markets with the chairman of the Panel and with the various associations represented on the Panel. The then Director-General of the Take-over Panel (Mr D. C. Macdonald) and the Deputy Chief Executive of The Stock Exchange (Mr J. R. Knight) were commissioned to draw up a plan for a voluntary body to supervise the securities industry. After further discussions, the Bank on 30 March 1978 was able to announce the setting up of the Council, under the chairmanship of Mr F. Patrick Neill, Q.C. It consisted of a Chairman and Deputy Chairman appointed by the Governor of the Bank, the Chairman of the Take-over Panel, Deputy Governor of the Bank of England, the chairman or other representative of the Accepting Houses Committee, the Association of Investment Trust Companies, the British Insurance Association, the Consultative Committee of Accountancy Bodies, the Committee of London Clearing Bankers, the Confederation of British Industry, the Issuing Houses Association, the National Association of Pension Funds, the Council of The Stock Exchange, and the Unit Trust Association. The Chairman of the Quotations Committee of The Stock Exchange is also a member. The overseas banks and overseas dealers in shares in London are represented and there is provision for the representation of other dealers in securities. Three lay members have been nominated by the Governor as representatives of the individual investor and the wider public interest. The Council meets once a quarter on a regular basis and on other occasions, as required. It has set up a Markets Committee and that committee operates in part through sub-committees. When the Council was set up, its principal objectives were described as follows:

(a) To maintain the highest ethical standards in the conduct of business within the securities industry.
(b) To keep under constant review the evolution of the securities industry, market practice and related Codes of

THE FUTURE OF THE CODE

Conduct and to scrutinize the effectiveness of existing forms of regulation and the machinery for their administration.
(c) To maintain arrangements for the investigation of cases of alleged misconduct within the securities industry and breaches of codes of conduct or best practice and to keep these arrangments under review.
(d) To initiate new policies and codes as necessary concerning activities in the securities industry other than those properly within the domestic province of each individual constituent member.
(e) To resolve differences on matters of principle between constituent parts of the securities industry.
(f) To consider the need for changes in legislation affecting the activities of the securities industry and to examine any proposals for such legislation.
(g) To ensure liaison with the European Commission on securities industry matters and the implementation of the EEC Capital Markets Code of Conduct.

The Department of Trade has designated the Council as an authority to supervise the implementation of the Code of Conduct referred to above, which relates to transactions in transferable securities. The EEC commended the Code to member Governments on 25 July 1977. The authority of the Council stems, as in the case of the Panel, from the commitment of the bodies represented on it to support its activities and any codes it produces, and to respect its rulings. The bodies represented on the Council recognize that the Council has the right to make recommendations bearing on any aspect of the activities of their members relating to the securities industry, although such recommendations have no legal force. The wide-ranging powers available to The Stock Exchange and the other sanctions which have been deployed by the Take-over Panel in recent years are available for use in appropriate cases. Other organizations represented on the Council are expected to examine their own procedures to ensure if necessary that additional action can be taken to assist the Council in making its recommendations effective.

The Markets Committee of the Council has taken over from

the City Working Party the responsibility for the amendment and revision of the Take-over Code. In effect the Council is the legislative body responsible for the Code and the Panel is the executive body that administers and interprets the Code. The membership of the Markets Committee includes those who were on the City Working Party. It is however chaired by the chairman of the Council in place of the chairman of the Issuing Houses Association and it includes the three lay members of the Council. The chairman of the Issuing Houses Association (Mr. G. G. Williams) and a small committee, in consultation with the Panel executive, will bring proposals to the Markets Committee. This follows the procedure adopted by the City Working Party which worked well in the past.

In its first year the Council was active in co-ordinating views on the clauses of the 1978 Companies Bill dealing with insider dealing and the Markets Committee disposed of a somewhat contentious issue on Rule 23. The next major task in this field is the revision of the Take-over Code. The Panel itself has been described as an arm of the Council and it makes a quarterly report to the Council on its work. The Chairman of the Council and a representative of the accountancy profession have joined the Panel. Otherwise the Panel and the Panel executive operate essentially as before. The decisions of the Panel on the interpretation of the Take-over Code are final and not subject to appeal. It was felt to be essential to maintain this position, if speed and finality of decision were to be retained. The advantages of self-regulation would be lost if a bureaucratic structure were to be created. The Appeals Committee of the Panel continues to hear appeals from decisions of the Panel of a disciplinary nature in the field of take-overs and mergers. The Appeals Committee will also hear appeals against disciplinary decisions of the Council.

Code Developments

FUTURE CASES OF MERGERS

There has for some time been an undercurrent of doubt whether mergers in general produce greater efficiency, and these doubts have been expressed more strongly in the last few years. Something of this was reflected in the tone of the Labour

Government's green paper entitled 'A Review of Monopolies and Merger Policy' (Cmnd. 7198 of May 1978). It is not clear that these doubts will have much direct influence on the number of bids. The Panel dealt with 148 announced offers in 1975/6, 199 in 1976/7, 225 in 1977/8, and 167 in 1978/9. A recovery in the economy would probably lead to more bids. The acquisitive instinct, the belief of the bidder that he can run the company bid far more efficiently than the existing board or the use of the take-over technique to acquire further plant and machinery may be only marginally affected by arguments that some mergers have not promoted efficiency. Doubts about the efficacy of mergers are more likely to be influential in the field of government action. If there were to be more frequent reference of certain types of take-overs to the Monopolies and Mergers Commission, this could have a discouraging effect on take-overs. If the employees of offeree companies came to have a say in individual take-overs, the result on balance would almost certainly be to reduce the number of successful take-overs.

FUTURE OF THE CODE

Whereas commercial law tends to protect the buyer against the seller, in take-overs it is the innocent seller (in the shape of a small shareholder in the offeree company) who has to be protected against the buyer (the predator endeavouring to gobble up unsuspecting companies). Subject to this, the Code endeavours to hold the balance evenly between the offeror and the offeree. Holding the balance can of course be interpreted differently by different people. If the general climate becomes less favourable to mergers, offerors and their advisers may regard some of the protection afforded by the Code to offeree shareholders as an interference with normal commercial operations and as tilting the balance against them.

Again, who is the typical offeree shareholder? There has long been a general awareness of the extent to which institutions have increased their shareholdings in public companies and private individuals have lessened theirs.[1] Reference to this development featured strongly in evidence presented to the

---

[1] See Ownership of Company Shares, in Economic Trends (September 1977).

Wilson Committee. In 1963 private investors held 58.7 per cent of ordinary shares. In 1975 the percentage had fallen to 36 per cent and it is still falling. In the same period insurance companies had increased theirs from 10.6 per cent to 16 per cent and pension funds from 7 per cent to 15 per cent. The question is sometimes asked whether the Code in future will pay less attention to the needs of the small private shareholder. The answer in the foreseeable future is almost certainly 'No'. First of all, private investors are still a sizeable element in company shareholdings, particularly in medium sized and small companies. Secondly they need to be protected more than institutions. Thirdly the position of the private investor often affects the form, rather than the substance, of the rules. Whereas, say, ten days would have to be given for an institution to consider a revised offer, the private shareholder in a remote part of the country is thought to need fourteen days; and the rule therefore provides for fourteen days.

It is likely, however, that the institutional shareholders will play an increasing part in Code revision. They may press for the Code to give a larger part to the wishes of shareholders in general meeting—a complex subject which is dealt with later.

The Code is not doing its job if there is not some criticism of its operation. 'Woe unto you, when all men shall speak well of you'. There are occasional murmurs against the Code that seem to stem from a feeling that the Panel executive is too close to events and exercises too close control. Perhaps those who feel that way would take the view that an SEC on the American model, even if tiresome in many ways, would be less effective. The Code upholds what a majority of the practitioners regard as sound ethical conduct but there must always be some who resent what they regard as restrictions on legitimate business transactions.

On a number of questions the solutions in the Code depend on a balancing of conflicting arguments, and views may be expected to change when conditions change. Shut-outs and shut-offs are both criticized from time to time, as are partial bids, and by implication the criticism can extend to the more tolerant attitude towards them of the Code in recent years. Again there has never been complete agreement that an offeror should be free to buy an offeree company's shares in the period before the public announcement of a bid. At various points, the Code requires shareholders to be provided with independent advice; and there is an unresolved problem whether the advice should be truly independent or whether it is best given by an adviser who is deeply knowledgeable but also involved to a greater or less degree in the board's decisions. The full effect of the provision in the current Companies Bill that directors must have regard to the interests of employees as well as of shareholders will take time to show itself. Institutional shareholders are expected to take special steps to inform themselves of the problems of the company. The Code requires that there should be equality of treatment in the provision of information to shareholders and the Code is primarily concerned with the offeree shareholder, although there are occasional complaints that the offeror shareholder may not always get a fair deal and ought to be consulted. The Stock Exchange Yellow Book (pp. 74/5) enumerates cases in which offeror shareholders have to be consulted, including reverse take-over where a small listed company mounts a bid for a large unlisted company, but offeror shareholders sometimes complain about what they regard as unfair treatment, for example in reverse take-overs where the directors of the listed company have a controlling interest.

FORM OF THE CODE

As regards the form of the Code, there are conflicting considerations. To preserve the flexibility of the Code, it can be argued that it can be expressed in broad general terms, so that everyone can see what the Code is trying to do and no one would get bogged down in a mass of detail. The Panel would then apply the principles so expressed to the circumstances of each case and would not pay much attention to past decisions. The contrary argument is that, while flexibility must be preserved in a constantly changing situation and there must be no slavish following of precedents, practitioners expect a measure of uniformity in the administration of the Code and want to know how the Code is being interpreted. Most practitioners prefer to know established practice in some detail rather than be told that each case will be handled in the light of the spirit of the Code. Rules and rulings have to be clear and definite, and they ought to be consistent, one with another. Practitioners would be quick to point to inconsistencies of policy if the Panel executive cast all precedents aside and dealt with each case as an unrelated exercise in the applications of general principles.

The Code is about one third longer than it was in 1972, but it is very much the same kind of document as before. Practice notes occupy more space, but for reasons already given they do not give rise to serious complaints. What seems to be needed is that the General Principles should retain their importance. There was a time when it seemed possible that they would be regarded as of historic interest only, leaving all developments to the Rules. Any tendency in this direction was halted in the 1976 revision when new General Principles were added. Also the Panel should continue to have regard to the broad intention of the General Principles and Rules and not engage in legalistic interpretation of the wording. Fortunately, the Panel has shown no inclination to take a narrow view of its functions.

It is undeniable that the discretion given to the Panel by the present Rules has increased with each successive revision. This might not work so well if the Panel was dealing with a vast clientele, but most of its business is conducted with a fairly narrow circle of merchant banks who have in effect agreed to accept the Panel's jurisdiction.

LICENSED DEALERS RULES

The existence, side by side, of the Code and the Licensed Dealers Rules has over the years given rise to few practical difficulties. Licensed dealers have to observe the Rules and the Department of Trade accepted that the Panel expected licensed dealers and others involved in take-over bids to observe the Code as well. The Code covered a much wider ground than the Rules. Save on one or two minor points of procedure, there was no conflict between the Code and the Rules.

In 1977 an offeree company complained to the Panel that the bidder had issued the offer document on the same day as he informed the offeree board of the bid, contrary to the Licensed Dealers Rules which required three days' notice. In the ordinary case, some time elapses between the intimation of a bid to the offeree board and the dispatch of the offer document. Rule 1 of the Code simply said that the offeree board must have the offer in the first instance. The Panel took the view that, in this particular case, the intention of the offeror was well known and that it was sufficient for the exempted dealer (the merchant bank acting for the offeror) to conform to the Code. On the other hand the Department has been inclined to hold the view, dating back to 1960, that it expected exempted dealers to observe the Licensed Dealers Rules.

There is no reason to believe that this difficulty will not be solved in the course of the revision of the Code and of the Licensed Dealers Rules. If practice under the Code and the Rules can be brought into line on the one or two points on which there is some divergence, the problem will vanish. The need for flexibility and for the exercise of discretion in the administration of take-over rules, because of the different forms that take-overs can take and the ever-changing pattern, means that the Code, administered by the Panel, suits the needs of the situation better than rigid statutory rules on the 1960 model.

Conclusion

The City Take-over Code and its administration by the Panel are generally considered to have proved to be effective in regulating take-over bids. One has only to compare the situation described in the earlier chapters with the present situation to realize the extent of the change that has been effected. The merchant banks and other City bodies accept the authority of the Code and its interpretation by the Panel. The Code and the Panel have survived quite a number of crises. The voices that tended to greet each successive crisis with the cry that the Panel now had its last chance have become fainter. Governments appear to accept that in this field self-regulation works better than State-regulation. This is an uncertain world and we must wait and see what the Wilson Committee has to say about the supervision of the securities market; but, as matters stand at present, the Panel seems to be securely established.

Much of the credit for this state of affairs must go to Lord Shawcross. The Panel is a strong body and forms a collective view: but inevitably the Chairman plays an important part in its deliberations. Lord Shawcross has had long experience in business, in the law, and in public administration; and is able to move confidently and effectively in work that spans all these fields of activity. A Chairman who was not a lawyer might have been fearful about insisting that the Panel should retain a simple procedure, and might not have appreciated what had to be done to ensure that the Courts would be satisfied that the procedures adopted were fair. Lord Shawcross has aimed at firm and clear-cut decisions and has that indefinable attribute that gives authority to his views. His skill with the pen resulted in the clear and persuasive presentation of Panel decisions. All these qualities have been of immense value, especially in the formative stages when the Panel had to fight for general acceptance.

One should, however, add that Sir Humphrey Mynors laid the foundations for what followed and the first annual report of the Panel is an excellent record of the constructive thought that was applied by Sir Humphrey Mynors, his colleagues and the secretariat to the multitude of problems that crowded in during the early days. Less in the public eye but playing a vital role have been the successive chairmen of the Issuing Houses Association, who chaired the City Working Party—Mr Michael Bucks, Sir Kenneth Barrington, Mr Peter Cannon, Mr J. M. Clay, Mr D. C. Macdonald and Mr I. G. Kennington.

X
PANEL ORGANIZATION

The Panel Executive

PROCEDURE

The reputation of the Panel in the City depends very considerably on the efficiency of the Panel executive in dealing promptly, fairly, and decisively with the large number of queries that pour into the office every day. From the outset, merchant bankers and others engaged in take-over activities have been encouraged to consult the Panel executive on the interpretation of the Take-over Code. Some of these queries may come in letters but a great many come in telephone calls. If the point is a difficult one, the Panel executive may ask for time to consider, but this is thought of in terms of hours rather than days. In the ordinary way of business the Panel executive deals with the agents of one side to the take-over—usually a merchant bank representing the offeror or the offeree. In this way the agent can be entirely frank. If, however, the course of action proposed by the executive or its interpretation of the Code is likely to affect the other side, then the executive insists on the other side being informed.

In a case in 1978 the Panel had occasion to point out that the Code is not a legal document and that it is no answer to a failure to consult the Panel Executive in a case of difficulty that a legal opinion had been obtained on the interpretation of a rule. 'The authority designated to interpret the Code is the Panel and it is the Panel executive that should be consulted in any case of doubt.'[1] In commenting on this passage, the *Financial Times* of

[1] Statement of 19 July 1978 on bid by Mooloya Investments for Customagic Manufacturing Company.

20 July 1978 remarked that 'this just about sums up the practical difference between self-regulating and SEC-type enforcement'.

A substantial part of the Panel's routine work consists in vetting formal offer documents and related papers. These do not have to be submitted in advance. Rule 20 says that, in order to facilitate the work of the Panel, copies of all public announcements and all documents bearing on a take-over or merger transaction must be lodged with the Panel at the same time as they are made or dispatched. In fact, if there is any point of doubt, a merchant bank is likely to show the offer document in draft to the Panel executive. Listed companies are required by the Listing Agreement to submit to the Quotations Department of The Stock Exchange the draft of any circular to be issued by the company to holders of its securities and a company is also expected to submit the draft of any circular to holders of securities other than its own, and this includes offer documents. This is another avenue through which the Panel executive may be consulted about a draft before issue. If an offer document or a comment to shareholders by the offeree board is considered not to conform with the Code, the board concerned has to issue a correction to shareholders or take some other agreed remedial action.

The volume of business handled by the Panel executive is illustrated by the following figures, which, however, do not include many queries with which the executive has to deal.

Year ended 31 March	Bids discussed which never materialized	Announced bids withdrawn before offer document	Offer documents circulated	Bids outstanding at end of period
1969	—	80	420	74
1970	100	29	363	61
1971	108	35	296	60
1972	113	43	393	81
1973	145	32	356	48
1974	140	20	266	26
1975	153	9	142	27
1976	87	9	139	28
1977	117	10	189	38
1978	127	11	214	20
1979	164	9	158	24

STAFFING

It was decided at an early stage that the Panel executive should for the most part be staffed by temporary secondments from City firms. It was felt that this would secure a higher standard of ability, since firms would be prepared to release good people for a short stint with the Panel; and this would also ensure that the Panel executive had a close knowledge of current operations.

The disadvantage of staffing the office by temporary secondments is that it could lead to a loss of continuity in administration. In practice the Panel has managed to secure the best of both worlds, as both the Deputy Directors-General (Mr Peter R. Frazer and Mr T. Peter Lee) are permanent members of the staff.

The Panel has been very fortunate in its Directors-General. Mr Ian Fraser (1969–72) was a director of Warburgs and had previously been with Reuters. To him fell the onerous task of establishing the authority of the Panel executive and he performed this task with great expertise, judgement and firmness. The City owes him a great debt for his outstanding performance as Director-General at a critical period. His analyses of the reasoning behind various parts of the Code are still of the greatest value. Mr Fraser is now chairman of Lazard Brothers. He was succeeded by Mr John Hull (1972–4), a director of Schroder Wagg and a barrister by training. He maintained the reputation of the Panel executive and, like his predecessor, established a position of authority by the quality of his rulings. Mr Hull left to become deputy chairman of Schroder Wagg.

The next Director-General was Mr Martin Harris (1974–7), a director of Price Waterhouse, who had previously advised the Panel on accountancy problems. Mr Harris was the first Director-General who was not a merchant banker and it says much for the very capable manner in which he performed his duties that it was never felt that he was at a disadvantage because he had not previously been involved in corporate finance work as closely as his predecessors. He brought to the Panel an acumen in financial and accountancy matters which has been of the greatest value.

Mr Harris was succeeded by Mr David Macdonald

(1977–9), formerly a director of Hill Samuel and a solicitor by training, who had a very successful career in merchant banking and who, at a comparatively early age, became chairman of the Issuing Houses Association. As such, he chaired all the discussions that preceded the 1976 revision of the Code. He brought to the Panel a thorough knowledge of take-over techniques.

The present Director-General is Mr Graham R. Walsh, who came from being a director of Morgan Grenfell and of Morgan Grenfell Holdings. An accountant by training, Mr Walsh brings to the Panel, like his predecessor, considerable experience in corporate finance work and he has been able quickly to make his mark on the day-to-day administration of the Code and on the revision of the Code.

The Senior Deputy Director-General, Mr Peter R. Frazer, has been involved in the work of the Panel since its inception. He is now a permanent member of the Panel executive and his involvement in the decisions taken over a long period is of great value to the Panel and to the merchant banking community as a whole. The other Deputy Director-General, Mr T. Peter Lee, is a solicitor by training and, subject to a brief period in other employment, has been with the Panel since 1972. Like Mr Frazer, he is now a permanent member of the Panel executive, and with changing Directors-General, they provide a valuable element of continuity.

Under the Director-General and two Deputy Directors-General, there is a Secretary and four Assistant Secretaries. The office is quite small. It has no reserve capacity and this means that in times of stress very long hours are worked. A merchant bank may have an important, contested bid only at intervals and it is prepared to work long hours at the crucial stages. The Panel executive can be under continuous strain, especially at times when there is marked take-over activity.

Those who have had dealings with the Panel executive have paid tribute to the speed and incisiveness of their rulings. The fact that all their rulings can be appealed against to the full Panel has never operated to blunt their willingness to make clear the executive's view on issues brought before them. In reply to the Department of Trade's questionnaire of July 1974, the Chairman and Deputy Chairman, as independent members of the Panel, rejected from their experience any suggestion of an 'old boys' club' in the administration of the Panel's affairs. They said that both the Panel and the executive interpreted the Code without fear or favour and in a very robust way.

The Panel

MEMBERSHIP

The Panel consists of a chairman (Lord Shawcross)[1] and a deputy chairman (Sir Alexander Johnston) nominated by the Governor of the Bank of England and the chairman of:

>Accepting Houses Committee
>Association of Investment Trust Companies
>British Insurance Association
>Committee of London Clearing Bankers
>Council for the Securities Industry
>Issuing Houses Association
>National Association of Pension Funds
>The Stock Exchange
>Unit Trust Association

The accountancy profession is represented by the President of the English Institution of Chartered Accountants. There is also a representative of the Confederation of British Industry. From 1968 to 1977 this was Sir Peter Menzies. The bodies represented on the Panel nominate substitutes so that a full attendance can be ensured even if a meeting is summoned at short notice.

PROCEDURE

Cases come before the Panel by way of an appeal against a ruling by the Director-General or the Director-General may consider that a case is sufficiently important, or closely enough related to a decision previously given by the Panel, that it ought to be brought directly to the Panel for a Panel ruling. When considering a case, the Panel is reluctant to take too narrow a view of its function. It would not, for example, necessarily restrict itself to the precise point that is the subject of an appeal.

[1] Lord Shawcross is resigning in the early summer of 1980 and Sir Jasper Hollom will become Chairman.

The Panel executive takes the day-to-day decisions but it is not to be regarded as having supplanted the Panel as the executive arm of the Code. The Panel is not simply a first court of appeal, followed by an appeal in disciplinary cases to the Appeal Committee. If, for example, the contents of an offer document came before the Panel on appeal from a decision by the Director-General on a particular point, the Panel would feel free to consider other points in the offer document—always subject to the parties being given more time, if they asked for it, to argue the matter further.

Disciplinary cases, where someone has broken the Code and some form of penalty may be required, come before the Panel, unless the breach is of no great significance and the Chairman considers that a word of protest or a warning by him or by the Director-General will meet the case. The Panel is unwilling to adjudicate on a case in the presence only of one party to a take-over. Both sides are invited to attend and to hear the representations put forward. On very rare occasions, one party may be allowed to advance considerations in the absence of the other party, where there is a sustainable argument that serious damage would be done if confidential information became known to the other side. The Panel is most reluctant to act on an ex-parte confidential statement because its findings are made known to both sides and usually published, and they ought to be related to facts and arguments known to both sides.

Where the Panel is hearing an appeal against a ruling by the Director-General, it is customary for the party that is appealing to submit a short paper beforehand and the Director-General may circulate a paper outlining the circumstances of the take-over and the reasons for his ruling. These papers are circulated beforehand to the Panel and to those who are appearing before it. Proceedings before the Panel are confidential and those who attend are warned that they must not repeat outside any information which they obtain in the course of the hearing. This is necessary to encourage everyone to speak frankly and fully. No permenent record of the proceedings is kept, though a tape recording is taken (and subsequently destroyed) to facilitate reference back to what was said at an earlier stage of the proceedings.

Throughout its existence the Panel has insisted that those

who appear before it or do business with the Panel executive must be completely frank—that indeed a scheme of self-regulation will not work unless there is complete frankness. Reference has already been made to this in relation to financial advisers (pages 122 and 123). In a wider context the need for frankness was emphasized in the statement on Norbury Insulation issued on 2 April 1971 and again in a statement issued on 5 April 1974 in connection with the St Martin's Property Corporation's bid for Hays Wharf.

In a typical case of a contested bid where there is an appeal against a ruling given by the Director-General on the application of the Code to a particular set of circumstances, the parties will be represented by their merchant banks and accompanied by members of the respective boards. The Chairman will explain for the benefit of the company representatives that the proceedings of the Panel are informal and that there are no rules of evidence, the procedure to be followed and the confidentiality of the proceedings. The Director-General goes through his paper on the circumstances of the case and the grounds for his ruling. Any member of the Panel or any of the parties may then question the Director-General on any point. The representative of the merchant bank that is appealing then says anything in amplification of the paper that has been submitted and he in turn may be questioned by the Chairman and other members of the merchant bank and company on the other side. The representative of the other merchant bank then adds anything he considers necessary and he in turn may be questioned by the Chairman and other members of the Panel or the other side. The Director-General then sums up and all withdraw except the Panel members. Normally, after consideration by the Panel, the parties are recalled and the Chairman announces the Panel's decision. A written statement of the decision and the reasons for it may be issued at once, or, if the issues are involved, the statement may be issued later. Like the Duke of Wellington, the Panel endeavours to do the business of the day in the day.

If the Director-General has referred a point to the Panel without giving a ruling himself, the Director-General will send a paper beforehand to the members of the Panel. Both sides to the take-over bid are then invited to attend with their advisers.

The Director-General opens the discussion, both sides are invited to add anything and everyone can question everyone else. The Director-General usually remains with the Panel during their deliberations. Representations by shareholders are presented in writing and are normally considered by the Panel in their absence.

If there appears to have been a breach of the Code the executive invites the person concerned to appear before the Panel for a hearing. The Director-General informs him by letter of the nature of the alleged breach and of the matters which the Director-General will present. He is sent a copy of the background note, outlining the circumstances of the case, which the Director-General sends to Panel members. He is told that in the ordinary way the Panel does not allow full legal representation (as to which see below) but that he may bring an adviser or advisers with him and that an adviser will be allowed to take such part in the proceedings as the Chairman may determine. At the hearing the Director-General outlines the facts as set out in his letter and the individual concerned then has an opportunity to reply. If any fresh issue is raised he is allowed to ask for an adjournment. If the Panel finds that there has been a breach, it may have recourse to private reprimand or public censure, or, in a more flagrant case, to further action designed to deprive the offender temporarily or permanently of his ability to enjoy the facilities of the securities markets. The Panel may refer certain aspects of a case to the Department of Trade, The Stock Exchange, or other appropriate body. No reprimand, censure, or further action will take place without the person concerned having the opportunity to appeal to the Appeal Committee of the Panel.

The Panel, having found that there has been a breach of the Code and decided on the requisite penalty, informs the party concerned of the decision and states that he may serve notice of appeal within the next forty-eight hours. The Panel normally suspends publication in full of its findings during this time. If there is no appeal, publication (if that is so decided) follows immediately. If there is an appeal, publication is further suspended until the decision of the Appeal Committee. The Panel recognizes that its authority in take-over matters can only be sustained if its impartiality is placed beyond doubt. Where a matter arising for discussion is likely to create a conflict of interest for any Panel member, the member arranges for his alternate to be empanelled.

It is the Panel's policy in the case of important or controversial matters to publish its conclusions and the reasons for them. In this manner its own activities are subject to public scrutiny. The Panel executive have a distribution list for public statements that involves the issue of about 300 copies. The Issuing Houses Association copies the statement to all its members. Other Panel copies go to the constituent bodies, to the Press and to a wide circle of interested bodies abroad. In the ordinary way, one cannot expect the newspapers to publish Panel statements on individual cases in full, since they may run to several foolscap pages in order to explain the circumstances and the exact points at issue. One is, therefore, dependent on the full statements, issued by the Panel, reaching all who are interested. The Journal of Business Law has performed a useful function by publishing in each quarterly issue an account of the more important cases.

REPRESENTATION

At hearings before the Panel, principals (whether companies, individuals, or their advisers) present their case in person. It is the practice to allow persons appearing to have present with them their professional advisers (such as merchant banks or accountants or solicitors who have been concerned in the conduct of the transactions under review). These advisers may play such part in the proceedings as the Chairman may on each occasion consider appropriate in the circumstances. On issues concerning the interpretation of the code, merchant banks normally take the lead and present the case of their client. It is not, however, the Panel's normal practice to allow representation by legal advocates. The issue does not really arise in contested bids where two merchant banks are taking opposing views on the interpretation of the Code. They are experts. The Panel is largely composed of experts and is the final authority on the interpretation of the Code. There is no obvious need for the assistance of non-experts, however gifted in advocacy.

The real problem over full legal representation arises in disciplinary cases where the consequences to the individual concerned may be grave. By full legal representation is understood a procedure under which a barrister or solicitor would lead his client in giving his evidence, cross-examine the Director-General and other parties and make a speech for his client at the end. The booklet containing the Code states:

> Proceedings before the Panel are informal and private. There are no rules of evidence. A verbatim record will normally be taken for the assistance of the Panel, but no permanent record will be maintained.
>
> Parties appearing before the Panel are permitted to bring with them any adviser that they wish and to call such witnesses as they may feel necessary. It is not, however, the Panel's normal practice to allow full representation by legal advocates.

As already indicated, these points are also explained by letter to an individual appearing in a disciplinary case.

The Courts have held explicitly that voluntary bodies, like the Panel, provided that they act fairly and are seen to act fairly, are the master of their own procedure and can decide whether legal representation is necessary in any particular case. In a case that came before the Court of Appeal in 1971,[1] the Master of the Rolls (Lord Denning) said that 'in many cases it may be a good thing for the proceedings of a domestic tribunal to be conducted informally without legal representation' and in the same case Lord Justice Cairns said: 'Where the tribunal is composed of intelligent laymen who have a great knowledge of the business concerned, I think that the employment of lawyers is likely to lengthen proceedings and certainly greatly to increase the expense of them without any certainty of bringing about a fairer decision.'

The facts in these cases are usually not complicated and the truth can be elicited by straightforward questions and answers. There has never been any suggestion that the Panel has wrongly convicted an individual of a breach of the Code. There have occasionally been cases where the Panel failed to get at the facts and failed, therefore, to nail down a breach of the Code: but that would not be corrected by providing an evasive defendant with legal representation.

A practice of allowing full legal representation in all disciplinary cases would entirely change the character of the proceedings. The cases are not sufficiently numerous for an appropriate

---

[1] *Enderby Town F.C.* v. *F.A.* (1971), Ch. 591.

legal procedure to be built up to which lawyers would adhere. Some barristers would bring to the Panel the habits they have learned in the Courts—reading aloud every document, examining witnesses at length, and making long speeches. The question would arise whether the Director-General should not also be represented by Counsel. The lengthening of the proceedings which would follow would affect the quality of the individuals who were prepared to sit as Panel members. The senior Panel members are busy people fully employed on their regular work. It would be impossible to get Panel members of the necessary high standing to sit on cases that went on for days. It is those appearing before the Panel who would suffer. These are issues on which different views can be taken but the Panel has adhered to the view that normally full legal representation is unnecessary and undesirable. This does not exclude the possibility that legal representation in some form would be allowed in particular cases presenting special features and, as already indicated, someone appearing before the Panel may bring a solicitor to advise him.

QUARTERLY MEETINGS

The Panel meets at three-monthly intervals to review the work of the Panel and of the Panel executive and to consider any general issues that arise. The Director-General prepares and circulates beforehand a report on the work of the previous quarter.

Appeals

There is an Appeal Committee. It is chaired by Lord Cross of Chelsea, a retired Lord of Appeal, and he sits with three members of the Panel who did not sit on the case when it was before the Panel. One of these members, so far as is possible, will be a representative of the body to which the party concerned is affiliated. From 1968 to 1976 the Chairman of the Appeal Committee was Lord Pearce and the City owe a great debt to Lord Pearce for his services at the formative stage of the organization. There is a right of appeal to the Appeal Committee where the Panel both finds a breach of the Code and proposes to take disciplinary action and in a case where it is alleged that the Panel has acted outside its jurisdiction. An appeal may also lie with leave of the Panel against decisions which, although not strictly of a disciplinary nature, inflict in the view of the Panel serious hardship on an individual or company. No appeal, however, lies against a finding of fact or against a decision of the Panel in the interpretation of the Code. The Panel postpones the issue of any public statement on the case till after the decision of the Appeal Committee.

The Appeal Committee do not normally hear new evidence. If the Appeal Committee considered there might be material new evidence which could not have been presented to the Panel, they they would remit the matter to the Panel for further consideration. Proceedings before the Appeal Committee are conducted in a similar way to those before the Panel. If the Appeal Committee dismisses the appeal, the findings of the Panel are published with the addition of a statement that there was an appeal but it was unsuccessful. The Appeal Committee may suggest some alteration in the Panel's statement of the case, which the Panel then considers. If the appeal is successful there may be no statement at all, unless the individual concerned wants one to be made. In the Leasco/Pergamon case, Mr Robert Maxwell was content that the Panel's statement should be issued forthwith, and the Appeal Committee issued a later and separate statement. The procedure was, however, exceptional.

XI

GOVERNMENT AND THE CODE

In the fifties the attitude of the Conservative Government to take-over bids was that on balance they were beneficial and that the need had not been established for any Government intervention in respect of the standards of conduct to be observed. Much of the debate that went on related to the merits of individual take-overs and this led to mergers of a certain size being brought within the ambit of the monopolies legislation in 1965.

The Licensed Dealers (Conduct of Business) Rules were issued in 1960. It was the intention of the Department to revise the rules from time to time, but such are the difficulties of changing statutory rules in a fast moving situation that no changes were made. Meantime there were the Notes (1959), Revised Notes (1963), and then there was the first edition of the Code (1968). The Labour Government, elected in 1964, showed no inclination to endeavour to control take-over procedures, if the voluntary system could be made to work successfully. This became clear in 1968, when the Code and the Panel were under attack.

The reorganization of the Panel in 1969 revolved round the question of how it was to assert its authority. It was arranged that the Panel would report to the Board of Trade any case where an offender was a licensed dealer and where public reprobation did not seem to be an adequate sanction, so that the Board of Trade could consider the possibility of action under the Prevention of Fraud (Investments) Act 1958. The Panel was assured by the Board of Trade that they would take into prompt consideration the facts relevant to the exercise of their powers which were disclosed in any such report by the Panel.

After the Panel was set up in 1968, it had a good working relationship with the Industrial Reorganization Corporation which had been established by statute in 1966. In the summer of 1968 the IRC supported George Kent Limited which was bidding against the Rank Organization for Cambridge Instrument Company Limited and this led to some press comment and criticism. In a press release dated 5 July 1968 the IRC said 'The Panel on Take-overs and Mergers has authorized IRC to say that in its view the IRC has conformed to the Code.' A few days later the Minister concerned said in reply to a parliamentary question that '. . . the Industrial Reorganization Corporation naturally regards itself as bound by the Code' (Commons Debates, 10 July 1968—Written Answers, col. 103).

The continuance of take-over bids, particularly by large companies, the general report of the Monopolies Commission on conglomerate mergers and the operations of the Industrial Reorganization Corporation all led to a demand for a statement of the Government's policy on mergers. In July 1969 the Government issued a guide to Board of Trade practice, under the title 'Mergers'. It gave the text of the City Code on Take-overs and Mergers and explained that 'the purpose of the Code is to ensure that all shareholders affected by a bid are treated fairly and to that end the Code enunciates general principles of conduct to be observed in bid situations and lays down rules based on these principles'. It went on to say that 'since the Licensed Dealers Rules are narrower in their scope than the City Code, the Board should, when giving permission for the distribution of a take-over circular, also draw the applicant's attention to the Code'. The guide entitled 'Mergers' was reissued in 1978 and repeated the above references to the Code. Those concerned with take-overs were referred to the Code, of which copies of the current edition could be obtained from the Issuing Houses Association.

There has, over the years, been close contact between the Panel executive and the Department of Trade on general questions of policy. The abortive efforts to revise and bring up to date the Licensed Dealers (Conduct of Business) Rules, 1960, led to queries by the Department of Trade about the reasons for various provisions in the Code: and the Department was also concerned from time to time to know whether the City Working Party was taking steps to deal with some practice which had been adversely commented on.

The Conservative Government, in its White Paper issued in July 1973, outlined its proposals for company reform. Those relating to insider dealing have already been mentioned. It was proposed also to deal with 'warehousing', which the White Paper defined as 'a situation in which a number of parties act in undisclosed concert, not sufficiently close to bring them within the existing provisions, each acquiring an interest in the equity of a company below 10 per cent (at which notification to the company was already required), thus enabling one or more of them to acquire by stealth a dominant position in the company'. Although the City Code had elaborated the concept of persons acting in concert, the Department found difficulty in putting this into statutory form and did not go beyond proposing that the percentage of acquired shares requiring notification should be reduced from 10 per cent to 5 per cent. The time allowed for notification was to be reduced. Directors' dealings were also to be reported more promptly. A company must also have the right 'reasonably to demand to know who are the beneficial as opposed to the nominal owners of its shares'.

The abortive Companies Bill of 1973 contained a number of provisions bearing on take-overs. There was to be speedier reporting of dealings by directors and by substantial shareholders (a substantial holding being reduced from 10 per cent to 5 per cent). A listed company could require a registered shareholder to say who was the beneficial owner of voting shares. Any new issue of equity shares by a listed company was not to have restricted voting rights. There were provisions directed against insider dealing.

On 19 November 1973 the Minister for Trade and Consumer Affairs (Sir Geoffrey Howe) said that 'clearly there were certain matters which required statutory powers and enforcement by means of an Act of Parliament, but equally clearly there were others which were more susceptible of remedy by means of a self-policing organization of the kind represented by the Take-over Panel' (Commons Debates 19 Nov. 1973 col. 920.)

The Fair Trading Act 1973 made a number of changes in the monopolies and merger legislation. It provided for the appointment of a Director-General of Fair Trading, heading an Office of Fair Trading, who, *inter alia*, advises the Department of Prices and Consumer Protection on the reference of mergers for investigations to the Monopolies and Mergers Commission, though the final decision on a reference rests with the Secretary of State. The Act deals at some length with the physical division of a merged unit if it is decided, after reference to the Commission, that the merger is against the public interest. It does not deal so aptly with the unwinding of the commonest form of merger and the one that concerns the Panel—where shares of the offeree company have been acquired. This depends on the application of a rather obscure paragraph in a schedule (Schedule 8 paragraph 15). The Panel executive keeps in touch with the Office of Fair Trading on general questions of policy. Obviously neither can discuss the details of individual cases that come before them.

One problem that exercised the attention of the Panel was the effect of a reference to the Monopolies and Mergers Commission of a bid, and more particularly a mandatory bid. Under powers taken in 1965, which were re-enacted in section 74 of the Fair Trading Act 1973, the Secretary of State could by order prevent action that might prejudice a reference to the Commission or prejudice the subsequent implementation of the Commission's recommendations. The Secretary of State could, for example, prohibit a merger or oblige a company to continue certain activities, or not to sell some of its assets, or forbid the acquisition of a company's shares or assets, or lay down conditions as to the acquisition of assets. Although these powers have on occasion been used,[1] the Department and the Office of Fair Trading prefer to obtain voluntary undertakings—e.g. an undertaking from the offeror that he, and possibly also those acting in concert with him, will not buy offeree shares during the period of the reference. The Department and the

---

[1] For example, in 1973 the proposed acquisition of Wilkinson Sword by the British Match Corporation was referred to the Monopolies Commission; and in Statutory Instrument no. 1137 of 1973 the British Match Corporation was not allowed to acquire further shares in Wilkinson Sword, if as a result Wilkinson Sword became a subsidiary of British Match Corporation, while the merger was under investigation.

GOVERNMENT AND THE CODE

Panel agreed that the simplest course, so far as the Code was concerned, was to insert in the offer document a condition that the offer lapsed if there was a reference to the Commission. This was done in 1974 under what is now Rule 9. Voluntary bids are often abandoned by the offeror, on a reference to the Commission. Where the offer is mandatory under Rule 34, the offeror is under an obligation to bid again if the Commission clears the bid (paragraph 11 of Practice Note 8). Strictly speaking, the offer period lapses on a reference to the Commission. The Panel would, however, regard Rule 38 as still in force, unless the offeror in a voluntary bid had completely abandoned it, since 'the board of the offeree company has reason to believe that a bona fide offer may be imminent'. Hence, an offeree board remains prevented during the reference from taking action, without the approval of its shareholders, which would frustrate a subsequent revived bid.

The Government and the Bank of England observed the provisions of the Code in relation to the purchase in January, 1975 by the Bank of England of the 20 per cent holding of BP owned by the Burmah Oil Company. A statement issued by the Panel on 23 January 1975, with the agreement of the Government and the Bank was in the following terms:

The Panel has had discussions with the Bank of England and the Board of BP regarding the purchase of BP's stock by the Bank of England which has been announced to-day. The Bank of England have undertaken to the Panel that while they hold this stock they will not exercise the votes attaching to it.

The Bank have also informed the Panel that it is not Her Majesty's Government's intention that this transaction should change in any way the existing arrangements between the Government and BP, and that accordingly while the stock in question remains in the Bank's hands Her Majesty's Government will not exercise a greater proportionate voting power in relation to other shareholders than they could have exercised hitherto.

Having regard to these assurances the Panel has ruled that no bid need be made to the public shareholders in BP.

In February 1975 the Department of Prices and Consumer Protection referred to the Monopolies and Mergers Commission a proposal that H. Weidmann A. G. of Rapperswil, Switzerland, a manufacturer of electrical insulating pressboard, should take over B. S. & W. Whiteley Limited of Pool-in-Wharfdale, Yorkshire, which was in the same line of business. It is no secret that the Department received with modified rapture the Commission's conclusion, after a four-month inquiry, that the proposed take-over would not operate against the public interest. The matter then came before the Take-over Panel, because Weidmann and three other Swiss companies, acting in concert and in possession of more than 30 per cent of the Whiteley shares, had in August 1974 acquired further shares amounting to more than 1 per cent and had thereby made themselves liable to make a mandatory bid under Rule 34 of the 1974 Code. Weidmann was not anxious to make a bid at the highest price of its recent share purchases and the Panel had power to waive the requirement to make a bid. The Panel heard the case on 1 December 1974 and relieved Weidmann of the obligation. The Panel pointed out that the bid, if successful, might have resulted in the transfer abroad of control of the sole manufacturer of electrical insulating pressboard in the United Kingdom. Weidmann accepted a condition that the 33.4 per cent holding of the Swiss interests should be reduced to not more than 25 per cent.

The Industry Act 1975 set up the National Enterprise Board with the function, *inter alia*, of extending public ownership into profitable areas of manufacturing industry. During the passage of the Bill through Parliament, the Panel discussed with the Department of Industry the application of the Code to the operations of the Board. The Department gave an assurance that the National Enterprise Board would observe the letter and spirit of the provisions of the Code 'in their entirety and without reservation'. In June 1974 the Secretary of State for Trade (Mr Peter Shore) announced that his Department proposed to carry out a review of the existing arrangements for the supervision of the securities market. The Department of Trade issued a questionnaire to interested parties, designed to ascertain the adequacy of the existing arrangements for the supervision of the securities market. For the most part those consulted expressed themselves as satisfied with the existing arrangements. The Panel's reply, dated January 1975, expressed confidence in the existing scheme of self-regulation. On the idea of a supervisory body, the Panel said:

GOVERNMENT AND THE CODE

It has been suggested that a statutory body dealing with City affairs should be interposed between Government and the self-regulatory bodies. No doubt, if the statutory body were simply intended to perform more efficiently the functions at present residing in Government Departments it might have certain advantages, although it would be preferable to improve the efficiency of Government Departments without establishing a new statutory body. But if, as seems more likely, the statutory body were to preside over the voluntary bodies and exercise powers over them, then it would be a mistake to imagine that the virtues of self-regulation could be preserved. There would be appeals to the statutory body and possibly from that body to the courts. Delays and uncertainties would result. The Panel's activities would suffer because it could not move swiftly and effectively. The interposition of a new body would reduce the sense of responsibility of those already supervising the conduct of take-overs and this might mean that leading people would be unwilling to undertake the work. It is easy on paper to get the best of both worlds, but much less easy in practice.

The next two years saw a number of developments designed to tidy up some aspects of the State's concern in this field. A Companies Bill was introduced in March 1976 and passed into law later in the year. Consultative documents were issued in July 1977 on The Future of Company Reports (Cmnd. 6888) and on Amendments to the Prevention of Fraud (Investments) Act 1958 (Cmnd. 6893) and in November 1977 on The Conduct of Company Directors (Cmnd. 7037). Later, in July 1978, the draft of a further Companies Bill was circulated under cover of a White Paper entitled Changes in Company Law (Cmnd. 7291). In addition to tightening up the statutory provisions relating to the form of company accounts and their filing with the Department, the Companies Act 1976 had a number of provisions (sections 23–7) designed to secure the disclosure of dealings. Directors have to report purchases of shares in their own companies within five, not fourteen, days: and the passing of the information to The Stock Exchange is speeded up. Shareholdings amounting to 5 per cent, not 10 per cent as before, have to be reported to the company and entered in a register, and companies are given powers to ascertain the beneficial owners behind nominee holdings. This of course is not effective against nominee holdings by overseas banks, and the disinclination of Swiss banks to disclose information is well known. In consequence of the passing of the Act, the City Working Party in September 1977 made an addition to Rule 31 to the effect that anyone who under the 5 per cent provision would have to notify dealings in the shares of the offeror or offeree during the offer period must report them to The Stock Exchange, the Panel and the press not later than the following day, naming the person dealing and the resultant holding.

Under the Restrictive Trade Practices (Services) Order 1976 (SI no. 98 of 1976) an agreement arising out of compliance with the Take-over Code or with a decision of the Panel is exempted from registration and from investigation by the Restrictive Practices Court.

There remained the problem of the boundary between State supervision and self-regulation and the relations between the two systems. On 7 October 1976 it was announced that the Government intended to set up a committee, under the chairmanship of Sir Harold Wilson, to enquire into the functioning of financial institutions in the UK and, *inter alia*, 'to consider what changes are required in the existing arrangements for the supervision of these institutions, including the possible extension of the public section'. The Wilson Committee was formally constituted on 5 January 1977.

Following discussions between the Secretary of State for Trade (Mr Edmund Dell) and the Governor of the Bank of England (Mr Gordon Richardson), Mr Dell announced on 21 October 1976 the results of the review initiated by his predecessor in June 1974. He said that the review had shown that the existing combination of statutory and self-regulatory control, although perhaps a good deal more effective than its critics admitted, could with advantage be improved in a number of respects. He had therefore decided, without pre-empting the study to be undertaken by Sir Harold Wilson's committee, to take a number of limited measures to improve the supervision and functioning of the present system. These measures were:

(a) a joint review body to be set up by the Department of Trade and the Bank of England. The details of the joint review body were announced on 22 December 1976. The joint chairmen are a Deputy Secretary of the Department of Trade and the Deputy Governor of the Bank and the other members are two officials

from each side. The terms of reference are: 'To keep under review the functioning of the securities market and the arrangements for its supervision; to identify any gaps or other deficiencies in the combination of statutory and self-regulatory control; and to make recommendations as appropriate to the Secretary of State and the Governor of the Bank of England.'
(b) the Bank of England to develop its surveillance of the securities industry with a view to improving the effectiveness of the existing self-regulatory machinery. This led to the setting-up of the Council for the Securities Industry.
(c) legislation to be introduced as soon as opportunity permitted to bring abuses, such as insider trading, within the scope of the law and to impose tighter restrictions on loans by companies to their directors. This was effected by the introduction of the Companies Bill 1978.
(d) as soon as opportunity permitted, the Prevention of Fraud (Investment) Act to be amended in order to bring up to date the Department of Trade's regulation of the statutory part of the securities system.

The Conservative Government which came into office in 1979 has expressed its belief in the efficacy of self-regulation for the supervision of the securities industry. It has brought into its 1979 Companies Bill provisions on insider dealing and loans to directors, being matters which are appropriate for legislation.

DEPARTMENT OF TRADE INSPECTIONS

Reference has already been made to the report of the Board of Trade inspectors on Pergamon. Since then there have been a number of inspections of cases in which the Panel has been involved. The Panel has on occasion pointed to the need for the examination by the Department of Trade of issues that have come before the Panel. There is no necessary conflict. The Panel is concerned with the administration of the Code, it has no statutory powers and it has to handle issues with expedition. Department of Trade inspectors appointed under section 165 of the Companies Act 1948 have usually the much wider remit of inquiring into 'the affairs' of a company and its subsidiaries, they have powers to require the attendance of the company's officers and agents and to take evidence on oath and their inquiries normally take a year or more. The inspectors may, therefore, unearth information that was not available to the Panel or the Panel executive.

The Panel has shown itself to be anxious to give such help as it can to inspectors. There is, however, a real difficulty in cases in which parties express an unwillingness to agree that the Panel should make evidence available to inspectors. The Panel has no legal powers and depends on witnesses speaking fully and frankly. They might not do so if they thought that what they had said would be passed to inspectors without their agreement. There is no check on the use that inspectors may make of information or of the comments they may make. There is no reason to believe that other bodies with confidential information (e.g. the Office of Fair Trading) would react in a different way. There is a statutory procedure for enabling inspectors to go to the High Court and require witnesses whom inspectors could not require to appear before them to give evidence to the Court (section 167(4) of the Companies Act 1948); but outside this provision the Panel is reluctant to provide confidential information to inspectors without the consent of the parties.

In the inspectors' report on the affairs of CST Ltd., one of Mr Christopher Selmes's companies, there was implied criticism of the Panel for not making information available to the inspectors, although there was objection from at least one party involved. The report also inferred that the Panel had not been thorough enough in its inquiries, although on a number of crucial issues the inspectors had been no more successful than the Panel in getting at the facts.

XII

LAW AND THE CODE

TAKE-OVER bids involve legal transactions of a more complex character than a straightforward purchase or sale of securities. A bidder makes a general offer to acquire shares, subject to certain conditions being fulfilled. The most important is the percentage of acceptances he must secure before he closes the deal. The proposed consideration may be cash or securities or a mixture of both. The cash may be provided by a merchant bank offering to buy from offeree shareholders any securities in the offeror company they receive as consideration. There may be legal problems arising out of the relations of directors with their own shareholders and with the shareholders of the other company.

There are no provisions of a general character in the Companies Acts about the techniques used in mergers or take-overs. There are, however, statutory provisions dealing with special aspects of the subject. Thus schemes of arrangement are regulated. Dealers licensed under the Prevention of Fraud (Investments) Act 1958 are subject to statutory rules which have already been described. Directors have to report dealings in the shares of their companies and may not deal in options. 'Warehousing' is also subject to a measure of publicity—the latest provision being the requirement in the Companies Act, 1976, that holdings of 5 per cent or more of voting shares should be reported to the company and the information made available for public inspection.

From the start, the fear was expressed, most commonly by solicitors, that the Code might clash with the law. This did not relate to the detailed provisions described above but to general obligations under company law. Thus the Law Society, in a memorium addressed to the Department of Trade in January 1975 in listing the advantages and disadvantages of self-regulation, referred to 'the danger of conflict between the rules or objectives of the regulatory body and the legal rights and duties of those to whom the rules apply'.

There were those who expressed a less pessimistic view and as things have turned out this has proved to be nearer the truth of the matter. Reference has already been made to Sir Milner Holland's comment on the 1969 revision of the Code that there need be no real conflict between the higher standards of conduct sought by the Code and the legal requirements. In relation to the common law rule that proper care should be shown in the drafting of company documents, Professor R. R. Pennington in a prescient comment on the Code in 1968, said that 'when the court comes to apply the rule to take-over documents, it will certainly be reinforced in imposing and defining the duty of care by the fact that the City institutions have recognized the need for it'.[1] The courts have found the Code a convenient statement of the best City practice. An early instance is to be found in the House of Lords' judgement in *Hinchcliffe* v. *Crabtree* [(1972) A.C. 730] and a later case in the judgements given in the Court of Appeal in *Dunford & Elliott* v. *Johnson & Firth Brown* [1 Lloyds Rep. (1977) 505 CA].

The need to include various provisions of the Code in offer documents has ensured that City solicitors took an interest in the Code and assisted in its various revisions. There are a number of points on which it is conceivable that the Code might in a particular case come into conflict with the law. The courts regard a board of directors as having a duty to look after the interests of the company. There is no appeal on merits from management decisions to courts of law. The Courts do not act as a kind of supervisory board over decisions, within the powers of management, honestly arrived at.[2] If, however, the question at issue is whether the board of a company had power to do what was at issue, the Courts would regard themselves as free to analyse a decision by the board of a company to the extent of taking a view whether, of various reasons for a decision, one or

---

[1] *Accountancy* (June 1968), p. 409.
[2] *Howard Smith Ltd.*, v. *Ampol Petroleum Ltd.* (1974), A.C. 821.

other reason was the substantial or primary reason. If that reason fell outside the interests that the law considers that the board should have regard to, a plea that the board had been following the Code would not avail. Again, one of the main objects of the Code is to see that the shareholders of the offeree company get fair play and at various points the Code imposes obligations on the offeror board in relation to the offeree shareholders. There is always the possibility of a clash between the offeror board's obligations to its own shareholders and to the offeree shareholders. Indeed General Principle 2 recognizes that.

The Panel has had well in mind the need to keep on the right side of the law! In relation to the abortive bid for Hay's Wharf, the Panel was careful to impose conditions on the board of St Martins which did not require ratification by the St Martins' shareholders. The Panel directed, and the board of St Martins undertook to the Panel, that until such time as the outstanding obligation was fulfilled by St Martins, the shares in Hay's Wharf held by St Martins should not be voted nor should St Martins deal in Hay's Wharf shares. The exercise of voting rights attaching to any shares held by a particular company is a matter for which responsibility is normally vested in the directors of the company by the Articles of Association. Likewise in the Ashbourne case, the Panel directed that the block of shares which had given rise to the bid obligation should not be voted in any circumstances and that the remaining shares held by the consortium should be voted so as to maintain the reconstituted board in office. These were matters for the directors.

Efforts have been made from time to time to invoke the assistance of the courts in connection with take-over bids. Here again the fear has been expressed that resort to the law might provide a ready means of nullifying the operation of the Code: but this has not so far proved to be a serious risk.

Guest, Keen & Nettlefold/Miles Druce. In 1972 Guest, Keen & Nettlefold made an unsuccessful bid at 150p for the ordinary shares of Miles Druce, which was the country's largest steel stockholders. GKN then built up its holding of Miles Druce shares till it and its associates reached 39.9 per cent. In June 1973 GKN applied to the European Community Commission for a clearance to make a bid for Miles Druce. In October 1973 the Commission rejected an application by Miles Druce for various preliminary measures of protection and on 14 March 1974 the Commission gave the clearance to GKN to go ahead with the bid, subject to the status quo being maintained while Miles Druce considered whether within the next three weeks it would appeal to the European Court against the decision of the Commission. GKN issued its offer document on 14 March. GKN offered 198p for the ordinary shares of Miles Druce. The offer was conditional on no court of competent jurisdiction blocking the bid, and the offer could not become unconditional before 8 April 1974.

On the morning of 20 March 1974 the Panel ruled

(i) that General Principle 4 required the directors of Miles Druce to obtain the approval of shareholders in general meeting before taking any step which would or might give rise to an order of a court of competent jurisdiction preventing the acquisition of shares by GKN; and
(ii) that at any such general meeting of Miles Druce, no votes should be cast in respect of any of the share capital of Miles Druce owned by GKN.

On the same day (20 March 1974) the European Communities Commission ordered GKN to withdraw its offer document and so preserve the status quo. GKN had understood that the Commission's order of 14 March did not go beyond preventing GKN from acquiring further shares. GKN announced that in response to its offer, it now (with the shares it already controlled) had over 50 per cent of the voting rights of Miles Druce shares. With the consent of the Panel, GKN withdrew its offer but announced that it would reinstate it on 8 April on the same terms. In the end Miles Druce did not appeal to the European Court. Share prices were falling and some institutional shareholders were understood to have indicated that they intended to accept the GKN offer. The reinstated offer was successful.

Ashbourne. Following the obligation to make a bid for all the remaining shares of Ashbourne, which Crest, Corporate, and their associates incurred by their purchase of Ashbourne shares, a shareholder of Crest instituted proceedings in the High Court in April 1974 in which he sought an injunction to restrain Crest from making a general offer until the proposition was considered by Crest shareholders in a general meeting. The Panel was made a party to these proceedings by leave of the Court. This was the first time that the Panel became a party in a Court case.

Subsequently separate proceedings were instituted in the High Court by Crest and Corporate against the vendors of the 1,700,000 shares bought, claiming rescission of the purchase contract on the ground of misrepresentation of the financial position of Ashbourne at the time of the purchase. Those proceedings were at one time adjourned, pending an effort to secure a settlement, and then resumed. Meantime the Panel felt obliged to endeavour to hold the position by a direction, dated 23 July 1974, reducing the consortium's representation on the Ashbourne board and restricting their use of voting rights. The consortium then sought to obtain an injunction to restrain the Panel from issuing the direction and obtained an interim injunction to that effect on 23 July. On 25 July Mr Justice Kilner Brown refused to grant an injunction before trial. He was satisfied that the attitude of the Panel had been conditioned by the well-being of the shareholders and not in criticism or condemnation of the plaintiffs. There was 'no question of discipline—no question of sanction'. The action by Crest and Corporate against certain Ashbourne directors who had sold them shares was settled out of court.

In regard to the action by the Crest shareholder, Mr Justice Templeman ruled on 27 November 1974 that 'so far as the Court is concerned there is no objection, and every advantage, in the Panel conducting such investigations as the Panel think fit. The Panel are to notify in writing what they would do, if the action was not in the way. Anything done by the Panel would not be contempt of Court... No statement should be issued by the Panel until the matter is mentioned to me...'

Babcock & Wilcox/Herbert Morris. Babcock & Wilcox in 1976 acquired from Amalgamated Industrials 37.7 per cent of the issued share capital of Herbert Morris, cranemakers of Loughborough, and became liable to make a bid for the remaining

63.3 per cent of the shares. Herbert Morris sought a restraining order in the US District Court at Baltimore on anti-trust grounds against Babcock & Wilcox proceeding with the bid. A temporary restraining order was granted on 4 October 1976, but this was vacated on 15 October and a longer-term injunction was refused.

Johnson & Firth Brown/Dunford & Elliott. On 8 November 1976 Johnson & Firth Brown announced the terms of an offer for the share capital of Dunford & Elliott. Johnson & Firth Brown had previously been given confidential information about Dunford & Elliott by the Prudential Assurance Company, in connection with a proposal that insurance companies and others should underwrite a rights issue by Dunford & Elliott. Dunford & Elliott then initiated an action in the High Court against Johnson & Firth Brown on the ground that there was an unauthorized use of information to the detriment of their shareholders: and asked for an injunction restraining Johnson & Firth Brown from proceeding with the offer pending the trial of the action. In the High Court the injunction was granted on 30 November 1976 but the Court of Appeal on 3 December 1976 reversed the decision on the ground that an injunction would not preserve the status quo since it might not be possible to proceed with the bid at a later date.

In January 1977 the Panel issued a statement that a board that contemplated legal proceedings in relation to an offer or prospective offer would be well advised to consult the Panel before action was taken, since in certain circumstances, problems might arise under the Code. This statement has been criticized in some quarters as failing to indicate how the Panel would in fact handle a case. The probability is that the Panel would be wary of seeming to attempt to deprive directors of their legal rights.

Graff Diamonds. The Panel normally postpones any investigation into the conduct of parties to a take-over if legal proceedings have already been set in train in respect of that conduct. On occasion the Panel has postponed its investigation on being told that one of the parties was contemplating legal action, but this can lead to an undesirable delay if the party in the end decides not to proceed. In 1978/9 in connection with an offer for the remaining shares in Graff Diamonds Ltd., the Panel investigated an allegation which had appeared in a newspaper and which was the subject of legal actions against the newspaper and against the Panel. On 1 March 1979 the High Court allowed the Panel to proceed with its investigations but did not allow its findings to be published, pending the conclusion of the action against the newspaper. The circumstances were somewhat unusual. The embargo on publication may have been linked with the fact that a libel action may be tried by a jury.

Schemes of Arrangement. The Code applies to schemes of arrangement made under sections 206 and 208 of the Companies Act 1948. In the definitions 'offer' includes, wherever appropriate, take-over and merger transactions, however affected. It is often not clear at the outset what form a merger will take. It would open the door to a disregarding of the Code if schemes of arrangement were regarded as outside the Code. The Panel executive is sent explanatory statements issued in connection with schemes of arrangment, scrutinize them and offer comments on them. Statistics about schemes of arrangment are included in the annual reports of the Panel. The statutory requirement (section 207) is that the circular to shareholders must explain the effect of the scheme of arrangement and whether the directors are to get any special benefits. The Code requirements supplement the statutory provisions and do not conflict with them.

The Code affects schemes of arrangement up to the point when the scheme is approved by shareholders and creditors of the offeree company at the statutory meetings of creditors and different classes of shareholders convened by the Court. One of the main purposes of the Code—as set out in General Principle 3—is to ensure that shareholders have in their possession sufficient evidence, facts and opinions upon which an adequate judgement can be formed. That duty is discharged by the time of the meetings of shareholders. This corresponds to the point of time in an ordinary take-over bid when sufficient acceptances have been received for the offer to become unconditional. The subsequent stage of sanction by the Court is one at which the Court is satisfying itself that the statutory provisions have been complied with, that the meetings were properly conducted and that the Scheme was such as a man of business would reasonably approve. For the Panel to intervene at that stage or in respect of events happening after the meetings of shareholders would clearly open up the possibility of an undesirable confusion of function with the overriding function of the Court. Difficulties do not arise in practice about purchases in the market, because schemes of arrangment are normally restricted to cases where the boards of the two companies agree on the merger. Purchases in the market, are, therefore, unlikely.

Disciplinary Cases. A different range of considerations arise in disciplinary cases. Like any other individual or organization, the Panel can, within the limits set by the law of libel, express its views on a course of conduct that has been pursued. Beyond that, agreement to accept the Panel's authority is required[1] and in the case of professional people that agreement can be given by the professional body to which they belong. In dealing with breaches of the Code outside these limits the Panel is always careful to ascertain that the party accepts the Panel's jurisdiction.

The Panel observes the rules of natural justice in its proceedings—in so far as that somewhat undefined concept has been given form and substance by the courts.[2] Thus it is laid down by the courts that:

(a) a person charged with a breach of the required standard of conduct should know the nature of the accusation made;
(b) he should be given an opportunity to state his case;
(c) the tribunal should act in good faith.[3]

The courts would probably accept that in a general inquiry, such as the Panel conducts, points may arise in the course of a hearing of which an individual has not had previous notice.[4] The Panel would give an adjournment if the person concerned wished time to consider new allegations made against him.

---

[1] *Abbot* v. *Sullivan* (1952) 1KB 189.
[2] In *Gaiman* v. *N.A.M.H.* (1971) Ch. 317, Megarry J., in commending 'Natural Justice' by P. Jackson, said that the ambit of natural justice was a subject worthy of further academic study.
[3] *Bryne* v. *Kinematograph Review Society Ltd.* (1958) WLR 784.
[4] See *Davis* v. *Carew Poke* (1956) 1 WLR 833.

XIII

INSIDER DEALING

In recent years, there has been a rise in the standard of conduct in security transactions expected of those in possession of items of confidential information likely to affect the price of a security. This has been happening in most countries with highly developed securities markets.

Developments in the United States have influenced policy elsewhere. The Wall Street Crash of 1929 and the subsequent depression led to official investigations into the conduct of the securities markets and cases were produced in which insiders with confidential information had made large profits at the expense of unsuspecting buyers or sellers of shares. The Securities Exchange Act 1934 endeavours to deal with this situation in three ways. An obligation is placed on directors and officers of listed companies (extended to all companies over a certain size) and on the beneficial owners of 10 per cent or more of share capital to disclose each month's dealings in the shares of their companies to the SEC and the stock exchange with a view to publication. Secondly the company or any shareholder can sue for the recovery of any profit made by an insider by buying and selling shares within six months. Proof of the use of inside information is not required, so the provision in effect prohibits short-term speculation by insiders. Thirdly 'short sales' by insiders are prohibited—sales by insiders who do not own the stock when they sell it or who cannot deliver it within twenty days. Under rule 10b–5 made by the SEC (in its original form in 1942), anyone who fails to disclose a material fact in relation to a dealing in securities may be sued by the other party to the transaction, may be the subject of an injuction at the instance of the SEC in the federal courts and may be exposed to criminal charges at the instance of the Department of Justice. The absence of any specification of the types of person caught under rule 10b–5 has led to its application to a wide range of employees and professional advisers of companies and to tippees.[1]

A number of points are worth noting in regard to US experience (a) As in the development of UK company law, the United States believed in the value of disclosure as a means of preventing malpractices. 'Insiders [in the USA] have to operate as if in a goldfish bowl' (Jenkins Committee: evidence. p. 1060). This was not, however, considered to be enough and those who favoured more direct action against insider dealing prevailed. (b) In the thirties it was believed in the United States that insider dealings had distorted share prices. While, therefore, insider dealing was condemned as unethical, there was also an inclination to say that the seller and buyer of a security should operate with equal knowledge—'market egalitarianism'. The Jenkins Committee was told that it was almost true to say that in the United States sales and purchases of securities by insiders had become contracts of the utmost good faith (as in insurance contracts) requiring disclosure of all material facts (Jenkins Committee: evidence. p. 1061). This view has not however gone unchallenged. Thus a committee of the American Bar Association, reporting in October 1973, said that 'although there have been intimations in judicial decisions that the law in this area was designed to achieve ultimate equality of information for investors (as distinguished from equal access to that information) we do not believe that the Securities and Exchange Commission has endorsed this philosophy and we do not think it should do so'.
(c) The emphasis is on material facts or special facts—particular pieces of confidential information that are price-sensitive—rather than on a body of information which in its totality might lead to a view on the value of a security. The draft

[1] Professor Louis Loss invented the convenient term 'tippee' for those who receive tips from insiders. In his authoritative book on Securities Regulation in the USA, Professor Loss in 1969 said: 'Having some respect for the English language, he does pray his readers, for at least a decent interval, not to join elements of the press in dropping the quotation marks' (vol. vi, p. 3561). Perhaps the decent interval can now be regarded as having elapsed.

code on federal securities, published by the American Law Association in March 1978, referred to an insider knowing 'a fact of special significance . . . that is not generally available', though admittedly this is defined in terms that give it a broad meaning.

(d) Great reliance is placed on civil actions by shareholders and others as a means of policing the insider dealing restrictions. In the United States an individual can initiate a legal suit at much less risk of financial loss than in this country. American lawyers are prepared to undertake work on a contingency basis—no cure, no pay—and American courts do not normally award costs against the unsuccessful party. A shareholder may also undertake a class action on behalf of himself and all other holders of the same security and this can make a legal suit very lucrative for a lawyer.

(e) The procedure by which the SEC can obtain an injunction and damages against an insider in the federal courts means that less reliance is placed on criminal proceedings initiated by the Department of Justice.

Events have developed more slowly in this country than in the United States. Section 12 of the Prevention of Fraud (Investment) Act, 1939, which enabled heavy sentences to be imposed on the pushers of worthless shares included a provision against 'any dishonest concealment of material facts'. Mr B. A. K. Rider, who has made an intensive study of insider dealing law, here and overseas, has argued that greater use should have been made of this provision (now section 13 of the consolidating Act of 1958),[1] but the Board of Trade and its successor departments regarded the need to establish dishonesty as severely restricting its scope and the Department had some support for this view in the attitude of the Courts.[2]

In 1945 the Cohen Committee on Company Law Amendment in their report (Cmnd. 6659) said that it should be generally realized that a speculative profit, made as a result of special knowledge not available to the general body of shareholders in a company, is improperly made. It is of interest that

[1] B. A. K. Rider and H. L. Ffrench: The Regulation of Insider Trading (1979). On the scope of the 1939 provision B. A. K. Rider: The Crime of Insider Trading: Journal of Business Law: January 1978 pp. 19–29.
[2] R. v. Mackinnon (1958) 3 All E.R. 657.

the report went on to say: 'We would add that some directors who would not themselves take advantage of inside information do not so clearly appreciate the impropriety of letting it be known to their friends that events as yet unknown to the shareholders have made the shares in the company an attractive purchase.' The Cohen Committee considered that the best remedy was the disclosure of dealings and recommended that there should be a register, open to inspection by shareholders, of directors' holdings of, and transactions in, securities of their company and of its subsidiaries. Effect was given to this recommendation by section 195 of the Companies Act 1948.

In 1962 the Jenkins Committee recommended a tightening up of the provisions for the disclosure of directors' dealings. Partly because of American experience, they also recommended that the provisions of section 195, relating to the disclosure of directors' dealings, should be extended to the beneficial owners of 10 per cent or more of the equity capital of listed companies. A director was not to speculate by dealing in options in securities of his company or group. Effect was given to these recommendations in the Companies Act 1967. The Jenkins Committee also proposed that a director who, in dealings in the securities of his company or group of companies, made improper use of a particular piece of confidential information which might be expected materially to affect the value of these securities should be liable to compensate anyone who suffered from his action. This was a general recommendation, though the Committee acknowledged that it presented difficulties in its application to Stock Exchange transactions. This has not been the subject of legislation. All this covers a much wider field than take-overs. The Cohen and Jenkins Committees were mainly interested in other aspects of inside knowledge, such as the impending conclusion of a favourable contract or the intention of the board to recommend an increased dividend.

Concern about the possible leakage of information about impending bids was expressed at an early stage in the post-war development of take-over bids. The 1959 Notes referred to the matter obliquely when they said 'Every effort should be made to avoid disturbance in the normal price level of shares until the relevant information has been made available' and the Notes stressed the need for secrecy in the stages preliminary to an offer and for a preliminary announcement to be made, if there were signs of a speculative market arising in the shares concerned. The 1963 Revised Notes reiterated the need for secrecy in preliminary discussions and said 'directors and others who have close associations with them should avoid any dealings in the shares likely to be affected and should exercise great care in connection with any transactions which may have been initiated but not completed when the talks begin'.

The 1968 Code prohibited dealings of any kind (including option business) in the shares of the offeror and offeree companies 'by any person who is privy to the preliminary take-over or merger discussions' during the preliminary period between the first idea of a bid and the announcement of the bid or the termination of the discussions (Rule 30). During the offer period, there could be dealings, subject to daily disclosure to The Stock Exchange and Press by parties to the take-over and their associates of purchases and sales of shares in the offeror or offeree companies and at what price. Apart from changes designed to correct ambiguities, those provisions of the 1968 Code remained substantially unchanged until 1972 when the offeror was freed from the obligation not to deal during the preliminary stages before the announcement of the offer.

Arising out of the Pergamon/Leasco inquiry, the Panel issued a report on the handling of confidential price-sensitive information by merchant banks. This was appended to the Panel's annual report for 1969/70. The report recommended what was already common practice in the larger merchant banks, namely, that the work of the corporate finance department, which handled take-overs, should be segregated from the investment advisory department. The report made a number of other detailed recommendations, designed to ensure that confidential price-sensitive information available in the corporate finance department was not available for investment purposes.

The Stock Exchange was concerned about the leakage of confidential information in so far as it operated unfairly for its members and for the investing public generally; the leakages they investigated went much wider than information related to take-overs. The Stock Exchange Council has the right under

The Stock Exchange Rules to request information from its members. It became normal for The Stock Exchange to conduct an investigation into dealings by brokers and jobbers and then (if the Panel was concerned) to hand the matter over to the Panel Executive for further investigation among the parties concerned and members of the public. Until 1976 The Stock Exchange Council normally restricted its inquiry to brokers and jobbers. In that year, a committee of the Council which was investigating matters concerning Scottish and Universal Investments Ltd. interviewed a number of witnesses, including directors and employees of Suits, and the Council published the report of the committee.

The Panel had been appointed to carry out a rather aggressive role and considered that it should be active against insider dealings in connection with take-over bids. The Panel had—and still has—an insurance policy against libel actions, which ensured that it was not unduly inhibited in publishing the results of its inquiries. It felt itself able to interview stockbrokers, merchant bankers, investment advisers, company directors and employees, and members of the public. The Panel executive has always been prepared to go and meet any witness on his own ground. It has been very rare for anyone to refuse to discuss matters: but it was obvious from the start that in the absence of statutory powers there were severe limits on the information that could be secured from a witness who, for whatever motive, was disinclined to give any real assistance, particularly a witness who stuck to an account of events which was tenable though concocted.

In April 1971 the Panel found that the conduct of the managing director of a quoted company deserved the most severe censure and doubt was expressed about his fitness to remain managing director of the company. He had bought shares in a company, for which his company made a bid, during the preliminary discussions: and he bought and sold shares during the bid period, including a period when his company was trying to withdraw from the bid, without disclosing these transactions. He had also not been frank with the Panel during preliminary investigations. In consequence he resigned from the board. An authorized member dealer of The Stock Exchange who effected the share transactions was suspended for a period.

Since then there have been one or two cases most years in which the Panel has found that a director or employee of a company has had share dealings while in possession of confidential information about a bid. This represents only a small proportion of the cases investigated by the Panel executive. It has always been difficult to identify cases where insiders have passed on tips to outsiders. The work has proved to be a substantial burden and not related to the main work of the Panel executive. The published cases have, however, kept in public view the wrongness of insider dealing, pending legislation on the subject. The work of the Panel has also illustrated a strong feature of self-regulation, in that it can apply the intention of its rules. The wording of Rule 30 would be quite inadequate as a legal expression of an offence of insider dealing but the Panel has refused to be tied to precise wording as distinct from intention.[1]

The sanctions at the disposal of the Panel are a public reprimand, the expression of views about suitability for directorships and other offices and arrangments under which the person concerned agreed to forfeit the profit he has made, usually by donation to a charity. In the case of professional people, there is the possibility of disciplinary proceedings by their professional body on the basis of the Panel's findings. The effect of a public reprimand is somewhat unpredictable. In one case in 1970 the Appeal Committee on an appeal substituted a private for a public reprimand, on the ground that the effect of a public reprimand might be out of all proportion to the gravity of the offence. The offender had pleaded ignorance of the Code due to prolonged absence from the country. Certainly there have been cases where a public reprimand has led to removal from the Commission of the Peace and other deprivations. On the other hand, in a case where reprimands were not made public because of the poor health of one of the individuals concerned, it was later held against the Panel that it had failed to alert public authorities overseas to possible malpractices. Latterly the Panel has been inclined to resort to public rather than private reprimands, unless very strong grounds are brought forward against a public statement. Where an

[1] See, for example, Panel statement of 15 December 1978 regarding transactions in the shares of Chaddesley Investments Limted.

individual refused to co-operate in inquiries, the Panel named the individual as having refused to help.

Over the years, a general view developed that insider dealing should be handled by the criminal law. 'Justice' published in 1972 a report on insider trading prepared by its sub-committee on company law. It recommended that dealings through a stock exchange by insiders in possession of confidential price-sensitive information should be made a criminal offence. Insiders would be prevented from engaging in short sales and short-term in-and-out transactions. In dealings outside a stock exchange, a person dealing with an insider who acted on material information which he did not disclose (or with someone acting on information supplied by an outsider) would have the same remedies in a civil action as if he had been the subject of deliberate misrepresentation. Insiders would be widely defined to include directors and employees of a company and any other person having access, professionally, to confidential information relating to the company. The City of London Solicitors Company reported in January 1973 in favour of insider dealing within a limited field being a criminal offence: and the City Company Law Committee recommended to the same effect.

In the course of 1971 and 1972 the Panel became increasingly conscious that, in its surveillance of market transactions in connection with take-overs, it was hampered not only by the use of nominee names but also by the absence of any statutory power to interrogate witnesses or demand the production of documents. Moreover, in so far as suspicious transactions might be carried out by tippees, the jurisdiction of the Panel over them and the obligation of such individuals to explain themselves to the Panel were not clear-cut. Further, no statutory defence of qualified privilege yet existed to protect statements the Panel made in connection with its investigations.[1] Although some insider dealing clearly was taking place, the Panel took the view that the incidence of such dealing had been much exaggerated. Many leaks seemed to be due to careless-

---

[1] The Committee on Defamation, under the chairmanship of Mr Justice Faulks, in their report (Cmnd. 5909 of 1975) recommended that a fair and accurate report of any adjudication, official report, statement or notice issued by the Take-over Panel, the Council of The Stock Exchange, or certain other bodies, should be given qualified privilege by statute (by a revised schedule to the Defamation Act 1952).

ness and inadequate security precautions. It remained a fact, however, that there was much public disquiet as to the alleged extent to which unpublished price-sensitive information in relation to companies was used by insiders for their own personal financial advantage. A great deal of this disquiet was no doubt emotive and unjustified but its very existence was damaging to the confidence upon which a securities market must be founded. The Panel, having in conjunction with The Stock Exchange carried out an exhaustive study of the whole problem during the course of 1972, reached the conclusion that insider dealing, properly defined, should be made a criminal offence and enforced in accordance with normal Companies Acts practice. A public statement announcing that the Panel and The Stock Exchange had so advised the Department of Trade and Industry, in connection with the Secretary of State's review of possible amendments to company law, was issued on 3 February 1973. The Panel believed that the mere enactment that insider dealing was an offence under the criminal law would be, as it had been in the United States, a very powerful deterrent to anyone who might otherwise be minded to make dishonest use of information obtained by virtue of his confidential relationship with a company.

In July 1973 the Conservative Government issued a White Paper on company law reform (Cmnd. 5391) which proposed, *inter alia*, that insider dealing should be a criminal offence. This was followed by a Companies Bill in December 1973, with clauses on insider dealing, which made no progress because of the fall of the Government. In April 1977 The Stock Exchange and the Panel issued a statement outlining measures designed to minimize leakages of confidential information. In August 1977 EEC published a code of conduct for transactions in transferable securities which *inter alia* condemned the improper use of confidential, price-sensitive information. In the autumn of 1977 The Stock Exchange Council published a model code for securities transactions by directors of listed companies. In November 1977 the Labour Government issued a White Paper on the conduct of company directors (Cmnd. 7037) which contained a section on the Government's legislative proposals on insider dealing. This was followed by the draft of a Companies Bill in July 1978 (Cmnd. 7291) and in November 1978 by the Companies Bill which followed the July 1978 draft. The Bill was in committee in the Commons when Parliament was dissolved in April 1979. In October 1979 the Conservative Government circulated the drafts of amendments to their 1979 Companies Bill, dealing with insider dealing and these were subsequently incorporated in the Bill.

The Justice report and the report of the City of London Solicitors Company canvassed the use of civil remedies before coming down in favour of the creation of a criminal offence. The statement issued by the Take-over Panel and The Stock Exchange in February 1973 laid little store on civil proceedings in combating insider dealing. It described them as 'expensive, time-consuming and in themselves an insufficient deterrent'. The Conservative Government's White Paper proposed that the law should confer a civil remedy on persons who could establish that by reason of the misuse of materially significant information they had suffered an identifiable loss. It also proposed that the law should preserve the present position whereby an insider using confidential information may be accountable to the company for his profit. The Companies Bill 1973 had a general provision making an insider liable to compensate those who could show that they had suffered a loss through his activities. The City Company Law Committee in a report dated 24 August 1976 considered that it was not practicable to operate civil remedies in respect of sales and purchases through The Stock Exchange, but recommended that in contracts outside The Stock Exchange a failure to disclose material information not known to the other party should entitle that party to rescind the contract or obtain damages. The accountability to the company of a director or employee for a profit made on the use of confidential information was to be confirmed in the legislation. The Companies Bill 1978 did not go beyond requiring an insider, dealing outside a recognized stock exchange, to reveal his connection with the company to the other party. Not much store seems to be placed on this device in the United States[1] and it did not feature in the 1979 proposals.

There has from time to time been some discussion of the precise grounds on which which insider dealing should be

[1] Loss, *Securities Regulation*, vol. iii (1961), p. 1463 and vol. vi (1969), p. 3600.

made a criminal offence[1] and there have been those who argued that on grounds of economic theory the case has not been made out. There is the straightforward moral argument that it is contrary to good business ethics that a man holding a position of trust in relation to a company should use confidential price-sensitive information for the benefit of himself or others. That line seems to have appealed to the Jenkins Committee and has featured strongly in the parliamentary debates. Insider dealing may also be condemned as reducing public confidence in the integrity of the securities markets. Thus the objective of the EEC code of conduct is to promote the effective functioning of securities markets and to safeguard the public interest.

It may also be said that the insider is acting unfairly towards the person with whom he deals and towards the company which had the information. Some economists would dispute this and in legal terms it is necessary to decide what information in the hands of the insider the other party is entitled to. The Justice report said roundly: 'we think that deliberate non-disclosure of material facts is just as wrong as deliberate misrepresentation'; but the repercussions on the law of contract generally have to be considered before one accepts the premiss that there must be full disclosure and equality of information in all cases. Most would agree that if companies are to provide more information it should be required as a general matter of company law and not via insider dealing legislation.

In defining the offence of dealing on the basis of confidential price-sensitive information the definition of 'insider' and of 'inside information' both present difficulties. If they are defined too widely, institutional shareholders, investment analysts and brokers and jobbers may find themselves inhibited from carrying on legitimate activities.

In the United States, the policy is to regard as an insider anyone who has inside information, but in the United Kingdom the policy has been to define insiders as directors, employees and professional advisers. The Companies Bill 1973 and the Companies Bill 1978, as introduced, treated substantial shareholders as insiders. This could present difficulties and the Labour Government (and later the Conservatives) in 1979

[1] See, for example, an article by Mr R. C. A. White, 'Towards a Policy Basis for the Regulation of Insider Dealing', *Law Quarterly Review* (Oct. 1974).

decided to exclude shareholders. The shareholder obtains information from the management and it is better to treat shareholders who possess inside information as tippees.

It is generally accepted that it is wrong for an insider to pass unpublished price-sensitive information to someone who will deal on the basis of this information, though this is not explicitly stated to be an offence in the United States legislation. As regards the nature of the information which the tipper passes on, the Companies Bill 1978, as introduced, seemed to catch only those who passed on the inside information and did not catch those insiders who gave a strong tip to buy or sell a share. This was eventually covered in 1978, and again in 1979, by referring to insiders who 'counsel' dealings in a security. As regards the tippee himself, the Companies Bill 1973 restricted the offence to a listed category of associates and to anyone who had an arrangement for the communication of information with a view to dealing. The 1978 and 1979 provisions were wider in scope and covered anyone who directly or indirectly obtained information from an insider with a view to dealing. A separate provision in 1973, 1978 and 1979 prohibited dealings on the bases of inside information by Crown servants, statutory authorities and members and employees of such authorities.

The Companies Bill 1978, as introduced, defined inside information as information which was price-sensitive and not generally available. In response to representations that this was too wide, the Government tabled amendments to define 'generally available' as meaning 'available on request to those members of the public likely to take an interest in it'. This meant that the Bill still covered not only company information but also outside information such as the prospective disposal of a block of shares, though to be within the provisions of the Bill the outside information has to come through insiders. In various quarters this was thought to remain too widely drawn. It was felt that if the risk to legitimate activities was to be minimized, the offence should be further restricted, for example by relating it to specific pieces of company information, knowledge of which should be confined to those who had to know it in order to perform their duties. This restriction was effected in the provisions tabled by the Conservative Government in October 1979.

There is agreement that liquidators, receivers, and trustees in bankruptcy should be able to carry out their duties without fear of being accused of insider dealing, likewise anyone who has not operated to make a profit or avoid a loss, e.g. under an urgent need for cash. The Companies Bill 1973 exempted a range of activities but subsequent Governments have been reluctant to go so far and the limited scope of insider information in 1979 lessened the need for exemptions. Governments have been unwilling to give statutory force to the exempted periods when directors may deal under The Stock Exchange's model code. The Stock Exchange's model code for directors has followed United States practice in discouraging short-term speculation in company securities by directors and officers of companies. This is not explicity provided for in UK legislative proposals.

For the future, developments on the continent may be important because of developments through EEC. In France it is an offence for company directors and others in possession of confidential, price-sensitive information to use that information, directly or indirectly, in dealings on the stock market. The Commission des Opérations de Bourse has wide powers of investigation. There is also a code of conduct covering dealers in securities. Germany has a code of conduct relating to insider dealing which has been adopted by stock exchanges, banks, and industrial and commercial concerns. Elsewhere, the main emphasis is on the disclosure of dealings. The EEC Capital Markets Code of Conduct contains a prohibition of insider dealing and in 1976 the Directorate for Financial Institutions initiated discussions whether there should be Community legislation on insider dealing.

Some inquiries lead to a dead end abroad. The case usually quoted is a Swiss numbered account, but if the beneficial owner of shares is a private company, the real owner may still elude inquiry. Something may be achieved by intergovernmental agreement but any moves in that direction will probably in the first instance be confined to tax evasion and suspected gross fraud. Meantime some companies have amended their articles of association to deprive nominee shares of voting rights where, on due cause shown, there has been a failure to reveal beneficial ownership.

The handling of cases presents difficulties in most countries. The preliminary investigations are usually made by the securities authority, which may be a self-regulatory body, an official organization or a Government Department. At a certain point the case may have to be handed over to the State prosecuting authority. The danger is that the investigation then begins *de novo*, with consequent delays.

The 1979/80 statutory provisions cover the main field. They leave some scope for the Take-over Code in respect of bids and for The Stock Exchange in respect of listed companies to have ethical standards expressed in more general terms and administered in a more flexible way.

Alongside the consideration of punitive measures, steps have been taken in this country to endeavour to prevent insider dealing. The Companies Act 1976 required a director to inform his company of the acquisition of its securities within four days, instead of fourteen days, and required the company to inform The Stock Exchange. Purchasers of 5 per cent (instead of 10 per cent) of voting rights had to inform the company. A company could require the disclosure of beneficial interests in its voting shares. Some of this was directed at take-overs as well as at insider dealing. The model code prohibited, subject to some exceptions, dealings by directors during the two months before the preliminary announcement of the company's yearly and half-yearly results. There was also an enlargement of the statutory disclosure provisions, including a requirement to inform the chairman or other designated director of proposed dealings, primarily in order that the chairman can warn of some exceptional matter, unknown to the director, which makes dealings undesirable at that particular time.

The Stock Exchange and the Panel have been concerned about the extent to which leakages of information and subsequent dealings in securities were due to insufficient attention to security. The existing rules required an offeree board to make a public announcement when negotiations had reached a point at which the board was reasonably sure that an offer would be made for the company's shares. The Stock Exchange and the Panel issued a joint statement on 14 April 1977 which *inter alia* urged that an announcement of the position should be made when negotiations or discussions were about to be extended to embrace more than a small group of people. Moreover the potential offeror was not to discourage the offeree board from making a statement; and in Practice Note 9 reissued in December 1978 an obligation was placed on the offeror to make a statement if it was his actions which contributed to rumour and speculation. In the April 1977 statement The Stock Exchange indicated that it would be prepared to halt dealing temporarily, if asked by a company because an announcement was being delayed and again if there was a significant price movement and no satisfactory explanation from the company was forthcoming. Experience since April 1977 has shown a greater resort to preliminary announcements of impending bids and a greater willingness by companies to ask for a temporary suspension of dealings.

XIV

SECURITIES AND EXCHANGE COMMISSION

THERE have been interesting developments in the regulation of take-over bids in Europe and the United States, Canada (notably Ontario), Australia, Hong Kong, Singapore, and elsewhere. However in dealing with the UK Take-over Code, it seems to be necessary to refer only to the United States Securities and Exchange Commission and to EEC developments. The suggestion is sometimes made that a Securities and Exchange Commission, modelled on the United States body of that name, should be set up in this country. A brief description of the American scene and of the role of the SEC may not, therefore, be out of place.

A common language and common traditions are apt to blind us to the extent to which conditions in the USA and in this country are different, making it dangerous to assume that what is good for the United States is good for the United Kingdom. There is no body in the United States which has the authority of The Stock Exchange in this country. The New York Stock Exchange does an enormous volume of business but it is only one of about a dozen stock exchanges. It deals with 3,000 listed securities. There is an active over-the-counter market in the United States with dealers in securities unconnected with any stock exchange. The shares of as many as 30,000 companies (some quite large) are dealt with in this way. In the field of Government, there is the division between federal and state authorities. Company law, in the United States, is a state matter. No federal body has the sweep of responsibility of the Trade and Industry Departments in this country.

The result was that when, in the thirties, the need for the

regulation of the securities markets was felt in the two countries, different paths were chosen. In the United Kingdom, the Board of Trade and the London Stock Exchange and other stock exchanges were able to cover the field; and the work done by the London Stock Exchange in the last half century in regulating the securities market has never had the full credit it deserves. In the United States, there was no voluntary body that could do what was needed and the field of responsibility of the federal departments was restricted. This resulted in the setting up of the Securities and Exchange Commission in 1934 to regulate dealings in securities and to take over from the Federal Trade Commission the administration of an Act of 1933 on new issues of securities.

Until comparatively recently, the contested take-over bid was not common in the United States. Mergers were effected by a statutory procedure which required the agreement of the management of the offeree company. To obtain the cooperation of the offeree management, the offeror would sometimes first buy shares in the market and seek to oust the existing board by means of what became known as a proxy fight. The merger would then be initiated under state law in the state of the offeree, and completed when a majority of the stockholders had given their consent. Contested bids of the sort with which the United Kingdom is familiar became more common in the sixties. Paper bids ('exchange offers') were regulated to the extent that the offer document was regarded as a prospectus. Cash bids ('tender offers') were not covered till the Williams Act of 1968. Exchange offers have become more common than cash offers because sophisticated paper deals could be worked out, also for tax reasons and because cash was not always available if the target company was large. Some would say that the Williams Act discouraged tender offers. America has little more than ten years' experience of bids of the kind we know on the scale that we know.

The Securities and Exchange Commission operates in a number of fields.

(1) The Securities Act of 1933 deals with new issues of securities. Where there is a public offering of securities for sale, the company must file with the SEC a statement giving a great many details about the company, part of which consists of a

detailed prospectus for public issue. There are civil and criminal penalties for material misstatements and omissions.

(2) The Securities Exchange Act of 1934 relates to dealings in securities already in issue. Companies listed on national securities exchanges, or having more than 300 shareholders, must file annual and other reports with the SEC and, if listed, with the stock exchanges. Letters and reports circulated to shareholders in connection with contested issues at shareholders' meetings—'proxy fights'—are subject to SEC supervision: indeed all proxy statements are so subject. In 1964 similar requirements were imposed on companies whose securities are not listed in stock exchanges but which are trading in the over-the-counter market. The activities of stock exchanges and brokers and dealers in over-the-counter business are subject to regulation by the SEC. The SEC can also regulate market practices, such as selling short and the use of credit to finance the purchase of securities. The SEC also has disciplinary powers over brokers, dealers, and their employees, and plays a part in the regulation of fees charged.

(3) The Williams Act of 1968 enables the SEC to make rules about the activities of offerors who make cash offers and the activities of those who oppose or support such offers.

(4) Various other Acts give the SEC powers in respect of public utility holding companies, investment companies, and investment advisers.

The general aim, in both the USA and the UK, is to see that the shareholder gets fair play and that he has all the facts he needs to reach a decision. But there are substantial differences in the ways thought necessary to secure this objective. American opinion considers that a shareholder should be allowed to sell shares to whom he likes at what price he likes, with in some circumstances the qualification that a controlling shareholder should see that the other shareholders get similar treatment. No one thinks the less of a controlling shareholder who sells out at a lower price to a congenial buyer, though he may be faced with a law suit by an aggrieved shareholder. If a controlling shareholder sells at a higher price than the other shareholders are likely to get, he may have an action taken against him. No difficulty is seen about partial offers—possibly because the minority shareholder is better protected by law than has been the case in this country. An offeror and his associates are not allowed to make market purchases of an offeree's shares during the currency of a paper offer. The directors of an offeree company are freer there than they are here in what they can do to frustrate an unwelcome bid. Until recently the SEC refused to allow profit forecasts to be issued though it has now moved away from that position.

Take-over battles can be more boisterous affairs there than here. A US publication gives the headings of some advertisements—'World's First Comic Prospectus. Read about Funny Money' and 'How Emerson Turned the Profit Corner and other Factual but Hilarious Stuff'—and adds demurely that 'attacks like these are aimed at discouraging security holders from tendering'. No one questions the value of the establishment of the SEC. It is universally agreed that it is now an essential part of the US securities organization. It seems to have managed to avoid the ossification that can affect an organization that has now existed for more than forty years. Its Enforcement Division is widely regarded as the most effective enforcement machinery in the US Government. The SEC is, however, primarily concerned with the disclosure of information to shareholders. There is nothing in the SEC rules or elsewhere corresponding to many of the provisions of the Take-over Code. In this country the SEC is sometimes described in lyrical terms which some Americans find it hard to relate to the realities of the situation as they know them.[1]

Professor Homer Kripke, of the New York University School of Law, has criticized the working of the Securities Act of 1933.[2] His general theme is that the SEC has undertaken the impossible task of trying to devise prospectuses that made highly complex company financial arrangements intelligible to the ordinary layman and that it would have been better to concentrate on making them meaningful for financial experts who could then have advised the ordinary layman. Professor George

---

[1] Thus in a BBC programme on 10 November 1972 a speaker said: 'On Wall Street to-day the SEC is a feared and respected body. It has a staff of 1,400, many of them lawyers, with powers to examine books, bar dealers from trading and to prosecute offenders. It ferrets out abuses with a missionary-like zeal and last year secured 89 criminal convictions for offences such as insider trading and worse, the sentences ranging up to 65 years in jail.'
[2] *Business Lawyer* (Jan. 1973).

J. Benston of the University of Rochester made a searching analysis of the operation of the Securities Exchange Act, 1934.[1] He believes that the extent to which fraudulent or misleading financial statements existed before 1934 has been much exaggerated, that the New York Stock Exchange and others were already securing a higher standard of reporting by companies before the Act was passed, that the financial disclosure requirements of the Act have had no measurable effect on the prices of securities, that the SEC has supported conventional accounting standards to an extent that makes company reports of little value to investors and that the riskiness of securities has not been reduced by the Act. Company frauds have not been reduced. These are responsible, well-regarded critics. Many practitioners would say that the SEC is extremely 'heavy-handed' in the whole matter of enforcement. It is difficult for an outsider to appraise the exact value of these criticisms nor is this the place to attempt to do so. They are mentioned because it is obviously wrong to regard the SEC as a 100 per cent success story.

Federal and State Departments and agencies like the Federal Trade Commission and the Securities and Exchange Commission perform some of the functions of official bodies in the United Kingdom though the work is more fragmented in the United States. There are self-regulatory bodies at work in the United States as in this country—for example, the New York and other US stock exchanges, the National Association of Security Dealers and the accountancy bodies. One important difference from the United Kingdom lies in the interaction between the official and the voluntary bodies. The Securities and Exchange Commission supervises and controls the operations of the voluntary bodies in ways that may be thought to deprive them of the independent vigour that a self-regulatory system can display.

There are various reasons why any statutory body in this country will not be likely to be on SEC lines. Some of these stem from the greater separation of powers in the United States between the legislature, executive, and judiciary. Others stem from the federal form of government. Mr Manuel F. Cohen, Chairman of the SEC from 1964 to 1969, made an interesting

[1] *American Economic Review* (Mar. 1973).

point during a visit to this country a few years ago. He said that the British had a very different attitude from that of Americans to the authority of a statute. In this country a statute was held to mean neither more nor less than it said. No sooner was legislation made in the financial field than some people became absorbed in finding ways round it. In the United States more attention was paid to the intentions of the legislators. Thus the Supreme Court has said that the Securities Exchange Act 'should be construed, like other securities legislation enacted for the purpose of avoiding frauds, not technically and restrictively but flexibly to effectuate its remedial purposes'.[1] The administering bodies have an interpretative function which allows them to do what the law was known to intend rather than to be bound by the letter of the law. All this makes statute law in the United States a far more flexible instrument to deal with ever-changing conditions than is the case in this country.

The older agencies of the US Government, such as the SEC, enjoy much more independence than a corresponding agency would have in this country. The rules the SEC makes have not to be approved by Congress. Congress has in some recent Acts tried to exercise some supervision over subordinate legislation by executive agencies, but this development is eyed critically by some constitutional lawyers. Nor have the rules to be approved by any Government Department. This difference between the American and the British use of statutory bodies was stressed by Professor Louis Loss, the recognized authority on US securities regulation, when advising the Australian Government on securities regulation.[2] This might suggest that in the United States rules can be made with great speed, but in fact procedures are slowed down by the need for extensive consultations under the provisions of the Administrative Procedures Act and other statutes aiming at more open government. In making its rules and in administering them, the SEC has to bear in mind that it is heavily dependent on the federal courts in implementing policy. Requirements have to be stated with precision and have to be obeyed to the letter, because enforcement rests with the Courts.

In the United States the courts also play a larger part in

[1] Mr Justice Goldberg in *Silver* v. *N.Y. Stock Exchange* 373 US 366 (1963).
[2] *Australian Securities Law Reporter*, Special Report, 20 Sept. 1973.

commercial and financial transactions than in this country. There is a tendency to rush to the courts for a remedy. The possibility of class actions[1] and the contingent legal fees system play a large part in the enthusiasm for litigation. When changes are contemplated or things go wrong, US boards of directors must be prepared for writs issued at the behest of aggrieved shareholders: and legal suits can occupy a long time. This is one of the reasons why, until recently, the contested take-over bid was comparatively rare in the United States. The SEC with its statutory powers and its own legal remedies, fits more congenially into the US commercial scene than it would in this country.

The SEC moves more slowly than corresponding procedures in the United Kingdom. Attention is often drawn to the fact that the SEC has a staff of about 2,000 and costs over £30,000,000. A company has in practice some ninety days in which to produce its annual report after the end of its financial year. The SEC gives an offeror ten days in which to report the result of an offer and an offeror has ten days in which to report dealings in offeree stock during the currency of a cash offer. More serious is the extent to which the processes become more involved. Offer documents are very long by UK standards—up to 250 pages—in order to comply with all the requirements. The greater complexity results in greater cost—probably twice what a take-over bid costs in this country. The SEC takes an average of about sixty days to deal with matters referred to it. The process is neither simple nor flexible nor speedy.

There is no reason to believe that a British statutory body would move any faster. Nor might its membership necessarily inspire confidence. There is a ritual element in the membership of these bodies in the United Kingdom—the statutory woman, the superannuated trade unionist, the academic full of financial theories but without practical knowledge of financial business. A statutory body thrust on top of the present self-regulatory voluntary bodies in the United Kingdom would have undesirable results. It would make it difficult, if not impossible, for the voluntary bodies to move speedily—certainly in regard to their rule-making functions, but also in relation to their day-to-day

[1] Cases where a shareholder can act for all the other shareholders holding the same class of share.

work. Fewer able people would be prepared to give their time to serve on bodies that moved slowly and had little real responsibility.

In the USA it was the States, not the Federal authorities, who between 1910 and 1920 first legislated in the securities field. They enacted 'blue sky' laws directed against promoters described as prepared to sell building lots in the blue sky in fee simple. This corresponded to the passing of the Prevention of Fraud (Investment) Act 1939 in this country. Following the slump of the early 1930s, Congress legislated on a federal basis, mainly to secure full disclosure of all material facts by those selling securities. Recently many of the States have intervened in this field again, usually in the interests of companies within their borders that are the subject of cash bids. There has long been controversy in the United States on whether the matter should be handled entirely by Congress on a federal basis or by Congress and the States.[1]

These State laws vary from state to state. Most require a proposed bid to be filed with the management of the offeree company and the state securities commission a specified period (ten days or more) before the offer is announced and sometimes there must be public disclosure of filing. During the filing period the target company can resort to defensive measures of the kind that would be disallowed in this country under Rule 38. Then there are requirements for the disclosure of information by the offeror about itself. Sometimes the bid can then go ahead, in other cases a hearing before the state securities commission may be demanded by the offeree board and in a few cases the commission has to be satisfied that the offer is 'fair and equitable'. Many states prescribe minimum periods for a bid to be open and allow offeree shareholders to withdraw their acceptance during specified periods. One state requires an offeror to purchase all shares tendered but most require the pro rata treatment of shareholders where more shares are offered than the offeror wishes to accept. Most states require the offeror to treat all shareholders alike in the price offered for shares, and some states specifically provide that controlling shareholders must not sell their shares to the offeror at a higher price than the offer price during the course of the offer.

[1] See, for example, L. Loss, op. cit., vol. I (1961) pp. 102–5 and D. C. Langevoort, 'State Tender-offer Legislation', *Cornell Law Review*, vol. 62 (1977), pp. 213–57.

In comparing the United States requirements with the provisions of the Take-over Code, one has to bear in mind the difficulty of making any general comparison because of the different laws in the different States. The withdrawal of an offer is a matter for the terms of the offer rather than for any general regulation. There has been little regulation of profit forecasts or asset valuation, save in so far as they may misrepresent the position. This is because profit forecasts were frowned upon, although latterly the SEC has been inclined to accept them and to seek to regulate them.[1] There is no general provision corresponding to Rule 21, under which an offer aiming at voting control must be conditional on the offeror acquiring over 50 per cent of the voting shares. Nor is there any requirement that an offer remain open for a period after the offer has gone unconditional (Rule 23). The idea of a mandatory bid is still at an early stage. There is no obligation to make a bid after acquiring specified percentages of shares (Rules 33 and 34); but there has been a proposal (still at a tentative stage) that any proposed purchase in defined circumstances, of more than some specified percentage of the share capital of a company should be treated as a tender offer and be open proportionately to all shareholders.

[1] For a detailed history of the attitude of the SEC to profit forecasts, see Appendix to the Report of the Advisory Committee on Corporate Disclosure submitted to the SEC in November 1977, pp. A265–329.

XV

EUROPEAN ECONOMIC COMMUNITY

MOST European countries have had for many years legal provisions enabling mergers to be effected somewhat on the lines of the UK schemes of arrangement. The take-over bid, in the sense of an appeal to shareholders over the heads of the board of the company, developed later in Europe than in the United Kingdom—in several countries not until late in the 1960s. The take-over technique has come to be used in some cases for agreed mergers, because of its relative simplicity compared with the statutory procedures. As in the United Kingdom, the need was felt for some supervision of take-over procedures. Some countries promoted legislation. Others relied on professional rules and codes of conduct. There are substantial differences in the requirements in different countries.

FRANCE

An offer for the shares of a public company has to be submitted, through a bank, to the Stock Exchange on which the shares are listed. The offer must conform to certain requirements laid down in regulations made by the Minister or by the Commission des Opérations de Bourse (COB) which supervises the exchanges. The Stock Exchange may discuss details of the offer with the offeror or his agent and at an early stage has to submit the proposal to the Minister for clearance in regard to monopoly implications or foreign ownership. Thereafter a draft of the offer document has to be sent to COB and to the offeree company and COB then supervises the issue of the offer documents by the offeror and a document indicating the attitude of the offeree company to his offer.

Regulations made by the Commission des Opérations de Bourse set out various general principles, covering some of the ground of the Code's General Principles. For the rest, the various regulations are mainly concerned with procedure.

There is not a sharp distinction between offers for control and partial offers, though normally a bidder must endeavour to secure at least 15 per cent of the issued share capital of the offeree company. The offeror has to indicate at the outset the minimum number of shares he must secure before the offer goes unconditional. The offeror must show to the Stock Exchange how the bid price has been calculated and give reasons. He must give an irrevocable undertaking to fulfil his obligations under the offer and this must be guaranteed by his bank. The Stock Exchange may require cash or securities to be deposited equal to the amount payable for all the shares in an open offer. An offeror can raise his price only once in the course of the bid, by not less than 5 per cent of the original price. The period for acceptance indicated by the offeror in the first instance cannot be extended unless there is a rival offer when the original offer can extend to the closing date of the rival. An offeror who has obtained the minimum number of shares set out in his offer can refuse to acquire any more. Where a company is about to acquire enough shares to be in control of another company it must report the fact to the Stock Exchange and then make an offer in a form agreed by the Stock Exchange—which may be an offer for a minimum number of shares or an offer to buy in the market the remaining shares at the price paid for the controlling block.

BELGIUM

Proposed offers must be submitted for approval to an official body, the Commission Bancaire. The Commission may request postponement because the material to be published is misleading or because the timing of the offer might upset the market or because its requirements are not being met. Belgium has no detailed rules. Much is left to the discretion of the Commission which publishes its rulings in its annual reports. On many points its rulings are in line with the UK Code. The Commission is not concerned with the merits of a bid.

If the Commission is of the opinion that a person or group of persons is seeking to acquire control by extensive purchases on the Stock Exchange, it can require them to make an offer for the remaining shares at the price at which the block of shares was acquired. Normally bids are only authorized if the offeror is endeavouring to seek control; but partial bids are allowed in some cases provided that their aim is not simply to thwart another offer. The conditions governing bids must be objective in character. The offeror must satisfy the Commission that sufficient funds will be available to pay for the cash element in a bid. The offeree board has to see the offer document before publication so that the directors can decide whether to comment on the terms but they are not obliged to express a view unless there are competing bids, in which case they have to compare them for the benefit of their shareholders. The Commission may prevent the offeror or offeree and their directors from dealing in the Stock Exchange during the offer period, if it fears the manipulation of market prices.

ITALY

In 1971 the Milan Stock Exchange—the most important of the ten stock exchanges in Italy—issued a code of conduct for take-over bids. It has much in common with French official regulations. Shareholders must be treated equally in regard to the disclosure of information and the terms of offers. Every effort must be made to preserve the confidentiality of the offer before it is announced. The normal minimum for a bid is 10 per cent of the issued share capital. An offeror can take up more shares than the number specified in the bid but he is not obliged to do so. If he obtains 90 per cent he must make an offer for the rest. The consideration must be cash or shares or bonds of a company listed on the Milan Stock Exchange. The offeror and the offeree company are strongly advised not to deal in the securities concerned or in others related to the offer. Proposals have to be submitted to the Executive Committee of the Stock Exchange which can refuse permission to proceed if the disclosure requirements have not been complied with. If there are violations of the code, the Executive Committee can publish the details and name the wrongdoer.

The Securities Markets Law 1974 set up the National Commission for Companies and the Stock Exchange (CONSOB).

The Commission supervises the operation of the securities market and the listing of securities. Various disclosure requirements have been imposed on companies. Companies that have more than 2 per cent of the share capital of a listed company must disclose the fact to the listed company, to CONSOB, and the Stock Exchange. Directors, auditors, and general managers of a listed company must reveal their holdings in that company and must hold them in registered form. It is early days to determine the degree of success that CONSOB will have or the eventual scope of its activities.

NETHERLANDS

The Netherlands Social and Economic Council—a semi-official body—issued rules of conduct in 1971 based on British practice. The conduct of offers is supervised by the Council's Committee for Merger Affairs. Most of the rules concern the preliminary stages and the content of the offer document. The offeree board must summon a shareholders' meeting during the offer period and give them all relevant financial and other information to help them decide whether to accept the bid. The offeror board must summon a meeting of their shareholders if new shares are being issued that exceed one quarter of the existing share capital. Information has to be given about the prices at which shares have been bought, but there is no obligation on the purchaser of a controlling block to make an offer at the same price to the remaining shareholders. After a partial offer has closed the offeror cannot for three years acquire shares at a higher price than the offer price.

GERMANY

There have been many mergers in Germany in recent years, altering considerably the pattern of German industry. They have, however, been very largely agreed mergers, with a large part being played by the banks which are substantial shareholders in industrial or commercial companies. In these circumstances there has not been the same need as elsewhere for rules dealing specifically with take-overs.

EUROPEAN ECONOMIC COMMUNITY

Article 2 of the Treaty of Rome gives, as one of the objectives of the European Economic Community, the harmonious development of economic activities and the interpenetration of capital markets in the Community. In pursuance of this objective, directorates of the Commission have been endeavouring to secure common rules on many aspects of commercial law. As part of this, they have been considering how to regulate public take-over offers. The hydra-headed nature of the Commission has led to a number of avenues being explored: and this is of great interest for the light it throws on the means by which take-over activities can best be regulated.

DRAFT DIRECTIVE

The Directorate for Internal Markets commissioned Professor R. R. Pennington of Birmingham University to draft a directive on take-overs and mergers. It was considered that, because the regulation of take-over procedures in the various community countries was at different stages of development, the acceptance of common rules would ensure that future developments in different countries proceeded along compatible lines. A draft directive, prepared by Professor Pennington in November 1973, was the subject of intensive study in the next two or three years. One difficulty was that if the common factors in the national regulations, where they exist, were taken as a basis, the result would not cover the field adequately or give sufficient guidance for the future. If, on the other hand, what seemed the best features of the various national regulations were taken and a complete code was constructed, there was going to be great difficulty in inducing countries to agree to modify their own regulations or, where reliance was placed on a voluntary code, in inducing them to replace that by legislation. Where there was little or no regulation, a country would be reluctant to adopt a detailed code. There was also the argument that take-over practice had not settled down to a pattern and the adoption of a detailed legislative code would take years and some of the code might then be out of date. The process of later modification would be slow. The provisions of the draft directive that was prepared owed much to the UK Code, but it has not made much progress against the doubts raised about the aptness of the procedure at this point of time.

CODE OF EXCHANGE CONDUCT

The Directorate for Financial Institutions considered that greater progress in the wider field of transactions in transferable securities could be made in the immediate future by ensuring that community state rules were comparable with each other rather than identical. This amounted to an ethical, rather than legislative, approach. In support of this procedure it was pointed out that most of the member states had a set of rules owing more to a voluntarily accepted discipline than to a strictly legal framework. In controlling a wide range of operations, in which the techniques were constantly changing, a code of conduct had the advantage, over a directive, of flexibility and could be adapted to types of behaviour or operations which were not at present foreseen. A recommendation could be adopted as community policy in a matter of months, whereas a directive could take several years.

The code was not, however, seen as a substitute for a directive, but as possibly preceding it. The code would facilitate the process of harmonization through directives, by making clear in advance the approach that the Commission would be adopting. The code was issued as a Commission recommendation, dated 25 July 1977. It covers a wider field than take-overs, namely conduct relating to transactions in transferable securities. One aim is to facilitate capital transactions between countries in the community. The intention is that Governments should obtain general acceptance of the code by those to whom it applies and that existing supervisory bodies should apply it, particularly in dealing with cases not covered by existing national rules or practices.

The code consists of principles and supplementary principles, corresponding very broadly to the distinction between general principles and rules in the UK Take-over Code. The principles stress the need to observe the spirit of the code. Information provided for shareholders must be complete and accurate. There must be equality of treatment for shareholders. There is a special responsibility on directors and managers to observe the code and avoid any action that might prejudice the rights of other shareholders or fair dealings in the shares of the company. Persons dealing regularly in the securities and mergers would be expected to observe the code, even if they have to forgo short term gains. Financial intermediaries are not to take advantage of confidential information and have to avoid prejudicing the interests of clients and other persons with whom they have a fiduciary relationship.

The supplementary principles are described as intended to supplement the general principles by making them clearer and illustrating them. They are very similar in their wording and there is nothing corresponding to the specific procedural rules in the UK Code. One group of supplementary principles spells out in greater detail the obligation of financial intermediaries to behave fairly. A second group enlarges on the need to provide accurate information publicly and speedily and so to cut down the time during which price-sensitive information is kept secret. It is contemplated that there should be one or more supervisory authorities in each state which would supervise the implementation of the Code at national level. Representatives of these supervisory bodies would form a liaison committee to advise the Commission on the development of the code in the light of the problems encountered in its application. The Department of Trade has designated the Council for the Securities Industry as a supervisory authority in the United Kingdom, along with the Department and the Bank of England.

In its report for 1972/3, the Panel expressed the hope that any European code would be sufficiently flexible to permit maximum scope for a voluntary self-regulating system within individual member countries. This wish has been granted. There are some requirements that a UK body would have phrased differently, but the code is broadly comparable with the Take-over Code and it should raise no problems for the UK other than problems likely to arise on the Take-over Code itself. In this longer term it is to be expected that the EEC will lean towards State regulation, rather than self-regulation. If there is to be greater uniformity in practice and a striving towards uniformity, the tendency will be to try to funnel cases towards the Community's organs, including the European Courts.[1]

[1] On this, see the evidence given on behalf of the Financial Institutions Directorate of the EEC to the Wilson Committee in October 1978 (*Second Stage Evidence*, vol. l, p. 77).

Notes on the Code

INTRODUCTION

THE Introduction to the Code points out that the Code has not, and does not seek to have, the force of law. It represents the collective opinion of those professionally concerned in the field of take-overs and mergers on a range of business standards.

Those who wish to have the facilities of the securities markets in the United Kingdom available to them should conduct themselves in matters relating to take-overs and mergers according to the City Code; those who do not so conduct themselves cannot expect to enjoy those facilities and will find that they are withheld. The privileges and disciplines described herein apply in the first place to those who are actively engaged in the securities market in all its aspects, but they will also apply to directors of public companies or persons or groups of persons who seek to gain control (as defined in the City Code) of public companies, and professional advisers (insofar as they advise on the transactions in question), even where they are not directly affiliated to the bodies who are responsible for this document.

The Introduction goes on to say that the authors of the Code are satisfied that sufficient advertisement has been given to successive editions of the Code to make it difficult to plead ignorance as an excuse for non-compliance.

The City Working Party points out that some of these general principles, based as they are upon a concept of equity between one shareholder and another, while readily understandable in the City and by those concerned with the securities markets generally, would not easily lend themselves to legislation. The City Code is therefore framed in non-technical language and is, as a measure of self-discipline, administered and enforced by the Panel on Take-overs and Mergers, a body representative of those using the securities markets. The duty of the Panel is the enforcement of good business standards, not the enforcement of law.

The Code is designed primarily to protect offeree shareholders and the scope of the Code is determined by the status of the offeree company. The Code is drafted with the take-over of listed public companies particularly in mind, but it also applies to the take-over of unlisted public companies. This is elaborated in Practice Note 1 which says that for the purposes of the Code public companies having no listing are treated in the same way as those having a listing. The only differences are that reporting to The Stock Exchange under Rule 24 about an unlisted company is not necessary and that part of Rule 25 which relates to the suspension of listing obviously does not apply to an unlisted company. Where the offeror is a private company and the offeree is a public company the Code applies to the whole transaction, whether the transaction involves all or only part of the capital of the company concerned.

Subject to one exception noted below, the Code does not apply to cases where the offeree company is a private company. The Panel does not expect to be informed, or to have documents submitted, in the case of a merger or take-over transaction between two private companies or in the case of a take-over of a private company by a public company. The exception is that, if a public company is bidding for a private company and it is in reality a reverse take-over since the private company is large and the public company small (the usual intention being to get the listing of the public company for the merged companies), then the Code applies. The test applied is whether, if the offer is successful, any person together with any acting in concert with him will come to hold 30 per cent or more of the voting rights of the public company.

The Code does not normally apply to the take-over of a company which is not resident in the United Kingdom, even though the company is listed on The Stock Exchange. For this purpose the United Kingdom includes the Channel Islands and Isle of Man. What matters is the status of the offeree company. A public company resident in this country which makes an offer for an overseas company is not subject to the Code, if the offeree company is outside the Code. By using the qualifying word 'normally', the right is reserved in an exceptional case to apply the Code to a non-resident company, but this is unlikely to occur in practice. An offer for a company in the Irish Republic is subject to the Code, if the company is listed on The Stock Exchange.

Neither the City Code nor the Panel is concerned with the evaluation of the financial or commercial advantages or disadvantages of a take-over or merger proposition, which must be decided by the company and its shareholders. The Introduction also points out that the Panel, as the administering body, works on a day-to-day basis through its executive, headed by the Director-General. The Director General or his Deputies are available at all times to give rulings on points of interpretation of the Code. Companies and their advisers are invited to make full use of this service. Consultations are confidential.

Definitions

ACTING IN CONCERT

Persons acting in concert comprise persons who, pursuant to an agreement or understanding (whether formal or informal), actively co-operate, through the acquisition by any of them of shares in a company, to obtain or consolidate control (as defined below) of that company. The phrase 'consolidate control' refers to the purchase of more than 2 per cent by a shareholder whose holding is between 30 per cent and 50 per cent.

Without prejudice to the general application of this definition the following persons are presumed to be persons acting in concert with other persons in the same category unless the contrary is established:

(1) a company, its parent, subsidiaries and fellow subsidiaries, and their associated companies, and companies of which such companies are associated companies, all with each other. For this purpose ownership or control of 20 per cent or more of the equity share capital of a company will be regarded as the test of associated company status;
(2) a company with any of its directors (together with their close relatives and related trusts);
(3) a company with any of its pension funds;
(4) a person with any investment company, unit trust or other fund accustomed to act on such person's instructions;
(5) a financial adviser with its client in respect of the shareholdings of—
   (a) the financial adviser; and
   (b) all the funds which the financial adviser manages on a discretionary basis, where the shareholdings of the financial adviser and any of those funds in the client total 10 per cent or more of the client's equity share capital.

There are references to persons acting in concert with an offeror in General Principles 9 and 13 and in Rules 8, 13, 17, 27, 32, 33, 34, 35, and 36. Its most important applications are in Rules 33 and 34.

For persons to be acting in concert, there must be (a) an agreement or understanding (whether formal or informal) leading to (b) active co-operation to obtain or consolidate control of a company by (c) the acquisition by any of them of shares in that company. It follows from the definition of acting in concert that there must be an understanding and active co-operation.

Then there are the categories of persons, set out in the definition, who are presumed to be acting in concert with other persons in the same category unless the contrary is established. In the interpretation of (1) above, there would ordinarily have to be a degree of management control over an associated company to bring it within the net. There is a certain amount of linking of these categories. Under presumption (2), a company is in concert with its directors, unless the contrary is proved and under (3) is in concert with its pension funds. The directors and the pension funds are regarded as in concert. Again the directors of a financial adviser would be regarded as in concert with the client of the adviser, by virtue of (2) and (5)(a). It is not usual to link presumptions (4) and (5).

If arrangements have been made to ensure that corporate finance work in an organization is isolated, it may be possible to rebut a presumption that associated activities are acting in concert, but this would apply to the period when an intended bid was confidential and would not apply when the facts of the bid and the relevant shareholdings were public knowledge. If a party presumed to be in concert deals after the bid has been announced it is difficult to rebut the presumption.

In a large group the number of directors in the parent company and in its subsidiaries and associated companies may run into many hundreds; but the assumption will be rebuttable in many of the cases. The concept relates to the offeror rather than the offeree. If a major shareholder in the offeree company indicates that he proposes to accept an offer and advises other shareholders to do the same, these actions do not in themselves make him in concert with the offeror. Members of an offeree board may, however, acquire shares in an attempt to secure control and so thwart an offer; and its members may render themselves liable to make a mandatory bid under Rule 34. In these circumstances the concept of acting in concert would apply.

ASSOCIATE

The term 'associate' appears only in Rule 31. It is not thought practicable to define associate in precise terms which would cover all the different relationships which may exist in a take-over or merger transaction. The term associate is intended to cover all persons (whether or not acting in concert) who directly or indirectly own or deal in the shares of the offeror or offeree company in a take-over or

DEFINITIONS

merger transaction and who have (in addition to their normal interests as shareholders) an interest or potential interest, whether commercial, financial, or personal, in the outcome of the offer. Without prejudice to the generality of the foregoing, the term associate normally includes the following:

(1) the offeror or offeree company's parent, subsidiaries and fellow subsidiaries, and their associated companies, and companies of which such companies are associated companies. For this purpose ownership or control of 20 per cent or more of the equity share capital of a company will be regarded as the test of associated company status;

(2) bankers, stockbrokers, financial, and other professional advisers to the offeror, the offeree company or any company mentioned in (1);

(3) the directors (together with their close relatives and related trusts) of the offeror, the offeree company or any company mentioned in (1);

(4) the pension funds of the offeror, the offeree company or any company mentioned in (1);

(5) any investment company, unit trust or other fund accustomed to act on the instructions of another associate;

(6) a holder of 10 per cent or more of the equity share capital of the offeror or offeree company. Where two or more persons act as a syndicate or other group, pursuant to an agreement or understanding (whether formal or informal) to acquire or hold such capital, they shall be deemed to be a single holder for this purpose;

(7) a company having a material trading agreement with the offeror or offeree company.

The term 'associate' does not apply to a banker whose sole relationship with a party to a take-over or merger transaction is the provision of normal commercial banking services or such activities in connection with the offer as confirming that cash is available or handling acceptances and other registration work.

CASH PURCHASES

References to purchases for cash and cash prices paid for shares is deemed to include contracts or arrangements for the acquisition of shares where the consideration consists of a debt instrument maturing for payment in less than three years. This definition was required because of efforts to avoid the consequences of cash purchases of shares by giving, instead of cash, short-term debt instruments.

CONTROL

Control is deemed to mean a holding, or aggregate holdings, of shares carrying 30 per cent or more of the voting rights (as defined below) of a company, irrespective of whether that holding or holdings gives *de facto* control. Early efforts to leave to the Panel the determination in individual cases of what was then called 'effective control' proved to be unsatisfactory. Definition here is essential because there is a variety of definitions of control under statutory law (see page 92).

DIRECTORS

References to directors are deemed to include persons in accordance with whose instructions the directors or a director are accustomed to act.

OFFER

Offer includes, wherever appropriate, take-over and merger transactions howsoever effected, including reverse take-overs, partial offers and also offers by a parent company for shares in its subsidiary, but offers for non-voting non-equity capital (this applies to most preference shares) do not come within the Code. It has been a matter of comment that the Code contains no definition of a take-over bid, unlike the Licensed Dealers (Conduct of Business) Rules, 1960. The explanation is that the Code is concerned with offers for securities and covers more than take-overs, for example partial offers. The definition of offer is very wide.

OFFEROR

Offeror includes companies wherever incorporated and individuals wherever resident.

OFFER PERIOD

Offer period means the period from the date when an announcement is made of a proposed or possible offer (with or without terms) until the first closing date or (if this is later) the date when such offer is declared to have become unconditional as to acceptances or to have lapsed.

VOTING RIGHTS

Voting rights means all the voting rights attributable to the share capital of a company other than rights exercisable only in restricted circumstances. However, the Panel should be consulted where rights exercisable only in restricted circumstances have in fact been exercisable for a long time, as it may consider the relevant shares to have voting rights for the purposes of the Code. The second sentence refers to preference shares, in cases in which they have had votes because of prolonged inability to pay dividends.

GENERAL PRINCIPLES

The 1959 Notes set out some general principles, followed by more detailed guidance on various procedural points. Developments in the sixties showed the need for guidance on broad lines. Take-over methods were constantly developing and changing. In a fast-developing situation, too great reliance on detailed rules would mean that the framers of the Code were always some steps behind those who were devising fresh techniques. The tendency would also be to observe the letter rather than the spirit of the regulations. Accordingly, in the 1968 Code, substantial reliance was placed on the General Principles, many of them new. At the same time the Rules were expanded and made more precise. The introduction to the 1968 Code said:

The organisations concerned on the City Working Party with the preparation of the revised Code considered it . . . to be impracticable to devise rules in such detail as to cover all the various circumstances which arise in take-over or merger transactions. Accordingly, persons engaged in such transactions should be aware that the spirit as well as the precise wording of these general principles and of the ensuing rules should be observed.

The General Principles in the 1968 Code remained more or less unchanged until the 1976 revision, when some discussion took place on the balance between General Principles and Rules. In the intervening years, the Rules had been elaborated, notably on the subject of mandatory bids, without any corresponding enlargement of the General Principles. There were those who felt that the main reliance should henceforth be placed on the Rules, and that the General Principles should be left more or less unchanged as a statement of the ideas out of which the Code had sprung.

In the event, two new General Principles were added in 1976. General Principle 13 states that, where a person has acquired control of a company, he must normally make a general offer to all other shareholders and that accordingly anyone who is acquiring control should ensure that he will be able to implement a general offer. General Principle 14 deals with voluntary bids and stresses the need to ensure, before a bid is announced, that the offeror can implement it. In 1976 a Rule about the responsibilities of directors in companies they control by reason of their shareholdings was elevated to be the second part of General Principle 11.

The Panel at an early stage decided that, if a Rule dealt precisely with a situation, it was not open to the Panel in a particular case to waive the Rule in favour of their interpretation of a General Principle covering the same situation. In such cases the General Principles could be resorted to only if the Rules could not be applied to the particular case.[1] The General Principles have, however, been rightly described as the corner stones of the Code and are of more widely ranging significance than the Rules. The Rules have to be interpreted in the light of the General Principles[2] and they apply to situations not covered by the Rules. The scope of the General Principles is not restricted by the scope of the Rules.

General Principle 1

THE SPIRIT OF THE CODE

It is impracticable to devise rules in such detail as to cover all the various circumstances which arise in take-over or merger transactions. Accordingly, persons engaged in such transactions should be aware that the spirit as well as the precise wording of these General Principles and of the ensuing Rules must be observed. Moreover, it must be accepted that the General Principles and the spirit of the Code will apply in areas or circumstances not explicitly covered by any Rule.

(Previous references at pages 55 and 72)

The earlier editions of the Code referred simply to the spirit of the General Principles and of the Rules. What may be regarded as the rather wider concept of 'the spirit of the Code' was introduced in the 1972 revision.

The following cases illustrate how the Panel has interpreted the spirit of the Code:

(1) In 1971 directors of a company favoured a lower rather than a higher bid. They had service contracts which were very onerous from the point of view of their company. They indicated that they would be prepared to agree to a modification of the contracts if the lower bid was accepted, but they were not prepared to do so if the higher bid was. This action might not have been conclusive

---

[1] Panel's statement of 2 Apr. 1971 in the Adepton case.
[2] Panel's statement of 24 Mar. 1970 in Trafalgar House Investments/Cementation.

enough to bring General Principle 4 into operation, but it clearly was against the spirit of the Code.
(2) There was nothing in the Code about a merchant bank that both acted as adviser for an offeror and agreed to pay cash for shares and loan stock which a shareholder in the offeree company received for his shares but did not want to hold. Nevertheless the Panel in the Ashbourne case felt able to consider what obligations towards offeree shareholders Brandts should be regarded as incurring as a result of an 'underwriting' agreement of this character.

Although the Rules are more narrowly drawn than the General Principles, the Panel has always felt free to interpret the reference to the spirit of the Rules as meaning that the Panel can have regard to the general intention of a Rule when dealing with a case not precisely covered by the Rule.

The Rules have always included provisions that the Panel could waive certain Rules in individual cases and the number of Rules in which the Panel is authorized to grant a dispensation has increased as time has gone on. This is necessary to secure a measure of flexibility in the administration of the Code. Normally no directions are given to the Panel how it is to administer its discretion: and this is another field in which the Panel endeavours to give effect to the spirit of the Code.

General Principle 2

LIMITATIONS ON DIRECTORS' ACTIONS

While the boards of an offeror and of an offeree company and their respective advisers have a primary duty to act in the best interests of their respective shareholders, they must accept that there are limitations in connection with take-over and merger transactions on the manner in which the pursuit of those interests can be carried out. Inevitably therefore these General Principles and the ensuing Rules will impinge on the freedom of action of boards and persons involved in such transactions.
(Previous references at pages 38, 88 and 149)

This had remained substantially unchanged since the 1968 Code. The Chairman of the Panel assured the Law Society in 1969 that, where there was a legal *duty* on directors or trustees which required them to accept a particular offer, they would not be penalized if they appeared to infringe the Code. The Panel would never seek to restrict the performance of legal duties: all that the Code sought to do was to impose some restriction on the way in which legal *rights* might be exercised.

General Principle 3

SUFFICIENT INFORMATION AND TIME

Shareholders shall have in their possession sufficient evidence, facts and opinions upon which an adequate judgement and decision can be reached and shall have sufficient time to make an assessment and decision. No relevant information shall be withheld from them.

(Previous references at pages 72, 77 and 153)

This dates substantially from the Notes and the Revised Notes. The second sentence was added in the 1969 revision of the Code. General Principle 3 should be read with Rule 15. In its 1977/8 report the Panel pointed out that, as each case had unique features, it was impossible for the Panel to detail what information should be made available in every circumstance. The need for full compliance with General Principle 3 is especially great in the case of agreed take-overs, since significant facts and arguments are not so readily made public as in a contested bid. The information supplied to shareholders should be up to date, for example in regard to borrowings.

Since the law regards a company as belonging to the shareholders, the Code is primarily concerned with the protection of the interests of shareholders. If company law was altered to take greater account of the position of the employees in a company, the Code would probably have to be amended to reflect the law.

The interpretation of General Principle 3 has largely revolved round cases where shareholders might be confused by what was said or done by directors and others. In 1971, a company, acting as financial adviser to another company which was the subject of a bid, agreed that a letter to shareholders advising acceptance of an offer could say that the financial adviser intended to accept the offer in respect of its holding. In fact, it then sold a substantial proportion of its shares (amounting to 15.9 per cent of the issued capital of the offeree company) on the market a few days later. The financial adviser continued to advise shareholders to accept the offer and gave an enforceable undertaking in respect of the remaining shares still in its possession. The Panel subsequently included in Practice Note 9 a statement that directors and financial advisers to a company who own shares in that company should not deal in such shares contrary to any advice they may have given to shareholders, or to any advice with which it can be reasonably assumed that they were associated, without giving sufficient public notice of their intentions.

The General Principle has not been interpreted to mean that, if a majority of the directors of an offeree company agree to make a recommendation about a bid, they must set out the views of a dissenting minority. Neither an offeror nor an offeree board should keep back something new, unexpected, or startling and then produce it to shareholders in the last few days of an offer period.

General Principle 4

FRUSTRATION OF OFFER BY A BOARD

> *At no time after a bona fide offer has been communicated to the board of an offeree company or after the board of an offeree company has reason to believe that a bona fide offer might be imminent shall any action be taken by the board of the offeree company in relation to the affairs of the company, without the approval in general meeting of the shareholders of the offeree company, which could effectively result in any bona fide offer being frustrated or in the shareholders of the offeree company being denied an opportunity to decide on its merits.*

(Previous references at pages 39 and 49)

This was intended to regulate some of the practices by which the boards of offeree companies had thwarted bids—for example by issuing shares to a favoured offeror in respect of assets acquired from him and so reducing the percentage holding of shares of a less favoured offeror and making it more difficult for a less favoured offeror to secure control. Another device, where a bidder was thought to be aiming to secure cash in the offeree company, had been to spend the funds to buy assets, possibly not easily realizable assets. Rule 38 sets out the provisions more precisely.

This, and the associated Rule 38, is the only Code provision that can be waived by shareholders in general meeting, though in certain circumstances described later the Panel has regard to shareholders' views in operating Rule 34. At an early stage, concern was expressed about the scope of the Principle. Did it prevent the board of an offeree company from endeavouring to secure a rival bid? The view was that a great deal of activity of this kind could take place without falling foul of the Principle which related to action which could effectively frustrate an offer. Then, if a director bought shares to keep them out of the hands of the offeror, was that against the Principle? Here again it was considered that the Principle was not intended to refer to market operations undertaken by a director on his own responsibility. The General Principle was in a more general form in the 1968 Code (the words 'in relation to the affairs of the company' did not appear). When the 1969 revision was under discussion, it was represented that this went too wide; and the words 'in relation to the affairs of the company' were therefore introduced.

Practice Note 9 points out that the declaration and payment of an interim dividend, otherwise than in the normal course, during an offer period may in certain circumstances be contrary to General Principle 4 and Rule 38 in that it could effectively frustrate an offer. Offeree companies and their advisers are therefore asked to consult the Panel before taking such steps.

In 1976 and 1977 there was much discussion whether the General Principle required the board of an offeree company to consult their shareholders before taking legal action which might have the effect of frustrating a bid. There are two difficulties about the application of the Principle to such cases. Directors may feel obliged to move with greater speed than would be practicable if an EGM of shareholders had to be summoned. Second, it may be difficult to explain the legal issues to shareholders, and shareholders may tend to apply their minds to the merits of the bid rather than to the merits of the proposed legal action. In January 1977 the Panel, without expressing a view on the application of General Principle 4 to those cases and without imposing any obligation on directors, advised them to consult the Panel Executive if they contemplated legal action to frustrate a bid, since such a move might have repercussions on the operation of the Code in respect of the bid. Presumably the Panel might endeavour to restrain a board that was simply endeavouring to thwart a bid, whereas it would be more sympathetic if there was a sound commercial reason for the suit. There is a strong body of opinion that would be opposed to any attempt to interfere with the exercise of legal rights by directors. On the whole past experience is not encouraging for boards that think of using a legal action as a weapon against a bid.

The General Principle and Rule 38 are considered to continue to operate during a reference to the Monopolies and Mergers Commission and the subsequent consideration of its report by Ministers, notwithstanding that the offer is formally abandoned on a reference to the Commission.

General Principle 5

PREVENTION OF A FALSE MARKET

It must be the object of all parties to a take-over or merger transaction to use every endeavour to prevent the creation of a false market in the shares of an offeror or offeree company.

The substance dates from the 1959 Notes. The aim is to protect shareholders and the general message is that rumours ought not to be allowed to run unchecked. The application of the General Principle is expanded in Rules 7 and 30 and is assisted by the requirement in Rule 31 that the offeror or offeree and associates should disclose dealings in shares in the offer period. If, for example, an offeror covertly sold shares in the offeree company in order to reduce their market value and so increased the attractiveness of his offer, this would create a false market, but it is considered that the requirement to disclose dealings makes this less likely. A more difficult case is where shares are being sold short in the offer period, with corresponding purchases after its conclusion. Because of the difficulty of identifying 'short' transactions and the restraints imposed by the speculative risk and the publication of the transactions, the Panel has not interfered in these cases. In a statement issued on 11 April 1979 in connection with the bid of Rockwell International Corporation for Wilmot Breeden (Holdings) Ltd. the Panel indicated that, where the market price of an offeree share was rising in anticipation of a higher bid, special care must be exercised in announcing that the offer would not be increased, if one of the objects of the announcement was to influence the market price and if there was a possibility that the offer price might in fact be increased.

Rule 73(b)(2) of The Stock Exchange Rules defines a false market as 'a market in which a movement of the price of a share is brought about or sought to be brought about by contrived factors, such as the operation of buyers and sellers acting in collaboration with each other, calculated to create a movement in price which is not justified by assets, earnings or prospects.' The Panel has sometimes given a rather wider meaning to the term 'false market' by applying it to buying or selling by an insider on the basis of confidential price-sensitive information. If the effect of insider dealing is to raise the price of a share nearer to its true value when the bid is announced, the market should perhaps be described as unfair to the outside buyer rather than false.

General Principle 6

COMPETENT INDEPENDENT ADVICE

A board which receives an offer or is approached with a view to an offer being made should in the interests of its shareholders seek competent independent advice.
(Previous references at pages 39 and 108)

The 1968 Code provided that the board should consider whether it should seek competent outside advice. The 1969 Code said that the board should normally seek outside advice. The present unqualified provision was introduced in 1976. The need to obtain competent independent advice applies not simply to offers but whenever a board is considering an issue of securities which could result in control of the company being transferred or consolidated. The advice may be given by a merchant bank or other professional adviser. The problems that arise are discussed in the notes on Rule 4.

General Principle 7

RIGHTS OF CONTROL

Rights of control must be exercised in good faith and the oppression of a minority is wholly unacceptable.
(Previous references at pages 46 and 77)

This General Principle stems from the widely held belief that minority shareholders are not as well protected under English law as under US and other codes of law. The matter engaged the attention of both the Cohen Committee and the Jenkins Committee and is the subject of provisions in the Companies Bill 1979. The corresponding General Principle in the 1968 Code was to the effect that, notwithstanding the legal rights of a majority, anything done to oppress a minority (in the general and not in the legal sense of the words) was wholly unacceptable. It was pointed out, before the 1969 revision, that the words in parenthesis were unnecessary, since the courts used the ordinary dictionary meaning of oppression (*Scottish Co-operative Wholesale Society Ltd.* v. *Meyer (1959) A.C. 324*).

Although the General Principle is expressed in wide terms, the Code deals only with take-overs and the General Principle is intended to secure that minorities are not treated unfairly in the course of or as a result of take-over transactions. This includes an offer by a parent company for shares in its subsidiary.

General Principle 8

EQUALITY OF TREATMENT

All shareholders of the same class of an offeree company shall be treated similarly by an offeror
(Previous references at pages 39, 64, 65, 72 and 73)

This is the core of the Code. It has been applied and interpreted in a number of Rules. The most obvious case in which the General Principle comes into play is where a potential offeror has paid a high price to obtain sufficient shares to give him control of a company. The Code says that in these circumstances he must make an offer for all the remaining shares at the highest price he paid for the shares in the last twelve months. In this way the premium paid for control is divided among all the shareholders. Some States in the USA take the view that control belongs to the company and that any premium paid for control should be the property of the company; but the view in the UK is that it belongs to the shareholders.

The concept of classes of shares is derived from the Companies Acts. There are three principal rights associated with shares—the right to a dividend, the right to vote at shareholders' meetings, and the right to a share of the company's assets on a winding-up. Any body of shares that carry different rights in any of these respects from other shares constitute a separate class. Exceptionally there may be different classes of shares although the shares carry the same rights—for example, if shares are issued to or for the benefit of employees. There are references to classes of shares in General Principle 9 and in Rules 21, 27, 28, 29, 33, and 34.

As regards the terms of a bid, proposals that cash be given for the holdings of directors having effective control and paper to the generality of shareholders, or vice versa, have in general not been accepted. An offer for voting shares should be accompanied by an offer for non-voting equity shares, but the values of the two offers need not be identical. See notes under Rule 21. One major field of difficulty was the application of the General Principle to cases where an offeror was making an offer and at the same time purchasing in the market. The Panel dealt with the matter at some length in its 1970/1 report.

There were several occasions during the year when an offeror who had announced a paper bid, which was or was likely to be opposed, sought to decide the contest by heavy purchases of offeree shares for cash in the market or outside it making later any upward revision to the terms of his paper offer which might be required. To the offeror his actions appeared unobjectionable on the grounds that Rules 29 and 31 [now Rules 30 and 31] permit any offeror to deal in offeree shares for cash subject only to (i) daily reporting of the amounts and price and (ii) upward revision of the offer if purchases are effected at above the offer value. At times, however, the technique appeared to the defending party to be in breach of General Principle 8 which requires all shareholders of the same class to be treated similarly by an offeror company. The breach appeared all the more grave when the offeror succeeded in buying control of the offeree company in the market while shareholders were still digesting the offer document with the result that frequently the more experienced or better advised investors were found to have realised their investment for cash while the remainder had to be content with the offer of less marketable paper.

The position in 1971 was that the Panel executive, when asked, ruled in all cases that offerors for paper were permitted to purchase unlimited offeree shares for cash provided that (i) the purchases were spread over a reasonable period of time and were not selective (or if selective were not selectively in favour of holdings critical to the outcome of the offer) and (ii) the reporting requirements were met and the value of the paper offer revised upwards if cash purchases were made at a higher price. A cash purchase of a 'critical' block of shares during a paper bid was, however, regarded as involving the offeror in an obligation under General Principle 8 to make a general cash offer for all the shares at the highest price paid for any of the shares purchased. What was or was not a critical block had to be determined in the circumstances of each particular case.

This question of the effect of cash purchases on a paper offer is now governed by Rule 33, introduced in September 1971. The Panel regards Rule 33 as having established 15 per cent as the critical percentage in all but very exceptional cases, such as where the sellers are directors or other insiders of the offeree company. Accordingly, where a bid is being made, a cash offer is required only where the cash purchases are 15 per cent or more of the relevant class of shares during the offer period or the previous twelve months.

As regards the price, the Code and the Panel have never sought to apply the General Principle with needling precision, because of the practical difficulties that would arise from such an approach. Thus a price obtained in the market to-day is regarded as the same as the identical price obtained later under a bid, although the purist would want to discount back the latter price. The incidence of taxation in individual cases is ignored. An offeror would not be required to make a paper offer as an alternative to a cash offer, simply because the incidence of capital gains tax would vary among offeree shareholders. Likewise in Rule 32, the price at which shares are purchased is the price at which the bargain was struck, although the purchasers may find that their net receipts per share vary because of differences in respect of brokers' commission.

Where shareholders are in different countries, an identical offer may represent different net receipts. In general, the Panel is opposed to tailoring bids to the special circumstances of shareholders and prefers to insist that the offeror makes the same offer to all. There have, however, been dispensations in exceptional cases. In one case, because of difficulties in including a loan stock element in an offer to US shareholders, they were treated differently from other shareholders. In another case, a controlling family was allowed to receive irredeemable unlisted loan stock of less value than the cash offered to other shareholders, on condition that the scheme was recommended by the independent directors and an independent merchant bank and approved by a majority of the non-family shareholders.

In its annual report for 1977/8, the Panel indicated that, even though the offer period may have ended, so long as the offer remains open for acceptance by shareholders the offeror should consult the Panel before it buys shares in the offeree company at above the offer price. The Code is primarily concerned with events that take place during the offer period and not with anything thereafter, but the Panel considered that General Principle 8, which is in general terms, should be more widely interpreted.

General Principle 9

NO LESS FAVOURABLE TERMS

> *If, after a take-over or merger transaction is reasonably in contemplation, an offer has been made to one or more shareholders of an offeree company, any subsequent general offer made by or on behalf of the same offeror, or any person acting in concert with it, to the shareholders of the same class shall not be on less favourable terms.*

(Previous references at pages 46 and 141)

General Principle 9 represents a particular application of General Principle 8. In 1968 there was only one General Principle, with the substance of General Principle 9 given as an illustration of parity of treatment. The division into separate General Principles was made in the 1969 revision. The procedure by which American Tobacco had secured control of Gallaher was thought to merit separate treatment of the particular technique employed. The subsequent general offer is the offer that was 'reasonably in contemplation'. The phrase 'reasonably in contemplation' is interpreted more widely than 'the consideration and discussion of any proposed offer' in Rule 30. A bid may be reasonably in contemplation even if a tentative decision to bid has not yet been taken. This matches up with the twelve months in Rule 33. A much later, un-related offer, would not be caught.

The scope of General Principle 9 is restricted by the extent to which the field has been covered since 1971 by Rule 33. Rule 33 provides that if an offeror and anyone acting in concert buys for cash shares in the offeree company carrying 15 per cent or more of the voting rights during the offer period or within twelve months before its commencement, then he must make a cash offer or give a cash alternative. The Panel may also require a cash offer or a cash alternative if in its view circumstances render this necessary in order to give effect to General Principle 8: and this has been used where an offeror was buying a significant number of shares, but fewer than 15 per cent of the voting rights, for cash, from directors and others inside the offeree company.

Unlike Rule 33, General Principle 9 does not require the selective purchases to have been for cash, nor does it require cash or a cash alternative in the general offer. Normally, the selective purchases will have been for cash and the obligation is to offer the other shareholders 'not less favourable terms'. The main field that remains for General Principle 9 is where an offeror buys a significant number of shares, but less than 15 per cent of the voting rights, from an outsider or outsiders. Except where the sellers are directors or other insiders of the offeree company the Panel does not normally require an offer to be in cash, or with a cash alternative, where the offeror acquires a large block of shares, but less than 15 per cent, just in advance of a bid, provided that the subsequent paper bid will, following its announcement, have a value at least equal to the cash price paid. The Panel might, however, say in a particular case that the paper was so unattractive, notwithstanding a temporary parity in value, that it did not constitute equally favourable terms. A prospective offeror buying shares and then proposing to make a paper bid has to bear in mind that the offeror's shares may fall in value when the bid is announced. General Principle 9 would also cover a critical acquisition of shares from insiders or outsiders, where the consideration was not in cash and where the offer seemed to be less favourable than the consideration paid for the acquisition of shares.

General Principle 10

INFORMATION TO ALL SHAREHOLDERS

During the course of a take-over or merger transaction or when such is in contemplation, neither the offeror, the offeree company nor any of their respective advisers shall furnish information to some shareholders which is not made available to all shareholders. This principle shall not apply to the furnishing of information in confidence by an offeree company to a bona fide potential offeror or vice versa, nor to the issue of circulars by members of The Stock Exchange (who are brokers to any party to the transaction) to their own investment clients provided such issue shall previously have been approved by the Panel.

(Previous reference at page 39)

The principle that all shareholders should be treated alike is fundamental to the Code. It would, however, be idle to deny that the General Principle causes some difficulty because of the efforts that

GENERAL PRINCIPLES

have been made to get institutional shareholders to take a more active part in the affairs of the companies in which they hold investments.

MEETINGS WITH SELECTED SHAREHOLDERS

Practice Note No. 2 refers to the desire of companies to hold briefings for selected shareholders to discuss an offer and it agrees that meetings with institutional investors have not been uncommon in the past. There is a strong possibility that, whatever the intention at the outset, fresh information will be forthcoming at meetings of shareholders at which directors of companies or their advisers express their views during a take-over or merger. Such information is not covered by a board responsibility statement within the provisions of Rule 14.

The Practice Note accepts that meetings with selected shareholders may be held, convened by the offeree board or the offeror, provided that the following safeguards are observed:

(a) a meeting should not be held until the offer document has been issued and the offeree company's board has published its views.
(b) All shareholders should be sent invitations to attend the meeting at least three days (Saturdays, Sundays and public holidays excluded) beforehand. In special circumstances the Panel may accept that paid press advertisements of a meeting are sufficient notice.
(c) The press and news agencies should be invited.
(d) If at the meeting any material new information is forthcoming or significant new opinions are expressed, a circular giving details should be sent to shareholders immediately thereafter: in the later stages of a take-over or merger it may be necessary to make use of paid newspaper space as well as a circular. The circular or advertisement should include the board responsibility statement. If such new information is not capable of being substantiated as required by the Code, e.g., a profit forecast, this should be made clear and it should be formally withdrawn in the circular or advertisement.

The emphasis is on meetings. No objection is normally taken to a visit to a company by a single institutional shareholder, provided, of course, that no new information is given. If the Panel is satisfied that no new information is likely to pass, no objection would normally be taken, in the case of an agreed bid, to a meeting of representatives of institutional shareholders to enable them to get to know those who will manage the new organization. The Principle is concerned primarily with the offeree shareholders. In the case of a cash bid, there is not the same objection to meetings arranged by the offeror about the offeror's business.

INFORMATION ISSUED BY ASSOCIATE BROKERS

On this subject Practice Note 2 says:

The Panel does not wish to prevent brokers who are associates in a take-over or merger transaction from giving to their own clients material on the companies involved in the take-over, but associate brokers should bear in mind the essential point that fresh information must not be restricted to a small group. Accordingly, such information should not include any statements of fact or opinion derived from information not generally available: in particular, profit forecasting (unless, and then only to the extent that, the offer documents contain forecasts) should normally be avoided. The brokers' associate status should be clearly disclosed. Clearance before release may in many cases be effected by telephone but where there is doubt a draft should be sent to the Panel. In all cases copies of the final version should be sent to the Panel.

PRESS, TELEVISION, AND RADIO

In its annual report for 1971/2, the Panel said that increasing use was being made of press, radio, and television for the advancement of rival views in contested bids. The Panel stressed the importance of the printed circular addressed to the registered shareholders. The circular alone could ensure total coverage of the body of shareholders. It could be comprehensive, read and reread and discussed with professional advisers. It unequivocally engaged the responsibility of its authors. Paid newspaper advertisements and organized press conferences had a role that was secondary to that of the circular: and the radio and television had further disadvantages because of the haphazard coverage and the lack of written records easily available to the public. On the question of information in television interviews, Practice Note 2 says:

Parties involved in take-overs or mergers should take particular care not to release fresh material in television or radio interviews or discussions. In view of the complexity of most financial issues and the difficulty of communicating these by broadcasting media in such a manner that the general public can readily understand, parties are in general advised not to discuss such issues on television or radio. A distinction may be drawn between the recording or televising of a straight interview, whether as part of a press conference or with a representative of the radio or television organisation, and participation in more general discussion programmes. The Panel deprecates anything which amounts to a confrontation between representatives of offeror and offeree companies or between competing offerors or which leads to any kind of gladiatorial combat. Where radio or television interviews of a straight kind are granted, those concerned would be wise to make it a condition that the sequence of the interview would not be broken by the interposition of comments or observations by others not made in the course of the actual interview itself, and that a transcript would be provided.

If any fresh information is made public as a result of such an interview, shareholders should be circularised and (where appropriate) newspaper space taken.

GENERAL PRINCIPLES

The revised version of Practice Note 9 issued in December 1978 contained further admonitions on the subject:

Directors and officials of companies and their advisers must take care when talking to the media that they do not inadvertently let slip information, e.g., concerning the content of profit forecasts or asset revaluations, which is not in a form in which it can be readily incorporated in a document sent to shareholders, nor allow themselves to give indications of future revisions or extensions when there is no absolute certainty. Advisers should warn clients of the care needed in this area when a bid situation develops.

General Principle 11

DUTIES OF DIRECTORS IN RELATION TO THEIR PERSONAL INTERESTS

Directors of an offeror or an offeree company shall always, in advising their shareholders, act only in their capacity as directors and not have regard to their personal or family shareholdings or their personal relationships with the companies. It is the shareholders' interests taken as a whole, together with those of employees and creditors, which should be considered.

Shareholders in companies which are effectively controlled by their directors must accept that in respect of any offer the attitude of their board will be decisive. There may be good reasons for such a board rejecting an offer or preferring the lower of two offers. The board must carefully examine its reasons for doing so and be prepared to explain its decision to its shareholders.

(Previous references at pages 43, 55, 68, 77 and 101)

The substance of this General Principle dates from the Notes and Revised Notes. The second paragraph was Rule 9 until the 1976 revision, when it was elevated to be part of General Principle 11. Directors who are invited to give shut-outs are expected to have regard to the General Principle.

In the Coral case in 1971 the Panel described the relationship between the two paragraphs as follows:

At first sight it may not seem entirely easy to reconcile [the two paragraphs] and certainly difficulty may arise in applying these provisions to the facts of particular cases. It is therefore appropriate for the Panel to state here the general way in which the provisions of the City Code in this context are to be applied. Whilst it is clear that the paramount duty of directors is to consider the interests of the general body of shareholders and in the advice they give or decisions they take, not to prefer their own interests or those of any special group or section, it is also the case that the control of companies lies with a majority of the shareholders rather than with a minority. The Panel will always be vigilant so far as it lies within its power to ensure that boards of directors which, through their own members or through associated family shareholdings control a majority of shares, do not exercise their powers as a board in order to oppress a minority or to force through some proposal which, properly considered, could not be regarded as for the benefit of the body of shareholders as a whole. But, whilst directors in their actions as such must disregard what they may consider their personal interests, it does not invariably and inevitably follow that in voting their own shares, which are no less their individual property because they are directors of the company as well as shareholders, they must defer what they conceive as their own interest as shareholders to that of a minority. The general position of directors is indeed not dissimilar whether they control a majority or only a minority of the voting shares. Directors controlling a minority of shares, which is the case with which [the first paragraph of] General Principle 11 is usually concerned, must of course not use their powers as directors in a way which promotes their own interests but is inimical to that of the majority. The possession of control over a majority of shares does not, however, diminish the powers of a director as such although it should make him the more careful that his actions are manifestly seen to be in accordance with his responsibilities. This said, it is, however, not inconceivable that whilst the duty of directors might require them to advise minority shareholders that some particular course would appear to be in their interest, where the directors come as individual shareholders to exercise their own personal proprietary rights in their shares they might, for their own part, act differently. Where a board, with or without associated or family shareholders, control a majority of the voting shares, the remaining shareholders must be deemed to be aware of the fact and, subject to the paramount requirement of good faith, must recognize that should any difference of view arise it must in the end be resolved by a decision of the majority. Any contrary view would, of course, give an overriding power to the minority and would also seem either to disenfranchise the directors' and associated shares or to mean that majority shareholders could not sit on the boards of the companies concerned, results which could hardly be thought on any view to be reasonable. [The second paragraph of General Principle 11] is in fact quite explicit in providing that this should not be the case. Majorities must not abuse their position, but minorities cannot dominate.

It will be observed that the General Principle requires directors to consider the interests of employees and creditors as well as those of the shareholders.

The difficult problems that can arise under General Principle 11 are illustrated by the case of W. Henshall and Sons (Addlestone) Limited which was the subject of a Panel statement on 3 July 1978. A company acquired just over 50 per cent of the Henshall shares and made an offer of 20p. per share for the rest. Another company then made an offer at 30p. which had the support of the Henshall board, but the first company said that it had no intention of accepting this offer. The board of Henshall then sought a Panel ruling that the first

GENERAL PRINCIPLES

company should accept the higher offer or that the Panel should allow the Henshall board to acquire assets in return for unissued shares which would have diluted the first company's holding below 50 per cent. This second proposal would have offended against Rule 38. The first company had control of Henshall and the remaining shareholders had to accept that their attitude was decisive.

General Principle 12

STANDARDS OF CARE IN DOCUMENTS

Any document or advertisement addressed to shareholders containing information, opinions or recommendations from the board of an offeror or offeree company or their respective advisers shall be treated with the same standards of care as if it were a prospectus within the meaning of the Companies Act, 1948. Especial care shall be taken over profit forecasts.
(Previous reference at page 39)

This has remained unaltered from the first edition of the Code in 1968. The substance of the General Principle is largely repeated in the opening sentence of Rule 14.

The Jenkins Committee (Cmnd. 1749 of 1962 paragraph 270) was troubled about the difference in the law relating to new issues and to take-over offers.

A prospectus is a document offering new shares or bonds for subscription in cash. Anyone may issue a prospectus as long as he complies with the provisions of the Companies Acts. These set out in considerable detail the information to be given and impose heavy civil liabilities and criminal penalties on persons responsible for issuing prospectuses containing fraudulent or reckless statements.

Take-over bids on the other hand come within the provisions of the Prevention of Fraud (Prevention) Act 1958 which restricts the channels through which take-over circulars and other offers to sell or buy securities may be distributed without express authorization. These channels are members of The Stock Exchange, other exempted dealers, members of recognized associations of dealers and licensed dealers. There are not the same detailed requirements for offer documents as in relation to prospectuses.

This is the reason for dealing with part of this field in the Code and for indicating the standards expected in take-over documents. In practice, errors in take-over documents are usually dealt with by issuing corrections to shareholders or in the Press.

General Principle 13

ACQUISITION OF CONTROL

Where control of a company is acquired by a person, or persons acting in concert, a general offer to all other shareholders is normally required; a similar obligation may arise if control is consolidated. Where shares are being acquired as a result of which a person incurs such an obligation he should, before making such an acquisition, ensure that he can and will continue to be able to implement the offer.

(Previous reference at page 107)

This General Principle was introduced in 1976. The mandatory bid was developed in the Rules and it was considered desirable to deal with the matter in general terms in the General Principles. The first part of the General Principle is spelt out in detail in Rule 34. The obligation to make a general offer relates to voting shares and other classes of equity shares. It does not necessarily extend to preference shares. The second part was new in 1976 and cases may arise under it.

General Principle 14

RESPONSIBLE ANNOUNCEMENTS

An offeror should only announce an offer after the most careful and responsible consideration. Such an announcement should be made only when an offeror has every reason to believe that it can and will continue to be able to implement the offer. Responsibility in this connection also rests on the financial advisers to an offeror.

(Previous references at pages 90 and 107)

General Principle 13 stresses that anyone who has it in mind to acquire shares which would involve him in making a general offer should ensure that he can implement the offer. General Principle 14 deals primarily with voluntary offers, though the reference to financial advisers should be regarded as covering mandatory as well as voluntary offers.

Some of the evidence before the Jenkins Committee related to the question whether an offeror should be required to show that he could honour the bid. Sir Charles Clore argued that there should be a legal obligation on the part of the offeror to arrange irrevocably for the full implementation of the consideration offered in the event of the offer becoming unconditional. The British Insurance Association considered that the bidder should be under an obligation to indicate the resources available to him for the purposes of the bid. *The Economist* said that where a bid was wholly or partly in cash, some evidence should be presented (such as a letter from a clearing bank) to show that the money was there to meet the bid. The Committee of London Clearing Bankers said that, before allowing its name to be used in connection with any bid, a bank (whether or not assisting with the finance) should satisfy itself that sufficient funds were available to carry through the transaction. On this point, the Jenkins Committee recommended that a take-over circular should contain a definite statement, in the form of a representation binding the offeror, saying what steps he had taken to ensure that the necessary cash would be available.

General Principle 14 links with Rule 18. General Principle 14 is wider than the Rule which specifically refers to confirmation in the offer document. At the time of the formal announcement of an offer, the position is governed by General Principle 14. Whether the offeror satisfies General Principle 14 in making an announcement of the offer, is primarily a matter for his judgement and that of his financial advisers. In most of the cases that come before the Panel, the argument is that unforeseeable circumstances have deprived the offeror of the financial ability to implement the offer. The Panel takes a serious view of any case in which it was shown that the offeror had entered into the transaction without adequate consideration for its financial implications. Thus in the bid by BSQ Securities for Court Hotels (London) the Panel in a statement dated 8 October 1975 said that it was not enough to have a reasonable hope that funds would be available. 'No firm announcement of an offer should be made unless those concerned have taken all reasonably prudent steps to satisfy themselves that the necessary funds will be available when required.'

RULES

Rule 1

The offer should be put forward in the first instance to the board of the offeree company or to its advisers.
(Previous references at pages 40 and 122)

This Rule is interpreted to mean that the offeror or his advisers should inform the board of the offeree company of his intention to bid, and the terms he offers, before the offeror announces the bid publicly or to the shareholders of the offeree company. The original intention, as indicated in the Notes and Revised Notes, was to try to channel the offer to the shareholders through the directors of the offeree company. 'Their Board is normally the best source of advice.'

Over the years there have been complaints from time to time that the offeror sometimes gives the offeree board the scantiest advance notice of an intention to announce a bid publicly. The Licensed Dealers (Conduct of Business) Rules, 1960, provide that 'the terms of the offer should be submitted to the offeree company at least three days before the offer is sent to the offeree shareholders'. This refers to the sending of the formal offer document to the offeree shareholders by the licensed dealer. In practice far more than three days usually supervenes between the communication of the terms to the offeree board and the posting of the offer document to the offeree shareholders. In 1977, the Panel had to consider a case in which it was argued that the offeror (Fruehauf Corporation) should have allowed at least three days to elapse between telling the board of the offeree company (Crane Fruehauf) of the bid and the dispatch of the offer document. In fact both took place on the same day. The Panel ruled that the Licensed Dealers Rules were not binding on the merchant bank acting for the offeror, because the bank was an exempted dealer. The general intention of the offeror had been known for a long time and had been the subject of a reference to the Monopolies and Mergers Commission. The probability is that the Code practice will be altered to conform with the Licensed Dealers Rules on this point, but with a proviso that the Panel may waive this requirement in exceptional cases.

Rule 2

If the offer or an approach with a view to an offer being made is not made by a principal, the identity of the principal must be disclosed at the outset.
(Previous reference at page 40)

The Code distinguishes between (a) an approach with a view to an offer being made; (b) the announcement of an offer; (c) the offer document, addressed to the offeree shareholders. This Rule deals primarily with (a) and (b). Rule 8 says than when an offer is announced the identity of the offeror must be disclosed. Later Rules deal with the contents of offer documents. The Licensed Dealers (Conduct of Business) Rules, 1960 require the identity of 'the purchaser' to be disclosed in the offer document: and the Code requirements give effect to the same intention at an earlier stage.

If sufficient cause is shown, the Panel may allow an approach without full details of the identity of the offeror, provided that this information is forthcoming very soon thereafter. For example, a foreign offeror may be faced with exchange control difficulties in financing the bid. In such circumstances he may wish to be able to make tentative enquiries without revealing his identity. In general, however, the Rule is strictly enforced and concessions are few. If the offeror was a shell company, the Panel would want to see that the real offeror was revealed.

Rule 3

A board so approached is entitled to be satisfied that the offeror is or will be in a position to implement the offer in full.
(Previous reference at page 40)

This relates to an offer which is wholly or partly in cash (compare General Principle 14 and Rule 18). It refers to an approach with a view to a bid. The offeree board is entitled to ask for proof from the offeror that the necessary resources will be available.

Rule 4

The board of the offeree company must obtain competent independent advice on any offer and the substance of such advice must be made known to its

> shareholders. *The Panel would not normally regard as an appropriate person to give such advice a person who has a substantial financial connection with the offeror or offeree company of such a kind as to create a conflict of interest for that person.*

(Previous reference at page 108)

Until 1976 the requirement to obtain competent independent advice applied only to offers made by a parent company for minority shareholdings in a subsidiary and other offers that were not completely at arm's length. The 1976 Code requires advice to be sought in all bids. Practice Note 9 goes further and says that the need to obtain competent independent advice applies not simply to offers but whenever a board is considering an issue of securities which could result in the control of the company being transferred or consolidated.

Before 1976 there was no specific requirement that the advice should be made known to shareholders. A common form of report to shareholders by an offeree board was that the board, which had been advised by AB Ltd., considered that the offer was fair and reasonable. Occasionally, this might conceal the fact that AB Ltd. had made reservations. The 1976 Code met this by providing that the substance of the advice by the competent independent adviser should be communicated to the offeree shareholders.

The adviser need not be a merchant bank. Accountants and stockbrokers sometimes perform the duty. Thus the auditors of the offeree company may act. Occasionally a solicitor or a consultant acts. The adviser would be expected, however, to be familiar with the UK securities market and this would ordinarily rule out overseas advisers. A good deal of consideration has been given to what constitutes independent advice. The Rule indicates that the Panel would not normally regard as appropriate a person who has a substantial connection with the offeror or offeree company of such a kind as to create a conflict of interest for that person. A substantial link with the offeror—as substantial shareholder, professional adviser, auditor or broker—is a disqualification. The risk of a conflict of interest is obvious.

As to links with the offeree, the position is more complicated. Prima facie, it might be thought that a substantial shareholder had no conflict of interest in advising other shareholders. If the shareholding is held by discretionary clients of the adviser and the management of their affairs is isolated from corporate finance work, no difficulty arises in most cases. Conflict of interest can, however, occur if the adviser's shareholding is not of long standing and has been put together for dealing purposes. Or it may be found that he is anxious for the repayment of a loan or wishes to sever his connection with the industry where the offeree operates. Any promise to commit a holding to an offer would of course create immediate doubts. A holding of 20 per cent or more is examined critically, and normally the percentage test is applied to the total shares for which an offer is being made where this is less than the total issued capital.

'Independent' means separate from the offeror or the offeree company. There is from time to time some discussion whether a rigorous test of impartiality should be applied. For example, is an adviser 'independent' in the sense of impartial if he has played a large part in devising an agreed bid. In some cases institutional shareholders will either form a view, independent of the advice given by the offeree board, or may obtain professional advice and sometimes this may be done with some publicity as when various pension funds asked a merchant bank to advise on Allegheny Ludlum's sale of a subsidiary to Wilkinson Match in 1977. This is of course different from the offeree board obtaining separate advice and paying for it.

If the normal adviser of the offeree board is regarded as disqualified on one of the grounds indicated above, the new adviser giving advice to the shareholders should operate on his own. The Panel would not agree that the original adviser should be associated with him.

The Panel's annual report for 1976/7 pointed out that independent advice was of particular importance in cases where the controlling shareholder was making an offer to the outstanding minority holders. In such cases the responsibility borne by the independent adviser is considerable and because of this it is essential that his independence from the parties involved should be beyond question. Another difficult case is where there is more than one class of equity (for example, voting and non-voting shares) and where the offers have to be comparable. The Panel would pay a good deal of attention to the views of the offeree company's adviser in deciding on comparability.

The Panel in its annual report for 1976/7, also considered cases in which it seemed desirable for the board of the *offeror* company to obtain independent advice for its shareholders. The Code does not require the board of an offeror company to seek independent advice on a proposed offer. There have been a few cases in recent years where, because of the unusual circumstances, for instance cross-shareholdings between the offeror and offeree companies and a number of directors common to both companies with shareholdings in each company, it seemed in retrospect that the interests of the offeror company's shareholders would have been better served if independent advice on the offer had been given to them. In these circumstances the offeror company will usually need to hold a general meeting, so that shareholders as a body have an opportunity to consider any advice given and in the light of that advice to authorize or reject the proposed offer. Where the offer is a reverse take-over (a transaction usually taken to mean one in which, if the offeree company were to become a wholly-owned subsidiary of the offeror, the offeror would need to issue more than 100 per cent of its present issued capital), the Panel has recommended that the offeror company should give serious consideration to obtaining independent advice on the offer and making the substance of that advice known to its shareholders.

The Rule gives no indication on what aspects of the bid the advice should be given but there has been little pressure for a more precise formulation of requirements. The advice does not usually enter into detail. If the adviser is not objecting to the offer, it is usually sufficient to say that he regards it as fair and reasonable for the shareholders or, where appropriate, for different classes of shareholders. His advice may take the form of associating himself with the advice of the offeree board.

Rule 5

When any firm intention to make an offer is notified to a board from a serious source (irrespective of whether the board views the offer favourably or otherwise), shareholders must be informed without delay by press notice. A copy of the press notice, or a circular informing shareholders of the offer, should, on the occasion of the first such press notice, normally be sent to shareholders promptly after the announcement.

Where there have been approaches which may or may not lead to an offer, the duty of a board in relation to shareholders is less clearly defined. There are obvious dangers in announcing prematurely an approach which may not lead to an offer. By way of guidance it can be said than an announcement that talks are taking place which may lead to an offer should be made as soon as two companies are reasonably confident of a successful outcome to negotiations.

In any situation which might lead to an offer being made, whether welcome or not, a close watch should be kept on the share market; in the event of any untoward movement in share prices an immediate announcement, accompanied by such comment as may be appropriate, should be made.
(Previous reference at page 40)

This Rule relates to early discussions about a bid. When the terms are settled Rule 8 comes into play. The substance of Rule 5 dates from the Notes and Revised Notes. From the start, it was felt that discussions about a bid should be announced as soon as practicable, in order to prevent the spread of rumours and resultant share movements. The phrase 'on the occasion of the first such press notice' was added in 1972, to make it clear that a special communication to shareholders was contemplated and not simply the offer document in due course. The Issuing Houses Association sent out a circular letter to its members on 5 December 1972, drawing attention to the need to send a copy of a press announcement or of a circular to offeree shareholders promptly after the announcement. If at the time of the announcement the offeror is still waiting for certain information before finally deciding whether to go ahead with the bid, this should be indicated in the announcement, preferably with an indication of what has still to be verified or investigated.

Much of the day-to-day work of the Panel executive, in interpreting the Rule, relates to the need for preliminary announcements, before there is a firm intention to proceed. The parties may be reluctant to reveal the present state of negotiations, although stories are flying about. In such a case the executive would usually be pressing for an early announcement of the state of play. There would sometimes be a discussion about the merits of an immediate statement, as against waiting until an offer in fairly definite terms could be announced. It can be argued that an announcement of negotiations which in the end prove abortive may cause speculative movements in share prices, since a statement that there are indeed negotiations in progress may lead to a further rise in the share price. The Panel believes, however, that, if prices are moving up and negotiations are in progress, the balance of advantage is in letting the shareholders of the offeree company know what is afoot. A rather general statement that talks are in progress, if not followed reasonably soon by the announcement of a bid, brings its own difficulties: but the Panel's view remains that the balance of advantage lies in making a statement at an early stage, if there is any risk of a leak. A very early statement need not give the terms of the offer; indeed these may not have been adequately discussed. A potential offeror may make a preliminary announcement for tactical reasons—to see what would be the reaction of the board of the other company or to see whether the Office of Fair Trading would be interested in relation to a possible reference to the Monopolies and Mergers Commission. In such a case the attitude of the Panel to the need for statements by the offeree board would depend on the circumstances.

Experience shows that the leakage of price-sensitive information is apt to occur when negotiations have reached a stage at which a fairly wide circle of people including, for example, advisers and possibly some shareholders, have to be informed what is afoot. In a statement issued in April 1977 by The Stock Exchange and the Panel, and repeated in Practice Note 9, the Panel indicated that it would expect an announcement to be made

(a) where negotiations have reached a point at which a company is reasonably confident that an offer will be made for its shares, or
(b) where negotiations or discussions are about to be extended to embrace more than a small group of people.

For its part, The Stock Exchange said that, where there were special reasons for a short delay in making an announcement, it was prepared to consider a request for a temporary halt in dealings. If there was a significant price movement and no satisfactory explanation or denial of knowledge was forthcoming from the company, The Stock Exchange would itself consider halting dealings temporarily.

Subject to what is said in connection with Rule 6 the onus lies on the offeree board to make a statement if (as is usually the case) it is the offeree shares that are moving up in price. A potential offeror should not attempt to prevent an offeree company from making an announcement at any time the offeree company considers appropriate.

Rule 6

Joint statements are desirable whenever possible, provided that agreement thereon does not lead to undue delay. The obligation to make announcements lies no less with the potential offeror than with the offeree company.

Rule 5 places an obligation on the offeree board to inform the company's shareholders of a bid or impending bid. Rule 6 places a similar obligation on the offeror. Rule 6 deals with the situation where an offeree may be slow in replying to approaches by the offeror and a situation may be building up where there will be a false market because of rumours. In such circumstances the offeror is under an obligation, having given the offeree board sufficient time to assess the merits of the offer, to announce how matters stand. This was more important before 1972 when an offeror could not buy shares while negotiations were going on: the announcement marked the stage at which the offeror could resume purchases.

Practice Note 9 says:

The Code imposes obligations to make announcements on the offeror as well as the offeree company. There are limitations on the extent to which it is practicable or fair to expect the offeror to assume responsibility for movements in the share price of the offeree company before any approach has been made and possibly before the tactical situation allows him to make any meaningful statement. Nevertheless the Panel would expect a potential offeror to use the utmost care regarding secrecy and the above guidance about widening the circle of people with knowledge would apply with equal force to a potential offeror. The Panel might also expect the offeror to make a statement when the potential offeree company is the subject of rumour and speculation and it is clear beyond reasonable doubt that it is the offeror's actions themselves (whether through inadequate security, purchasing of offeree company shares or otherwise) which have directly contributed to this situation.

Rule 7

The vital importance of absolute secrecy before an announcement must be emphasized.
(Previous references at pages 159 and 163)

This Rule is more like a General Principle than a Rule. As pointed out in Practice Note 9, it should be an invariable routine for advisers at the very beginning of discussions to warn clients of the importance of secrecy and security. Attention should be drawn to the Code, in particular to Rules 7 and 30.

The matter has not been left simply on the basis of emphasizing the need to avoid disclosure by those who know in advance of the bid. An addition to Rule 30, made in 1976, stressed the need not to pass confidential information to any other person, unless it was necessary to do so. The wider the circle, the greater the risk of a leak of information.

In 1970 the Panel ruled that, where a cash alternative is to be provided which involves underwriting, underwriters may be informed of the impending offer immediately before the formal announcement, provided that they are expressly warned of the confidential nature of their advance information.

By 1978 practice had been developed as expressed in Practice Note 9.

Where a proposed offer is agreed and it is intended to provide a cash alternative by way of underwriting, assuming no announcement has been made, the offeree company should request The Stock Exchange to grant a temporary halt in dealings before the impending offer is mentioned to any sub-underwriters. In the case of an offer that is not agreed, and hence a temporary halt is unlikely to be practicable, a restricted number of sub-underwriters may be informed of the offer immediately before its announcement, provided they are expressly warned of the confidential nature of the information.

Quite a wide range of individuals may be consulted before a bid is announced—large shareholders in the offeree company, brokers, jobbers, and others. In view of the risks of disclosure, the Panel and Stock Exchange, in the statement issued on 14 April 1977 indicated the desirability of a public announcement in the circumstances referred to in the note on Rule 5.

An addition made to Rule 30 in 1976 stressed the need for those in possession of confidential information so to conduct themselves as to minimize the chances of an accidental leak of information. Intelligent observers can deduce that a bid may be in the offing, if they see that unusual visits or unusual meetings are taking place.

Rule 8

When an offer is announced, the terms of the offer and the identity of the offeror must be disclosed. The offeror must also disclose any existing holding in the offeree company which it owns or over which it has control or which is owned or controlled by any person acting in concert with it.

All conditions (including normal conditions relating to acceptances, listing and increase of capital) to which an offer or the posting of it is subject must be stated in the formal announcement.

(Previous reference at page 70)

The purpose of the Rule is to ensure that the basic facts are made available as soon as the offer is announced. An important condition may be the need for approval of the offer by the offeror's shareholders. This arises if the effecting of the bid involves an increase in the offeror's authorized share captial or if The Stock Exchange's Yellow Book requires reference to shareholders.

All conditions to which the offer is subject must be stated and Practice Note 9 goes on to say that these should not be framed in a manner that leaves their fulfilment to the subjective judgement of the board of the offeror, since this creates unnecessary uncertainty. An offeror may be fearful that further enquiries will disclose a worse financial position than he envisaged and he may wish to be the judge of that. The Panel would not, however, wish to encourage an offeror to enter into a bid, with market consequences, until he had investigated the position and intended to go through with the bid.

Experience has shown than an insistence on hard objective tests is not always practicable and that some latitude has to be allowed. It is normally acceptable for an offer to be expressed as being conditional on statements or estimates being appropriately verified. The offeror may state that a decision not to refer the offer to the Monopolies and Mergers Commission is to be on terms satisfactory to the offeror. More generally, in special circumstances it may not be practicable to specify all the factors on which the satisfaction of a particular condition may depend. This applies especially to official authorizations, the granting of which may be subject to additional material obligations to be fulfilled by the offeror.

Companies and their advisers are expected to consult the Panel before issuing any announcement containing conditions that are not entirely objective.

In the case of a mandatory bid the only condition allowed in an offer document under Rule 34(2) is the lapsing of the offer under Rule 9 on a reference to the Monopolies and Mergers Commission. All other conditions have to be implemented beforehand.

Rule 9

Where an offer comes within the statutory provisions for possible reference to the Monopolies and Mergers Commission, it should be a term of the offer that it shall lapse if there is a reference before the first closing date or the date when the offer becomes or is declared unconditional as to acceptances, whichever is the later.

Except in the case of an offer under Rule 34, the offeror may, in addition, make the offer conditional on a statement being issued that there will not be a reference.

Where the law requires any proposed offer to be given prior clearance before it may be implemented by, for example, the European Commission under the Treaty of Paris, the offer document should not be despatched until such necessary clearance has been obtained.

(Previous references at pages 140 and 141)

If a proposed take-over or merger is referred to the Monopolies and Mergers Commission, the Secretary of State indicates the period, not exceeding six months (but with power to extend, on cause being shown), within which the Commission must report. Thereafter the report is considered by the Department of Prices and Consumer Protection and the Office of Fair Trading—a stage that may take weeks or months—and an announcement of the Government's decision is then made. When the offeror hears of the reference, he may decide that he wants to abandon the bid. If the Government decide that the bid can proceed and the offeror still wishes to go ahead several months are likely to elapse before the bid can be mounted again. Economic conditions may change, share prices may change and any underwriting arrangements will have to be renegotiated. It was decided in 1974 that the simplest course was for an offer (other than a mandatory offer) to be abandoned if there was a reference to the Monopolies and Mergers Commission and that an offer that could be the subject of a reference should contain a condition to this effect.

The Rule also provides that the offeror may make it a condition of an offer (other than a mandatory offer) that an official statement has been issued that there will be no reference. The Department of Prices and Consumer Protection is under no statutory obligation to issue a statement of this kind and the decision whether to make a reference may, for a variety of reasons, be seriously delayed. In practice, however, the Department does endeavour to indicate at a fairly early stage in the offer period whether a reference is to be made. No serious difficulty is being encountered in connection with a condition of this kind in offer documents. The offeror may state that the decision not to refer must be on terms satisfactory to him. If there is a possibility that a bid may be referred to the Monopolies and Mergers Commission and no indication of the Department's intentions has been received, the offeror should not quickly declare the bid unconditional even if he is assured by acceptances of over 50 per cent of the voting rights. He should wait till the Department shows its hand or at least till the twenty-first day after the posting of the offer.

The need to get an EEC clearance arises in the case of coal and steel undertakings falling under the authority of the Commission in Brussels. The need to get a clearance before the offer document is issued may involve considerable delay. The British Steel Corporation's announcement of an offer for Lye Trading Company Limited was issued on 3 May 1974. The offer document went out on 16 October 1974. This part of the Rule applies to mandatory bids as well as to other bids. It has sometimes been found to be best to deal with these EEC cases by extending the period of twenty-eight days under Rule 10 between the announcement of the offer and the issue of the offer document.

In the United States the Hart-Scott-Rodino Act 1976, which came into force in September 1978, requires proposed take-overs and mergers affecting companies of $10,000,000 or more assets or $100 mn or more annual net sales and substantial business in the USA to be reported to the Federal Trade Commission and the Anti-Trust Division of the Justice Department. If the anti-trust authorities have not taken action within thirty days (fifteen days in the case of an offer in cash) the offer can go ahead. In such a case the Panel will allow an offeror to exceed the twenty-eight days between the announcement of an offer and the issue of the offer document. Anyone who might trigger a Rule 34 obligation would be expected to clear the position with the US anti-trust authorities before doing so.

RULES

Rule 10

The offer document should normally be posted within 28 days of the announcement of the terms of the offer and at the same time, or as soon as practicable thereafter, the board of the offeree company should circulate its views on the offer, including any alternative forms of consideration offered. The Panel should be consulted if the offer document is not to be posted within this period.

Where there has been an announcement of an offer (as opposed to an announcement that talks are taking place which may lead to an offer) the offer cannot be withdrawn without the consent of the Panel.

(Previous references at pages 55, 60, 87, 89 and 97)

ISSUE OF OFFER DOCUMENTS

In its earlier versions, the Code required the offer document and the views of the offeree board to be circulated 'as soon as practicable' after the announcement of the offer. The practice of the Panel executive to expect the offer document to be circulated within twenty-eight days was recognized in the 1976 Code.

VIEWS OF OFFEREE BOARD

As to the circulation of the views of the offeree board, Practice Note 9 says:

Rules 8 and 10: (1) The language used in documents and press statements should clearly and concisely reflect the position being described. The word 'agreement' should be used with the greatest care and, in particular, statements should be avoided which may give the impression that directors have committed themselves to certain courses of action (e.g. accepting in respect of their own shares) when they have not in fact done so.

(2) If offeree directors advise their shareholders that they intend to accept an offer but there are qualifications to that intention then words such as 'present intention' should be used.

Where an offeree board is unable to agree on its views on an offer, the majority are not obliged to publish the views of the minority. The minority directors are, however, expected to make a public statement about their views on the offer for the information of the shareholders.

WITHDRAWALS OF OFFERS

The Rule deals with withdrawals of offers after the announcement of an offer but before the dispatch of the offer document.

From the early days, it was recognized that irresponsible bids should not be encouraged by allowing easy withdrawal. Since the offeror could deal in the market, there were dangers in allowing announcements followed by withdrawals. Circumstances in which the Panel may allow the offeror to withdraw an announced offer include:

(a) if a competitor has already posted a higher offer;
(b) if both offeror and offeree boards decide that they do not wish an agreed bid to proceed;
(c) if the offeror makes his bid conditional on recommendation by the offeree board and the offeree board opposes the bid;
(d) in a contested bid, if the offeror board wishes to withdraw and the offeree board does not object.

If an offeror wishes to withdraw but the offeree wishes him to proceed, the Panel is unlikely to agree to withdrawal, except in most unusual circumstances. Such cases include those in which the financial position of the offeror or offeree turns out to be radically different from what it was understood to be when the offer was announced and where it has not been a condition of the offer that the relevant statements or estimates should be appropriately verified. It may appear that the offeror is not now able to finance the offer, notwithstanding the provisions that the Code contains to guard against this contingency. The Panel in such a situation must consider what is practicable and to what extent the offeror is culpable for failing to foresee the course of events.

In any situation where withdrawal is allowed by the Panel but they feel that one of the parties (usually the offeror) has acted irresponsibly or without due and proper consideration in making his announcement, the Panel will consider whether the conduct of that party or of his adviser merits censure. The Panel has made it clear that a change in general economic, industrial, or political circumstances would not normally justify the withdrawal of an announced offer. To justify unilateral withdrawal some circumstance of an exceptional nature would normally be required.

Rule 11

Where directors (and their close relatives and related trusts) sell shares to a purchaser, as a result of which the purchaser is required to make an offer under Rule 34, the directors must ensure that as a condition of the sale the purchaser undertakes to fulfil his obligations under Rule 34. In addition, except with the consent of the Panel, such directors should not resign from the board until the first closing date of the offer or the date when the offer becomes or is declared unconditional as to acceptances, whichever is the later.

(Previous references at pages 55, 68, 79 and 96)

The requirement that directors, who have effective control of a company by reason of the size of their shareholdings, should not sell unless the purchaser agrees to make a comparable offer to the remaining shareholders goes back to the first version of the Code. It is an obvious application of the principle that all shareholders must be treated alike, and that shareholders having effective control should not be allowed to hog the premium on the share price which control gives. Since 1972 this requirement has been overtaken by the obligation which Rule 34 places directly on a purchaser who comes to have effective control (interpreted as 30 per cent) to extend an offer to the remaining shareholders: but the obligation on the directors who sell shares which give effective control has been left as an additional safeguard. In respect of other classes of equity shares, the selling directors must obtain from the purchaser a commitment to make a comparable offer but the exact terms can be left for later determination.

The second part of the Rule arose out of cases, notably Ashbourne, where the purchasers of a controlling interest secured control of the board before they had fulfilled the obligation to make a bid for the remaining shares. The existing directors may have to retain any qualifying shares for a period. To meet exceptional cases, there is a provision that the Panel may consent to resignation by a director. The obligation placed on the offeror under a mandatory bid about representation on the offeree board is contained in Rule 34(6).

Rule 12

Any information, including particulars of shareholders, given to a preferred suitor, should on request be furnished equally and as promptly to a less welcome but bona fide potential offeror.

This Rule does not mean that a less welcome suitor is entitled to ask to be given all the information supplied to the favoured suitor. He should specify the questions to which he requires answers. It is in answering these questions that the offeree board must observe the Rule. If one bidder already has information about the offeree company which he has obtained in the course of business, e.g. through representation on the offeree board, a second suitor is not necessarily entitled to that information. It has not been 'given' to the first party. It is for the offeree board to judge whether an offer is bona fide before giving information. If the first offeror owns over 50 per cent of the shares and a rival offeror comes along, it can be argued that the rival has no right to ask for information.

There are cases where the offeree board may legitimately say that information can be safely provided to one suitor but could not be provided to another because it would be commercially damaging to provide it. For the Rule to apply, there must be two in the field, one of which is preferred. If a potential offeror has been given certain information and has decided not to make an offer, the Rule does not apply when a secured potential offeror appears.

Rule 13

There must be included in every offer document:
(1) a statement as to whether or not any agreement, arrangement or understanding exists between the offeror or any person acting in concert with it and any of the directors, or recent directors, shareholders or recent shareholders of the offeree company having any connection with or dependence upon the offer, and full particulars of any such agreement, arrangement or understanding; and
(2) a statement as to whether or not any securities acquired in pursuance of the offer will be transferred to any other person, together with the names of the parties to any such agreement, arrangement or understanding and particulars of all securities in the offeree company held by such persons, or a statement that no such securities are held.

When the regulation of shut-outs was abandoned in 1976 this rule was introduced (from the Yellow Book) as a safeguard against any side deals between offerors and offeree directors that might not be covered by Rule 36. Problems arise in regard to the need to publish the conditions attached to irrevocable commitments, the arrangements between joint offerors for the financing of the bid and other matters. The Panel's bias is in favour of publication.

Rule 14

Any document or advertisement addressed to shareholders in connection with an offer must be treated with the same standards of care with regard to the statements made therein as if it were a prospectus within the meaning of the Companies Act, 1948. This applies whether the document or advertisement is issued by the company direct or by an adviser on its behalf. Each document or advertisement addressed to shareholders of the offeree company must state that the directors of the offeror and/or, where appropriate, the offeree company (including any who may have delegated detailed supervision of the document or advertisement) have taken all reasonable care to ensure that the facts stated and opinions expressed therein are fair and accurate and, where appropriate, no material facts have been omitted and also state that they jointly and severally accept responsibility accordingly. If it is proposed that any director should be excluded from such a statement, the Panel's consent is required. Such consent is only given in exceptional circumstances and in such cases the omission and the reasons for it must be stated in the document or advertisement.

A copy of the authority on behalf of the board of the company for the issue of such document or advertisement must be lodged with the Panel.

While this Rule requires a high standard of accuracy in all documents connected with a take-over bid, the need for directors to make a statement accepting responsibility applies principally to documents addressed to offeree shareholders by the offeror or offeree board.

In Practice Note 9 the Panel said:

Rules 14 and 16. Since the quotation in circulars or press advertisements of press comments relating to an offer will necessarily carry the implication that the comments are endorsed by the board, such press comments should not be quoted unless the board is prepared, where appropriate, to corroborate or substantiate them and the directors' responsibility statement is included.

The reference to 'press comments' is illustrative of the case that is most likely to arise. If a broker's circular was quoted, the board would similarly have to accept responsibility for the truth of the statements quoted.

Practice Note 9 contains the following further commentary on Rule 14:

Rule 14(1) Press releases, paid newspaper advertisements and documents sent to shareholders must identify clearly and prominently at their start from whom they originate. Shareholders should not be left in any doubt as to their source. Paid newspaper advertisements should also include the directors' responsibility statement unless the information published is all contained in a circular to shareholders which includes such a statement.

(2) The statement that no material facts have been omitted is considered to extend to any material changes in any information previously published by or on behalf of the relevant company during the offer period (including in particular details of shareholdings under Rule 17 and service contracts under Rule 19).

(3) Acceptance forms, withdrawal forms, proxy cards or any other forms connected with a take-over or merger should not be published in newspapers.

The Panel applies strictly the rule that all directors must accept responsibility. Only in highly exceptional circumstances is the Panel prepared to waive the requirement for an individual director. Absence or, prolonged tours overseas and the difficulty of getting in touch are not accepted as excuses unless it can be shown that contact is impossible.

The statement that directors are responsible 'jointly and severally' is intended to show that the board as a whole accepts responsibility and each director individually. What is not clear is whether it makes a director responsible for the negligent acts of his co-directors. The Yellow Book (page 186) has a somewhat different form of responsibility statement for prospectuses: in take-over bids the Rule 14 form should be followed.

It may sometimes be inappropriate for a director who has sold a large stake in advance to the offeror, or who is associated with the offeror, to play any part in advising shareholders on the merits of the bid. It is, however, his duty to accept responsibility for the facts contained in the document, particularly relating to his own shareholding. If a director is in disagreement with his colleagues, the Panel would not require the director to subscribe to the board's responsibility statement, so long as he published his views on the offer either in the offer document (subject to his colleagues agreeing to this) or in a circular to shareholders or in a press statement.

Where the offeror is a foreign company with a two-tier board structure, acceptance of responsibility by the members of the management board, as distinct from the supervisory board, has been accepted in some cases.

Rule 15

Shareholders must be put in possession of all the facts necessary for the formation of an informed judgement as to the merits or demerits of an offer. Such facts must be accurately and fairly presented and be available to the shareholder early enough to enable him to make a decision in good time. The obligation of the offeror in these respects towards the shareholders of the offeree company is no less than the offeror's obligation towards its own shareholders. In particular, whether or not the consideration in an offer is cash, information should be given about the offeror (including the names of its directors).

The offeror will normally be expected to cover the following points in the offer document and the board of the offeree company should, insofar as relevant, comment upon such statements in a letter to its shareholders:

(1) its intentions regarding the continuation of the business of the offeree company;
(2) its intentions regarding any major changes to be introduced in the businesss, including any re-deployment of the fixed assets of the offeree company;
(3) the long-term commercial justification for the proposed offer; and
(4) its intentions with regard to the continued employment of the employees of the offeree company.

(Previous references at pages 44, 97 and 113)

Rule 15 begins with requiring disclosure of all the facts necessary for an informed judgement on the merits or demerits of an offer. *Inter alia*, this encourages a company to provide profits forecasts, as they will help shareholders to reach an informed judgement, though the Code does not require a company to forecast profits.

In June 1977 the Panel criticized directors of an offeree company who, in an agreed bid, had failed to indicate the extent to which cash shown in the last balance sheet had since been invested in securities.

INFORMATION

The information that an offer document should contain is to be found in a number of places. These requirements are set out in Appendix B.

FUTURE INTENTIONS

In recent years, both The Stock Exchange and the City Working Party have been concerned to secure more precise statements about future intentions. Thus the offer document must state clearly the intentions of the offeror regarding the future business of the offeree company. If it is the intention to carry on the business in its present form then a statement to this effect would be sufficient, but details of any proposed major re-organization would have to be set out. In particular, any proposal for disposing of part of the business would not only have to be disclosed, but where conditional contracts had been entered into, detailed financial information showing the effects of such disposals would be required.

Similarly, in regard to employees, it was considered not to be sufficient to say vaguely that their rights would be safeguarded. The Panel in its Annual Report for 1972/3, said:

... Rule 15 in requiring that shareholders must be put in possession of all the facts necessary for the formation of an informed judgment as to the merits or demerits of an offer, provides in particular that an offeror must state its intentions in regard to the future of the offeree. The Panel is concerned that this provision of Rule 15 is not adequately observed by some offerors. Not only is it essential that offerors fulfil their obligations in this respect but it is the duty of the directors of offeree companies, in the case of agreed take-overs or mergers, to insist that they do so. The intentions of the offeror as to the future conduct of the offeree's business, and the likely effect of any such intentions on the future livelihood of the offeree company's employees, may be a significant factor for shareholders in deciding whether or not to accept an offer. The Panel regards this requirement of Rule 15 as a most important provision of the Code and, in this connection, it welcomes the requirements in the latest edition of 'Admission of Securities to Listing', published by The Stock Exchange, for more detailed information in offer documents with regard to the intentions of the offeror as to the future of the offeree's business and the continued employment of its employees.

The Panel regards the requirement that the offeror should indicate its intentions about the continued employment of the employees of the offeree company as including subsidiary companies, where in many cases most of the workers are to be found. Since 1976 the offeree company has been expected to comment on the offeror's statement of intentions.

Rule 16

Without in any way detracting from the necessity of maintaining the highest standards of accuracy and fair presentation in all communications to shareholders in a take-over or merger transaction, attention is particularly drawn in this connection to profit forecasts and asset valuations.

(1) Notwithstanding the obvious hazard attached to the forecasting of profits, any profit forecasts must be compiled with the greatest possible care by the directors whose sole responsibility they are.

When profit forecasts appear in any document addressed to shareholders in connection with an offer, the assumptions, including the commercial assumptions, upon which the directors have based their profit forecasts, must be stated in the document.

The accounting bases and calculations for the forecasts must be examined and reported on by the auditors or consultant accountants. Any financial adviser mentioned in the document must also report on the forecasts. The accountants' report and, if there is an adviser, his report, must be contained in such document and be accompanied by a statement that the accountants and, where relevant, the adviser have given and not withdrawn their consent to publication.

Wherever profit forecasts appear in relation to a period in which trading has already commenced, the latest unaudited profit figures which are available in respect of the expired portion of that trading period together with comparable figures for the preceding year must be stated. Alternatively, if no figures are available, that fact must be stated.

(2) When valuations of assets are given in connection with an offer the board should be supported by the opinion of a named independent valuer and the basis of valuation clearly stated. The document should also state that the valuer has given and not withdrawn his consent to the publication of his name therein.

(Previous references at pages 39, 55 and 113)

NO REQUIREMENT TO MAKE PROFIT FORECAST

Any estimate of profits after those set out in the last audited annual accounts or a published interim statement is a profit forecast. It can, therefore, relate to a period that is now past or largely past or to some period in the future. Nothing in the Code requires an offeror or offeree company to make a profit forecast. However, as the Panel pointed out in its Annual Report for 1969/70 and again in the report for 1977/78, there are occasions when directors would be withholding essential information from their shareholders if they were to abstain from giving a forecast of the results likely to be announced in the near future, especially where this relates to a period which may lie largely in the past. On the other hand, there are industrial and commercial activities in which the future is, by the nature of things, so uncertain as to render prognostication unwise. As indicated below, a company may have to confirm or deny a profit forecast made shortly before the bid was announced, since it will be in the minds of shareholders and may be used by Press commentators. Directors who have made a forecast cannot subsequently repudiate it.

The Rule emphasizes that the responsibility for profit forecasts rests solely with the directors. The responsibility of accountants does not go beyond a critical and objective examination of the accounting bases and calculations for a profit forecast and verification that the forecast has been properly computed from the underlying assumptions and data (economic, commercial, marketing, and financial) and is presented on a consistent basis. Profit forecasts depend on subjective judgements and are subject to inherent uncertainties: and the directors must take a view on these matters.

NEED FOR CARE IN PREPARATION

From the start, the authors of the Code attached importance to care in the compilation of profit forecasts in an endeavour to ensure that shareholders were not given misleading information. The Panel believes that directors' opinions on the immediate future profitability of a company are the most important single element in the formation of the decision whether to invest in the company or to disinvest. If forecasts were forbidden, uncorroborated statements for which no-one would be answerable might pass by word of mouth to selected shareholders. The Panel is anxious that profit forecasts should be prepared with care and a due sense of responsibility.

WHAT IS A PROFIT FORECAST?

Although a great deal has been written about profit forecasts, they are normally short and simple. An offeree company wishing to stave off an unwelcome bid, or an offeror who is offering a share exchange, will report that the profits before taxation for the present financial year, based on management accounts for what has passed and management estimates for the future, will be approximately £x million. Then the assumptions on which the forecast is based are set out, usually in fairly general terms. Paragraph 7 of Practice Note 3 refers to various other matters that might usefully be included in a forecast of profits, such as a forecast of turnover; but this is not always practicable.

Paragraph 6 of Practice Note 3 says:

It should be appreciated that even when no particular figure is mentioned certain forms of words may constitute a profit forecast. Examples are 'profits will be somewhat higher than last year' and 'the profits of the second half-year are expected to be similar to those earned in the first half-year' (when interim figures have already been published). It is impossible to generalise but broadly whenever a form of words puts a floor under (or, in certain circumstances, a ceiling on) the likely profits of a particular period or whenever a form of words contains the data necessary to ascertain an approximate figure for future profits by an arithmetical process, the Panel takes the view that there is a profit forecast which, except to the extent that in exceptional circumstances specific dispensation has first been obtained, must be reported on in accordance with this Rule. In cases of doubt professional advisers are strongly urged to consult the Panel in advance.

The following are examples of statements that are not normally regarded as profit forecasts:

1. Dividend forecasts, unless they are accompanied by an estimate as to dividend cover.
2. Statements in general terms of the benefits likely to arise out of a reorganization following a merger.
3. An outline of steps that are being taken to recover turnover.

The Rule applies to profit forecasts made after an offer has been declared unconditional, if there remain some shares which might be the subject of action by the offeror under Section 209 of the Companies Act, 1948.

PROFIT FORECASTS OUTSIDE THE OFFER PERIOD

Practice Note 3 says (paragraph 2):

The fact that a forecast has already been made outside a take-over or merger situation (e.g., in an interim statement or annual report) does not in any way reduce the requirement for it to be reported on if it is repeated in a document issued in such a context. If such a forecast is in existence it may well be of material importance to repeat it in the document (having it examined and reported on in accordance with this Rule), since, even if it is not referred to in the document, it is likely to be mentioned by financial commentators and thus made an important factor in shareholders' decisions.

The Panel would expect a forecast already made before the bid to be confirmed, amended or withdrawn in the offer document (with reports, as necessary, by the auditor, consultant accountant and financial adviser), if the forecast had been made fairly recently (say within three months) or was very significant. Where it was debatable whether the statement amounted to a forecast, factors that would weigh in deciding whether it should be reported upon would be if it had been a significant factor in the negotiation of the terms of the offer or if the bid was a contested one.

Practice Note 3 also says (paragraphs 3 and 5):

> An estimate of profits for a period which has already expired should be treated as a profit forecast within this Rule unless the figures for the whole of the relevant period are up to publication standard, i.e., they have received the same degree of examination and carry the same degree of authority as normally apply to published but unaudited interim or preliminary final results of the company in question. Any profit figures which have not been prepared to such a standard must be examined and reported on in the manner described in this Rule. Where figures of publication standard are incorporated in a forecast for a longer period the report should, of course, cover the whole period.

If a forecast, duly reported on, is included in a document, except with the consent of the Panel, any document subsequently sent out by that company in connection with that offer must contain a statement by the directors that the forecast remains valid for the purpose of the offer, and that the financial advisers and accountants who reported on the forecast have consented to the extended use of their reports.

ASSUMPTIONS

The Panel has devoted a long Practice Note (4) to the need to indicate clearly the assumptions on which profit forecast is based. Paragraph 10 of Practice Note 3 suggests that where a profits forecast is given in a press announcement the assumptions on which the forecast is based should be given.

REPORTING

The Rule requires the accounting bases and calculations of any profit forecast to be examined and reported upon by the auditors or consultant accountants. Any financial adviser mentioned in the document must also report on the forecast. The only exception is that where the consideration is cash an offeror's forecast does not require corroboration. The Panel enforces the reporting requirement strictly against constant pressure to relax it on a variety of grounds, including expense and loss of time.

It is sometimes argued that it is difficult to get accountants to report in time for the offer document, but in practice this has not proved to be a real problem. The Panel would be reluctant to be influenced by this kind of argument.

The Rule requires the auditor or consultant accountant to report on the accounting bases and calculations for the forecast. Although the accountant has no responsibility for the assumptions on which the forecast is based, the Panel in paragraph 5 of Practice Note 4 indicates that the accountant or financial adviser should comment in their reports on any assumption which appears to them to be unrealistic or on the omission of any assumption which appears to them to be important. Where income from property is a material element in a forecast that part of the forecast should normally be examined and reported on by a valuer.

ASSET VALUATIONS

The second part of the Rule applies to property but it also covers other assets such as ships. The most obvious application of the Rule is where an offeree board produces a valuation of the company's property in order to argue that the bid price is too low. Very exceptionally the offeror board may produce an asset valuation of the offeree's property, and in such a case it should be clearly indicated whether the offeree has co-operated in its preparation, e.g. by giving access to the property being valued. There may be exceptional cases where it is more in accord with the facts to value property on a going-concern basis, rather than at open market value which assumes disposal. Valuers often include in a valuation a clause to the effect that only the client may refer to the valuation. This clause should not be included in valuations to be used in bid documents, since the other side may legitimately want to comment on it. The Panel has given detailed guidance on asset valuations in paragraph 5 of Practice Note 5, relating to property companies. This does not apply to companies whose trading activity is to build houses and sell them off. They can value their properties at open market value in the state existing at the date of valuation. Paragraph 8 applies to office block developments where there are rent reviews and other complications. It does not apply to companies where land is their stock in trade.

Where a valuation of assets is given in any document addressed to shareholders the valuation certificate should be made available for inspection together with an associated report or schedule containing details of the aggregate valuation. Where the Panel is satisfied that such disclosure may be commercially disadvantageous to the company concerned, it will allow the report or schedule to appear in a summarized form. In certain cases the Panel may require any of these documents to be reproduced in full in a document sent to shareholders (Practice Note 5, paragraph 9). The report should give full details in respect of each property or (if this is too onerous or commercially harmful) at least a schedule identifying the properties and giving individual valuations.

DOCUMENTATION

It is not necessary for copies of accountants', valuers', and other financial advisers' letters reporting on forecasts to be lodged with the Panel.

Rule 17

(1) The offer document must state:

  (a) the shareholdings of the offeror in the offeree company;
  (b) the shareholderings in the offeror (in the case of a share exchange offer only) and in the offeree company in which directors of the offeror are interested;
  (c) the shareholdings in the offeror (in the case of a share exchange offer only) and in the offeree company which any person acting in concert with the offeror owns or controls (with the names of such persons acting in concert);
  (d) the shareholdings in the offeror (in the case of a share exchange offer only) and in the offeree company owned or controlled by any persons who, prior to the posting of the offer document, have irrevocably committed themselves to accept the offer together with the names of such persons.

(2) The document of the offeree company advising its shareholders on an offer (whether recommending acceptance or rejection of the offer) must state:

  (a) the shareholdings of the offeree company in the offeror;
  (b) the shareholdings in the offeree company and in the offeror in which directors of the offeree company are interested;
  (c) whether the directors of the offeree company intend, in respect of their own beneficial shareholdings, to accept or reject the offer.

(3) If in any of the above categories there are no shareholdings then this fact should be stated.

(4) If any party referred to above has dealt for value in the shares in question during the period commencing 12 months prior to the beginning of the offer period and ending with the latest practicable date prior to the posting of the offer document, the details, including dates and prices, must be stated. If no such deals have been made this fact should be stated.

References in this Rule to shareholdings include, where appropriate, holdings of securities convertible into equity share capital and any rights to subscribe for such capital.

(Previous reference at page 70)

The substance of this Rule goes back to the first edition of the Code in 1968. It has, however, been tightened up in successive editions. In 1969, if no purchases of shares had been made within six months (now twelve months) before the date of the offer document, a definite statement to this effect had to be made. In 1970 shareholdings in the offeree company by anyone acting in concert with the offeror had to be disclosed. In 1971 purchases had to be disclosed up to twelve months instead of six months before the announcement of the offer and up to the issue of the offer document. The reference to 'directors' is interpreted to include their spouses and children under the age of 18, as in section 30 of the Companies Act 1967 and as interpreted by The Stock Exchange for the purpose of the disclosure of shareholdings in a prospectus. Under the definition of 'directors' at the beginning of the Code persons, in accordance with whose instructions the directors (or a director) of a company are accustomed to act, would be deemed to be directors—this again follows the Companies Act. The Rule refers to shares. It is however regarded as requiring disclosure of the taking or granting of an option (including the purchase or sale of a traded option) by anyone whose shareholdings and dealings have to be disclosed. The Rule refers to shares in which directors are 'interested'. The word is also used in the Companies Act 1967; and section 28 of the Act, which is rather long for quotation here, gives some assistance in its interpretation. The authors of the Code have so far resisted any effort to define the term more closely. If there has been a recent rights issue and a director sold his rights, this is a transaction for value and falls to be disclosed.

The Panel applies the Rule strictly, which is in keeping with the way in which it has been extended in scope over the years. A director must reveal dealings for twelve months, even if he was not a director for that period. When, as part of the transaction leading to an offer being made, some or all of the directors of the offeree company resign, the terms of the Rule apply to them and their shareholdings. Dealings should be disclosed in the offer document in the usual way (Practice Note 9).

There are, however, circumstances in which the Rule cannot be applied inflexibly. The inclusion in relation to the offeror of persons acting in concert presumptively brings within the Rule the directors of a parent company, subsidiaries, fellow subsidiaries, and associated companies. In large groups this can affect many hundreds of individuals and the Panel is prepared, on application, to consider whether any useful purpose is served by bringing them all within the Rule. If good reason is shown, the Panel may be prepared to see the holdings of a director and those of his wife and family trusts aggregated together and not shown separately.

Similarly, on occasion there may be very large numbers of share transactions and the Panel is prepared to consider whether some of these transactions can be grouped together provided that no significant deals are thereby concealed. The Panel would normally require dealings during the period beginning three months before the announcement of the offer to be set out individually. Purchases and sales should not be netted and the highest and lowest prices paid should be stated. A full list of all dealings should be sent to the Panel and should be made available for inspection. (Practice Note 9).

The Rule does not require the director of an offeree company to say more than whether he intends to accept or reject the offer. If there are alternative considerations he is not obliged to say which he is accepting.

Rule 18

Where the offer is for cash or includes an element of cash, the offer document must include confirmation by the financial adviser or by another appropriate independent party that resources are available to the offeror sufficient to satisfy full acceptance of the offer.

(Previous reference at page 40)

The substance of this Rule has remained unchanged since 1968 and its interpretation has presented relatively few problems. The Rule relates to the offer document and is concerned with the consideration, not with any incidental obligation that may arise out of the way in which the operation is being conducted. The financial adviser should satisfy himself that his client has negotiated formal facilities to cover the offer, such facilities being clearly available to the offeror subject to their terms which may include conditions of a normal banking nature. Alternatively, the adviser may satisfy himself that the offeror has free cash resources to cover the offer.

Where anyone has, by the acquisition of shares, incurred an obligation under Rule 34 to make a bid for the remaining shares, Rule 34(5) requires that the announcement of the offer should also include confirmation that the necessary resources are available to implement the bid. As regards bids that do not fall under Rule 34, the only provisions in respect of the period before the issue of the offer document are that:

(a) General Principle 14 places a general obligation on an offeror and his financial adviser to have every reason to believe, before announcing an offer, that he can implement it.
(b) Rule 3 entitles the offeree board, when approached about an

offer, to require to be satisfied that the offeror is or will be in a position to implement the offer in full.

The 'financial adviser' will normally be a merchant bank. If the offeror is himself a clearing bank or a bank of similar standing, a separate confirmation of the availability of funds is not required. The reference is to 'financial adviser or another appropriate independent party', and the Panel has accepted licensed dealers and stockbrokers. A small dealer offering to confirm for a large company would not normally be accepted.

Occasionally, the provision of cash is subject to the fulfilment of certain conditions. For example, the funds may be provided under a US loan agreement subject to various standard US conditions. In exceptional circumstances, with the consent of the Panel, a conditional form of confirmation may be allowed (Practice Note 9). Practice Note 9 points out that the party confirming that resources are available will not be expected to produce the cash if the offeror fails to do so, provided that, in giving confirmation, it acted responsibly and took all reasonable steps to assure itself that the cash was available. The Rule does not apply beyond the offeror's obligations. For example, the Rule does not apply to a merchant bank or stockbroker who 'underwrites' the paper offer—i.e. undertakes to purchase for cash shares acquired by an offeree shareholder under a share exchange scheme.

Rule 19

Documents sent to shareholders of the offeree company recommending acceptance or rejection of offers must contain particulars of all service contracts of any director or proposed director with the offeree company or any of its subsidiaries (unless expiring or determinable by the employing company without payment or compensation, other than statutory compensation, within 12 months): if there are none, this fact should be stated. If such contracts have been entered into or have been amended within 6 months of the date of the document, the particulars of the contracts amended or replaced should be given; if there have been no new contracts or amendments, this should be stated.

Offer documents on behalf of the offeror should state, except in the case of a cash offer, whether its directors' emoluments will be affected by the acquisition of the offeree company.

The substance of the Rule goes back to the first issue of the Code in 1968 and indeed to the Notes of 1959. The Rule has, however, been elaborated over the years, in the light of experience. The subject is of great interest to directors and to shareholders. This interest is reflected in the detailed guidance which the Panel has felt it to be necessary to give in Practice Note 6 which should be consulted.

Rule 20

In order to facilitate the work of the Panel, copies of all public announcements made and all documents bearing on a take-over or merger transaction must be lodged with the Panel at the same time as they are made or despatched.
(Previous references at pages 41 and 126)

Practice Note 9 says:

Copies of paid advertisements (with a list of the newspapers in which they are published) and of any material released to the press by parties to a take-over or merger should be lodged with the Panel at the time of publication.

Rule 21

No offer, which, if accepted in full, would result in the offeror having voting control of the offeree company, shall be made unless it is a condition of such offer that the offer will not become or be declared unconditional as to acceptances unless the offeror has acquired or agreed to acquire (either pursuant to the offer or by shares acquired or agreed to be acquired before or during the offer) by the close of the offer shares carrying over 50% of the votes attributable to the equity share capital.

No offer for equity share capital may be declared unconditional as to acceptances unless, in addition to complying with the foregoing, the offeror has aquired the right to exercise over 50% of the voting rights of the offeree company. Classes of non-equity capital need not be the subject of an offer.

Where a company has more that one class of equity share capital, a comparable offer must be made for each class; the Panel should be consulted in advance if more than one class carries votes. An offer for non-voting equity capital should not be made conditional on any particular level of acceptances in respect of that class unless the offer for the voting capital is also conditional on the success of the offer for the non-voting equity capital.

This Rule does not apply to offers required to be made under Rule 34 which are subject to the special provisions set out therein.
(Previous references at pages 39 and 178)

Where an offeror has made a bid which, if accepted in full, would give him statutory control of the offeree company, he cannot make his offer unconditional (i.e., acquire shares under the offer) unless he has acceptances in respect of—

    (a) over 50 per cent of the votes attributable to the equity share capital and
    (b) over 50 per cent of the voting rights of the offeree company.

Shares other than equity share capital may have votes, such as preference shares or convertible preference shares, but the offeror must secure half of the voting equity as well as voting control. If the offeror is not able to meet these requirements, he has probably not offered an adequate premium for control. Shareholders are also entitled to know in a clear-cut way whether or not statutory control is passing to the offeror. The Panel is not prepared to waive the 50 per cent requirements.

Many of the problems that arise in the administration of Rule 21 turn on the interpretation of the terms used.

Equity share capital: as in the Companies Acts (for example, in section 154 of the Companies Act 1948) this means issued share capital but excluding any part of the issued share capital which, neither as respects dividends nor as respects capital, carries any right to participate beyond a specified amount in a distribution.

It follows that a preference share is not equity capital if the amount of the dividend that may be paid in any year is fixed and if the holder cannot receive more by way of capital repayment than the nominal value of the share. The fact that preference shares may have voting rights in a shareholders' meeting does not make them equity share capital (though shares with exercisable voting rights would have to be counted in deciding what percentage of voting rights an offer had obtained).

Then convertible loan stock has to be considered. Where there are conversion or subscription rights capable of being exercised during an offer period, the 50 per cent conditions relate to 50 per cent of the potential equity share capital and voting rights respectively, e.g., existing voting shares and any voting shares which would be issued on exercise of all such conversion or subscription rights. In any case where the right of conversion or subscription ends during an offer period, thereafter the offeror may not declare his offer unconditional as to acceptances until he has more than 50 per cent of the then existing equity and voting rights taking into account shares actually issued on exercise of such conversion or subscription rights. If the conversion terms are manifestly unattractive in current conditions the Panel may waive the need to include the convertibles.

Non-equity capital: preference shares restricted as above.

Classes of equity capital: a common distinction is between classes carrying different voting rights or in certain circumstances between ordinary shares and shares created under an executive incentive scheme.

Voting and non-voting equity capital: this is linked with the definition of voting rights. An offer for non-voting equity capital should not be made conditional on any particular level of acceptances in respect of that class, unless the offer for the voting capital is also conditional on the success of the offer for the non-voting equity capital.

If, in addition to ordinary shares, there are other shares (e.g. preference shares) with excercisable voting rights, an offer would normally have to be made for these shares as well as the ordinary shares. The reason for this is that the offer for the ordinary shares would have to be in terms which required the offeror to obtain not only 50 per cent of the ordinary shares but also 50 per cent of the voting rights before declaring the bid unconditional.

Occasionally in an agreed bid an offeror may indicate to the offeree board the amount that he is prepared to pay for the business and leave it to the offeree board to suggest how the total should be divided between different classes of shareholders. This can cause difficulties if the offeree directors hold many offeree shares of a particular class since the fairness of the split may be called in question. Much then depends on the offeree board's financial adviser being accepted as impartial.

The question whether an offer made for one class of equity share is 'comparable' with that made for another class of equity share can raise difficult problems. It usually arises in connection with voting and non-voting ordinary shares. The obvious yardstick is the market price of the two classes of shares, though it is sometimes argued that the market for one class (usually the voting shares) is restricted or distorted by special factors. If individuals, other than the offeror, have been buying voting shares at the market price, that suggests that the price is acceptable. Fortunately, an offeror usually wants the profits of the company as well as control and if he has made purchases of voting and non-voting shares at market prices these prices may be acceptable as a guide to comparability.

In general, the type of the consideration should be the same, if they are to be regarded as comparable. Thus the Panel would not normally agree for one offer to be in cash and another to be in paper.

'Agreed to acquire' refers to acceptances of the offer in respect of shares which the offeror has contacted to purchase but has not yet paid for. When it comes to deciding whether an offeror has acquired or agreed to acquire 50 per cent of the voting rights, the only rights that count are those that the offeror himself holds or has contracted through the offer to hold. Holdings by persons acting in concert who have not yet accepted the offer do not count. Nor do irrevocable undertakings to accept an offer that had not yet been implemented. Nor do acceptances that are still subject to the fulfilment of conditions—for example an acceptance by the board of a shareholding company that requires to secure the consent of its shareholders to part with the shares and has not yet done so. When an option to buy shares is exercisable when an offer becomes unconditional, shares acquired in this way can only come into the reckoning of the total shares to which the 50 per cent applies if the offer went unconditional before the end of the offer period.

If all the conditions have been fulfilled, including acceptances by the percentage indicated in the offer document, then on the closing day the offer becomes unconditional without any further action by the offeror.

The Code is concerned with the control of public companies, which is normally exercised through voting equity shares. Offerors are not obliged to make offers to acquire classes of non-equity capital because their rights afford them adequate protection and their value should not be impaired by a change of control.

Rule 22

An offer must initially be open for at least 21 days after the posting of the offer and, if revised, it must be kept open for at least 14 days from the date of posting written notification of the revision to shareholders; an acceptor shall be entitled to withdraw his acceptance in any case after the expiry of 21 days from the first closing date of the initial offer, if the offer has not by such expiry become or been declared unconditional as to acceptances; such entitlement to withdraw shall be exercisable until such time as the offer becomes or is declared unconditional as to acceptances. If an offer is revised, all shareholders who accepted the original offer must receive the revised consideration.

No offer (whether revised or not) shall be capable of becoming or being declared unconditional as to acceptances after 3.30 p.m. on the 60th day after the date the offer is initially posted nor of being kept open after the expiry of such period unless it has previously so become or been declared unconditional. An offer may be extended beyond that period of 60 days with the permission of the Panel which will normally only be granted if a competing offer has been announced.

In any announcement of an extension of an offer the next expiry date must be stated.

Except with the consent of the Panel, all conditions must be fulfilled or the offer must lapse within 21 days of the first closing date or of the date the offer becomes or is declared unconditional as to acceptances, whichever is the later.
(Previous references at pages 40 and 103)

Rule 10 provides that the offer document should normally be posted within twenty-eight days of the announcement of the terms of the offer. Rule 22 deals with the course of events after the posting of the offer document. Rule 22 endeavours to ensure that an offeree shareholder is given adequate time to consider an offer document while at the same time ensuring that the offeree company does not have the offer hanging over its head for too long a period. The Rule applies to alternative forms of consideration, as it applies to the main offer, subject to certain points referred to in the note on Rule 23. The days referred to in the Rule are calendar days including Saturdays, Sundays, and holidays. From time to time the suggestion is made that the reference should be made to working days, but the change has not been made, primarily in order to keep the Rule simple.

The effect of the conditions (a) that an offer cannot go unconditional as to acceptances after sixty days from the posting of the offer document and (b) that the offeree shareholders must have fourteen days to consider any revised offer is that a revised offer cannot ordinarily be made later than forty-six days after the posting of the original offer document. By similar reasoning, an offeror cannot purchase shares in the market at a higher price than his offer price after the forty-sixth day, since that would require a revised offer at the higher price. The only exception is where an offeror, who has not shut off his offer, buys a block of shares which, with shares already in his possession or accepted under the bid, takes him above 50 per cent and the offer becomes or is declared unconditional. As the offer must then be open for acceptance for a further period of at least fourteen days, the requirement of the fourteen days' notice is met. The offeror would, of course, have to offer any higher price paid for these shares to those who had accepted the bid.

An announcement that a dividend could be retained by an offeree shareholder where previously it was to go to the offeror, amounts to a revised offer. In Practice Note 9 it is pointed out: 'There is no obligation to extend an offer the conditions of which are not met by the first closing date.'

To what extent should an offeror be bound by statements that he will not improve his offer? The offeror may say this in order to clarify the position or to induce shareholders to take the plunge and accept the offer. If the offeror makes categorical statements as to his intentions in documents sent to shareholders or at the later stages of a bid, the Panel is not ordinarily prepared to allow a change of mind. Thus in Practice Note 9 it is said:

> In general, an offeror will be bound by any positive statement which it makes as to the finality of its offer. If expressions such as '... the offer will not be further improved...' or 'our offer remains at xp. per share and it will not be raised...' or 'the offer will close on... and will not in any event be extended beyond that date' are included in documents sent to offeree company shareholders, or are used by a company's directors, officials or advisers and not withdrawn immediately if incorrect, the offeror will not normally be allowed subsequently to go back on what has been said.

Thus, when an offeror had announced that his bid would not be further increased, he was not allowed to revise his offer to enable accepting shareholders to retain a special interim dividend declared by the board of the offeree company. If the offeror had the agreement of the offeree board to a continuation of his offer, the Panel would, however, probably allow it. This is in line with Panel practice in administering Rule 35, where an offeror who has failed may on occasion be allowed to make a fresh offer in less than twelve months if the offeree board agrees.

If the offer does not become unconditional as to acceptances within twenty-one days of the first closing date of the initial offer, then (until such time as the offer becomes unconditional as to acceptances) an acceptor can withdraw his acceptance. Whether the right of withdrawal applies to irrevocable undertakings to accept an offer, depends on the terms of the undertaking. An offer *becomes unconditional* as to acceptances if the conditions as to acceptances are fulfilled. The offer document usually mentions 90 per cent acceptances as automatically involving unconditional acceptance. At that figure Section 209 of the Companies Act, 1948 comes into operation and the offeror can obtain 100 per cent ownership. The offer may *be declared unconditional* as to acceptances if the offer document provided that the offeror could so declare on acceptances over 50 per cent but under 90 per cent.

In relation to the 60-day period, the word 'declared' is somewhat ambiguous, since it may be taken to refer to the offeror's decision or to his announcement of that decision. To clarify the position, Practice Note 9 states:

> The requirement that no offer shall be capable of becoming or being declared unconditional as to acceptances after 3.30 p.m. on the 60th day after the date the offer is initially posted should be interpreted to mean that a public announcement as to whether the offer is unconditional as to acceptances or has lapsed should be made not later than that time.

In a statement issued on 29 January 1973, in connection with the take-over bid by Babcock and Wilcox for Woodall-Duckham, the

Panel said that it attached great importance to the 60-day Rule. It was most undesirable to extend the period of uncertainty which the 60-day period already involved and which was likely to disrupt business activities and be worrying to management, staff, and employees.

The Babcock and Wilcox offer document was issued on 30 November 1972. The offer had to be declared unconditional or lapse by the sixtieth day after the offer was posted, namely on 29 January 1973. As the offeree shareholders had to have 14 days to consider a revised offer, any revised offer had to be issued by 15 January 1973. On 16 January Woodall-Duckham made a profit forecast and on 22 January said that an increased dividend would be paid for 1972. It was by then too late for Babcock and Wilcox to make a revised offer. The Panel refused to waive the Rule, on the ground that a good deal of information about Woodall-Duckham's prospects was already available and that it had not been shown that there had been deliberate delay for tactical reasons. The profit forecast did not constitute a new, unexpected, and substantial factor, the publication of which had been deliberately delayed for purposes of tactical advantage. The Panel did not consider it desirable to permit a new offer to be made.

The Panel did, however, imply that, if it were satisfied that an offeree had for tactical reasons held back important information until it was impossible for the offeror to make a revised offer under the 60-day rule, the Panel might give permission for the offeror to put out a new offer and extend the offer period beyond 60 days.

In 1976 the Rule was made slightly less restrictive by providing that the Panel *normally* allows an extension only if there is a competing bid. It is, for example, conceivable that an offeror at a very late stage may indicate a revised higher price which the offeree board would be willing to recommend to shareholders.

If a subsidiary has made the offer and the parent subsequently improves on it, this is a revised offer and not a new offer in terms of the 60-day rule. Under Rule 35, an offeror who has failed in a bid cannot normally make a fresh offer until twelve months have elapsed.

Rule 23

(1) After an offer has become or is declared unconditional as to acceptances, the offer must remain open for acceptance for not less than 14 days after the date on which it would otherwise have expired, except in the event that the offer becomes or is declared unconditional as to acceptances on or by an expiry date and the offeror has given at least 14 days' notice in writing to the shareholders of the offeree company that the offer will not

> be open for acceptance beyond that date. Such notice shall not be capable of being enforced in a competitive situation.
>
> (2) If, once an offer is unconditional as to acceptances, it is stated that the offer will remain open until further notice, 14 days' notice should be given before it is closed.

(Previous references at pages 21, 111 and 178)

Dating back to the Notes (1959) and the Revised Notes (1963), it has been accepted that, after an offer has become unconditional as to acceptances, there should be a further short period during which uncommitted shareholders can decide whether to accept the offer. The Notes pointed out that this was particularly important where the acceptances were between 50 per cent and 90 per cent, and uncommitted shareholders could see that they would be minority holders without the protection of Section 209 of the Companies Act, 1948, which applies only to a minority of 10 per cent or less.

The Rule seeks to protect the reluctant acceptor. A shareholder may not wish a bid to succeed; but if it is likely to succeed, he may wish to get out and not remain in a minority under the new management. He wishes, therefore, to be in a position to accept the offer after the bid has succeeded and the offer has gone unconditional. The Rule provides that an offeror may deny offeree shareholders the extra 14 days for acceptance (i.e. exercise a 'shut-off') if (i) an expiry date has been fixed and by that date the offer has become or been declared unconditional as to acceptances and (ii) at least 14 days' notice has been given to the offeree shareholders that the offer will not be open for acceptance beyond that date. A shut-off must be sent, by notice in writing, either to each offeree shareholder or at least to each shareholder who has not so far accepted the offer. As an alternative, it can, however, be included in the offer document or a revised offer document. If the offer is open for 21 days, the notice has to be given within 7 days of the issue of the offer document. It is not enough to give 14 days' notice of a shut-off—e.g. to announce seven days before the expiry date that the offer will not be available beyond seven days after the expiry date. As the Rule is worded the notice must be given at least 14 days before the expiry date.

If matters had been left on that basis, it might have been anticipated that a great many offerors would have issued a shut-off notice in their offer document. The Panel has, therefore, imposed further conditions. The shut-off must be explicit and without qualification. For example, where an offeree was understood to be producing a revised profits forecast, the offeror was not allowed to say that the shut-off would be cancelled if the figures were substantially different from those already produced. Further, a shut-off is irrevocable. The expiry date cannot be postponed nor can the offeror reopen the offer or part of the offer at a later date. The only circumstance in which an offeror might be allowed to change his mind (e.g. to re-introduce a cash alternative) would be if the offeree company agreed to this course. This accords with the Panel's practice under Rule 35. These conditions are designed to prevent a shut-off being used as a tactic to try to force shareholders to make a response.

These arrangements apply equally to offers where an alternative consideration is offered, usually a cash alternative to the offeror's paper: and for the purpose of a shut-off each may be treated separately. Thus it is quite common to shut off an underwritten cash alternative (e.g. an offer by a merchant bank to buy for cash securities of the offeror which offeree shareholders will receive in exchange for offeree shares) after 21 days. while the paper alternative runs on. A cash alternative provided by a third party by way of underwriting a paper offer presents special problems for an offeror and a concession has been made. The offeror may find it costly to negotiate an underwriting of his paper offer for (say) 40 days—the period from the date of the announcement of the offer to 14 days after the offer goes unconditional—instead of 21 days or 26 days. For this reason, an offeror may limit the alternative cash offer to 21 days or some other limited period, and this will be the shut-off notice for the purposes of Rule 23(1). Thereafter, unless the offeror has used language likely to be interpreted as meaning that the cash alternative will not in any circumstances be renewed, the offeror is permitted to procure a new cash alternative offer which will be part of an extension or revision of his proposals.

Practice Note 9 summarizes the position as follows:

(1) In general, the provisions of these Rules [22 and 23] apply equally to alternative offers. However, where an alternative offer is provided principally by third parties (typically a cash underwritten alternative) a statement limiting the availability of the alternative to a period approximating to that of the arrangements on which it is based, will be considered to be a satisfactory notice for the purposes of Rule 23(1). Thereafter, unless the offeror has used additional embellishment which is calculated to persuade the offeree company shareholders that the cash alternative will not in any event be renewed, the offeror will be permitted to procure a new cash alternative offer to be made as part of a revision and/or extension of the proposals.

If a second bid appears, it would be unreasonable to allow the second offeror to announce a shut-off of his offer, in whole or in part. The reason is that those who have accepted the first offer may have difficulty in extricating themselves from the first offeror and should not be deprived of the opportunity to get the second offer in its full form.

Practice Note 9 expressed the matter as follows: '(2) No Rule 23 "shut-off" notice of any offer (including a third party alternative) may be given between the time when a competing offer has been announced and the competitive situation has ended.'

As regards the first offeror in a competitive situation, Practice Note 9 says:

(3) Where a 'shut-off' notice of a third party alternative has been given before the competitive situation arises, the offeror may still end the alternative on its stated expiry date although, as explained in (1), it may not be bound to do so. Where any other 'shut-off' notice has already been given or an offeror has indicated, before a competitive situation arises, that it will not revise its offer, an offeror can choose not to be bound by these statements and to be free to extend and/or revise its proposals provided:
   (a) that notice to this effect be given as soon as possible and in any event within four dealing days of the announcement of the competing offer and that shareholders are informed in writing at the earliest opportunity; and
   (b) that any offeree shareholders who accepted the offer after the date of such statements be given a right of withdrawal extending over eight days from the date of posting the notice under (a).

The final section of the Rule was inserted in 1976 and is intended to give shareholders time to consider their position when they hear that an offeror has decided to close the offer, after going unconditional and placing no immediate time limit on late acceptances. The Panel's annual report for 1978/9 pointed out that the shut-off notice might be given in a public announcement and not simply in an offer document.

The Rule illustrates the fact that simplicity of administration is not easily achieved if exceptions are allowed. The Rule would be much simpler if shut-offs were not allowed; but no doubt there would then be fewer cash alternatives.

Rule 24

By 9.30 a.m. at the latest on the dealing day next following the day on which an offer is due to expire, or becomes or is declared unconditional as to acceptances, or is revised or extended, the offeror shall announce and simultaneously inform The Stock Exchange of the position and shall also state the total number of shares (as nearly as practicable):

   (1) for which acceptances of the offer have been received;
   (2) held before the offer period; and
   (3) acquired or agreed to be acquired during the offer period.

(Previous reference at page 40)

The purpose of this Rule is to report to shareholders and to the market generally the precise position of an offer which has run its course. It also discourages offerors, in doubt about the success of their offer, from fudging the results in the hope that later posts will bring in some more acceptances. The main requirement is that the information required by the Rule must be given in all cases on the next business morning following the day when an offer expires. Where an offer has become or been declared unconditional before the expiry date, the information is given at that time. Where an offer has manifestly failed, the offeror sometimes wishes to avoid an announcement to that effect and an indication of the number of acceptances he has received, but an announcement in the terms of the Rule has to be made.

Where the consideration offered takes more than one form (e.g. shares or cash), the Rule does not require the offeror to make a split of acceptances between the different forms of consideration. In practice, many offerors do publish details and the offeree board may press them to do so. Where an offer is revised or the time of acceptance extended beyond the expiry date of the original offer, an offeror has to give the information, as on the date of the revised offer or extension, at the time of the revision or extension. He is, of course, under an obligation to give the information again when the revised offer or extension expires.

If there is an alternative form of consideration (say, cash) which is not open to acceptance beyond a date that is earlier than the date for the offer generally, then an announcement under the Rule is also required on the dealing date next following the day on which the alternative form of consideration is due to expire (Practice Note 9). In order to discourage bullish statements of a vague character by offerors, which may stampede offeree shareholders into hasty acceptance, Practice Note 9 also provides: 'If, during an offer, any statements, either orally or in writing, are made by the offeror or its advisers about the level of acceptances to the offer, an immediate announcement should be made in conformity with this Rule.'

This, however, is not interpreted as preventing an offeror from making a simple statement that the offer is now unconditional. He may wish to state this immediately after he has got the necessary acceptances. As with Rule 18, the Rule does not apply to the acceptances of a cash alternative provided by underwriters.

Rule 25

(1) If the offeror is unable within the time limit to comply with any of the requirements of Rule 24, The Stock Exchange will consider suspension of dealings in the offeree company's shares and, where appropriate, in the offeror's shares until the relevant information is given.

(2) If the offeror, having announced the offer to be unconditional as to

acceptances, fails by 3.30 p.m. on the relevant day to comply with any of the requirements of Rule 24, then immediately thereafter any acceptor shall be entitled to withdraw his acceptance. Subject to the second paragraph of Rule 22, this right of withdrawal may be terminated not less than 8 days after the relevant day by the offeror confirming (if that be the case) that the offer is still unconditional as to acceptances and complying with Rule 24.

(3) For the purpose of Rule 23 (1) the period of 14 days referred to therein will run from the date of such confirmation.

This penalty Rule emphasises the importance that the authors of the Code attach to the implementation of Rule 24. In fact the application of Rule 25 has never arisen. There is the possibility that, if the acceptances are just over 50 per cent and the offeror has failed to comply with Rule 24, withdrawals under sub-paragraph (2) of Rule 25 might bring the acceptances below 50 per cent. So far this has not happened. Probably the lesser of two evils would be for the offer to remain unconditional.

In the event of a late compliance with Rule 24, the fourteen days for which the offer must remain open under Rule 23(1) runs from the date of confirmation that Rule 24 has now been complied with and that the offer is still unconditional.

Rule 26

The obligations of the offeror and the rights of the offeree company shareholders under Rules 21–25 must be specifically incorporated in the offer document. Where an offer is unconditional as to acceptances from the outset, Rule 21 is inappropriate and Rules 22–25 should be applied as necessary.

Rules 21–5 represent obligations of the offeror and rights of offeree shareholders. By specifically including them in the offer document the contract between the offeror and the offeree shareholder becomes subject to the fulfilment of these conditions which are thus given legal force. An offer may be unconditional as to acceptances if it is made by an offeror who already holds over 50 per cent of the voting rights (Rule 34(3)) or who is making a bid for non-voting shares not tied to the offer for voting shares (Rule 21) In such a case, the following provisions of Rules 22–5 apply to an offer document:

(a) under Rule 22, the minimum 21 days for an offer and either a statement regarding possible revision (with the necessary 14 days for acceptance) or a statement that the offer will not be revised;

(b) under Rule 23, either a statement regarding possible extension or a statement that the offer will not be extended;
(c) under Rule 24, a statement that the details of acceptances of shares held or acquired will be announced on the next working day following the last day of the offer (at 9.30 a.m. to The Stock Exchange, if a listed company).

Rule 27

The Panel's consent is required for any partial offer.

In the case of an offer which would result in the offeror holding shares carrying over 50% but less than 100% of the voting rights of a company, such consent will not normally be granted if an offer for the whole of the equity share capital of the offeree company has already been announced, or if the offeror or persons acting in concert with it have acquired, selectively or in significant numbers, shares in the offeree company during the 12 months preceding the application for consent. Any such offer must be conditional upon approval of the offer by shareholders in respect of over 50% of the voting rights not held by the offeror or persons acting in concert with it.

In the case of an offer which would result in the offeror holding shares carrying not less than 30% and not more than 50% of the voting rights of a company, such consent will be granted only in exceptional circumstances and in any event not unless the board of the offeree company recommends the offer. Any such offer must be conditional upon approval of the offer by shareholders in respect of over 50% of the voting rights not held by the offeror or persons acting in concert with it. Where such an offer is made the precise number of shares offered for must be stated and the offer may not be declared unconditional as to acceptances unless acceptances are received for not less than that number.

In the case of an offer which would result in the offeror holding shares carrying less than 30% of the voting rights of a company, consent will normally be granted.

Partial offers must be made to all shareholders of the class and arrangements must be made for those shareholders who wish to do so to accept in full for the relevant percentage of their holdings.

Where a company has more than one class of equity share capital a comparable offer must be made for each class.

In the case of a partial offer the offeror and persons acting in concert with it may not purchase shares in the offeree company during the offer period nor, in the case of a successful partial offer, may the offeror or persons acting in concert, except with the consent of the Panel, purchase such shares during a period of 12 months after the end of the offer period.

(Previous references at pages 40, 56, 108 and 121)

Earlier versions of the Code prefaced the provisions governing bids for less than 100 per cent of the voting shares of a company with the statement that partial bids were undesirable. The ground for this view was that, when the effective control of the company was at issue, shareholders should have an opportunity to use all their shares to oppose the change or to get the proffered price for all their shares if they did not like what was happening. The position of minority shareholders in the UK is not sufficiently strong for arrangements to be approved which leave shareholders in a minority whether they want it or not. With a full bid it is for each shareholder to decide whether he wishes to remain in a minority whereas in the case of a partial bid he is very unlikely to have that choice. Since 1974 the Code has moved away from this position. Partial bids are common in other countries and it was thought to be unreasonable to frown on them in a comprehensive fashion if the offeror had good reasons (such as limits on the funds at his disposal) for not making a full bid.

Rule 27 says that the consent of the Panel is required for any partial offer. The Rule indicates that the Panel's consent will not normally be given if an offer for the whole of the equity has already been announced or if the applicant or persons acting in concert with him have acquired in the previous 12 months shares in the offeree company selectively (e.g. from controlling directors) or in significant amounts. A shareholder who already holds more than 50 per cent of the voting rights and who wishes to obtain further shares by a bid has the choice of making an unconditional bid for all the remaining shares or of making a partial bid. In this latter event, his bid is subject to all the restrictions on partial bids.

There are four general restrictions on partial offers.

1. Any partial bid where the offeror aims to secure more than 30 per cent of the voting rights must be conditional on approval of the bid by shareholders holding over 50 per cent of the voting rights not under the control of the offeror and persons acting in concert. This requirement applies even in cases where the offeror already holds more than 50 per cent of the voting rights. Approval is normally signified by an entry in a box on the acceptance form. Approval of the bid is regarded as separate from acceptance. An offeror cannot treat acceptance of the bid as tacit approval — the approval must be specific and separate. It was envisaged that a shareholder might disapprove of the bid but complete the acceptance form in case it went through.

2. The offer must be open for acceptance by all holders of the class of share for which the offer is being made and if too many acceptances are received they must be scaled down *pro rata* for all accepting shareholders. This has been a feature of arrangements since the

original 1959 Notes and the Licensed Dealers (Conduct of Business) Rules, 1960.

3. Where a company has more than one class of equity share capital, a comparable offer must be made for each class.

4. The offeror or persons acting in concert must not purchase shares in the offeree company during the offer period or (if the partial bid is successful), without the consent of the Panel, for twelve months after the end of the offer period. In other words, the offeror must not avoid making a full bid and then try to complete the acquisition of control by the purchase of a number of shares, which means that all shareholders are not being treated alike. The offer period begins with the announcement of the intention to make a bid, but the Panel would regard it as a breach of the intention of the Rule if the offeror purchased shares after he had decided to make a partial bid.

As indicated, the Panel does not normally allow a partial bid to be made, if a full offer from another source exists or is known to be pending. Where a partial offer is running and a full offer is launched in competition, the Panel will normally allow the partial offer to continue, though it might look askance at extensions or revisions other than conversion into a competing full offer. The Rule differentiates between different types of partial offer. The percentages relate to the total holdings of the offeror and persons in concert with him, after the partial bid has succeeded. The percentages therefore include existing holdings in the offeree company.

OVER 50 PER CENT BUT LESS THAN 100 PER CENT

As already indicated, the Panel would not normally consent to such if there is already an offer in the field for the whole of the class of shares in question. One reason for this is the difficulty which the offeree shareholders are likely to find in comparing the value of the two offers. Nor would consent normally be granted if the offeror had been buying shares selectively or in significant numbers in the previous twelve months. In such a case, the bid has the appearance of being a step towards full control by selective purchases, followed by a partial bid, which means that all shareholders are not being treated alike.

In sanctioning a scheme of arrangement, Mr Justice Brightman on 22 September 1977 drew attention to the desirability of shareholders being warned in partial bids that an offer of this kind can lose for the shareholders a voting position of value. This has now been dealt with in the revision of Practice Note 9 issued in December 1978. Where a partial offer could result in the offeror holding shares carrying over 50 per cent but less than 100 per cent of the voting rights in the offeree company, the offer document must contain prominently a statement advising shareholders that, if the offer succeeds, statutory control will pass to the offeror who will be free to exercise that control and acquire further shares without incurring any mandatory offer obligations under the Code. Rule 21 applies to these bids and it is accordingly necessary for the offeror to secure acceptances from sufficient shareholders to secure that the offeror has over 50 per cent of the voting rights before he declares the offer unconditional. This fits in with the restrictions on bids between 30 per cent and 50 per cent outlined below.

30 PER CENT TO 50 PER CENT

The Panel is reluctant to give consent to a bid for this order of percentage—only in 'exceptional circumstances' and with the recommendation of the offer by the offeree board. It follows that such bids are exceedingly rare. It should be noted that the Rule requires that the precise number of shares sought must be stated and that the offer may not be declared unconditional unless acceptances are received for at least that number.

UNDER 30 PER CENT

These are normally allowed. The bidder could have bought 29.9 per cent in the market or by selective purchases without restriction.

EXTENSION OR REVISION OF OFFER

Partial offers are subject to the Rules applicable to offers generally. This if an offeror says that an offer will lapse after a specified date unless it has by then become or been declared unconditional as to acceptances, he cannot thereafter extend the time for which the offer is open. Again, if the offeror says that he does not intend to raise the offer, he cannot thereafter revise it.

SWITCH TO FULL OFFER

A partial offer may be converted into a full offer

(a) if there is a subsequent competitive full offer;
(b) if the offer document has not been issued, but subject to satisfaction that the value of the full bid to the offeree shareholder was greater than the value of the partial bid;
(c) much more doubtfully, after the issue of the offer document.

Conversion to a full offer would not be allowed if the offeror had said that the value of the offer would not be increased or had given a shut-off notice. The new full offer must be open for a period of 21 days and not for the 14 days that applies to a simple revision. Withdrawals could not take place until 21 days after the first closing date of the full offer, not 21 days after the first closing date of the partial offer. A full offer made in consequence of a subsequent competitive full offer is restricted by the competitive offeror's 60-day period.

PURCHASES IN THE MARKET

The prohibition on purchases applies even if the offeror had already over 50 per cent of the voting rights before making the partial offer and even where a partial bid is competing against a full bid.

Rule 28

Where an offer is made for more than one class of share, separate offers must be made for each class and the offeror should state, if it intends to resort to compulsory acquisition powers under section 209 of the Companies Act 1948, that the section will be used only in respect of each class separately.

Under section 209 of the Companies Act 1948, if the holders of 90 per cent of the shares have accepted a take-over bid, the remainder can have their shares compulsorily acquired by the offeror and they have a corresponding right to be bought out. The Jenkins Committee pointed out that the prescribed conditions should be separately fulfilled in respect of each class of share and Rule 28 which dates from the 1968 Code gives effect to this.

The Rule is applied rigidly. Rarely has a single offer been allowed for more than one class of share. One offer may be allowed where, for example, deferred shares are created in connection with an offer and issued *pro rata* to ordinary shareholders to save stamp duty.

The second part of the Rule was inserted because it had been argued than in law section 209 could be applied globally, even if separate offers had been made for each class of share.

Rule 29

(1) Where an offer is made for equity share capital and the offeree company has convertible securities outstanding, the offeror must make appropriate arrangements to ensure that the interests of the holders of the stock are safeguarded and in particular that the existence of a conversion option over a period of time is adequately recognised. Taking this into account, the offeror should make an appropriate offer or proposal to the stockholders.

(2) The board of the offeree company must obtain competent independent advice on any offer or proposal to the stockholders and the substance of such advice must be made known to its stockholders.

(3) Whenever practicable the offer or proposal should be despatched to stockholders at the same time that the offer document is posted to shareholders, but if this is not practicable the Panel should be consulted and the offer or proposal should be despatched as soon as possible thereafter.

(4) The offer or proposal to stockholders required by this Rule may be carried out by way of a scheme to be considered by a stockholders' meeting.

(5) If an offeree company has warrants, options or subscription rights outstanding the provisions of this Rule apply mutatis mutandis.

Loan stock or debentures which are convertible at some stage into ordinary shares have presented a problem since the early days of the Code. The value of the conversion rights varies greatly, depending *inter alia* on the terms of the conversion and the level at which ordinary shares stand. The Panel would normally expect holders of convertible loan stock to be offered either (i) a consideration based on the conversion rights and related to the offer for the equity captial or (ii) a convertible loan stock with conversion rights into the offeror's equity broadly on the same basis as applicable to the existing stock. It is, however, for the advisers to the offeree company and not the Panel to express a view whether, having regard to the offer for the voting shares, the offer for the convertible is 'appropriate' and whether 'the existence of a conversion option over a period of time is adequately recognized'.

Thus, the Panel would not investigate a claim by debenture- or warrant-holders than an offer was inadequate, if a competent independent adviser, acting for the holders, has said that the terms are appropriate. It has never been felt to be reasonable to have a rule requiring an offeror in all circumstances to make an offer in cash for convertibles or to bring forward any conversion date. At the same time the position of the stockholders must not be worsened.

The Rule requires the offeror to make an appropriate offer or proposal to the stockholders and to dispatch it to the stockholders at the same time that the offer document is posted to shareholders. If this cannot be done for some reason, the Panel must be consulted and the offer should be dispatched as soon as possible. A holder of convertible loan stock has no rights under section 209 of the Companies Act 1948, though the abortive Companies Bill of 1973 would have given him such rights. The trust deed setting up a loan stock may contain some provisions on what is to happen to a loan stock in the event of a take-over—for example it may say that if an offeror secures over 50 per cent of the voting rights attached to the equity capital a holder of convertible stock may convert within a specified period after the take-over.

The matter is dealt with by rules rather than by relying on the alteration of trust deeds, because it is difficult to deal with existing trust deeds and because an offeror is more directly bound by a rule than by a trust deed of the offeree company.

The offeree is sometimes reluctant to go to the expense of obtaining competent independent advice; but the Rule is mandatory in terms and gives no discretion to the Panel which always insists on advice being obtained.

Rule 30

All persons concerned with the consideration and discussion of any proposed offer must treat the information related to the potential offer as secret and must not pass it to any other person unless it is necessary to do so. Furthermore, such persons must conduct themselves so as to minimise the chances of an accidental leak of information.

No dealings of any kind (including option business) in the securities of the offeree company by any person, not being the offeror, who is privy to the preliminary take-over or merger discussions or to an intention to make an offer may take place between the time when there is reason to suppose that an approach or an offer is contemplated and the announcement of the approach or offer or the termination of the discussions.

No such dealings shall take place in the securities of the offeror except where the proposed offer is not deemed price-sensitive in relation to such securities.

Without prejudice to the generality of the foregoing, a person shall be regarded as 'privy to the preliminary take-over or merger discussions or to an intention to make an offer' if, assuming he has received relevant information, either

(1) he is a director or employee of one of the companies involved in the proposed offer; or

(2) he is a professional adviser either to one of the companies involved in the proposed offer or to any director or employee of such a company; or

(3) that information was received in the context of a confidential relationship and it was necessary that he received such information.

The spouse and the close relatives and related trusts of such a person would be deemed to be in the same position as such person.

(Previous references at pages 80, 145 and Chapter XIII)

Rule 30 has to be considered with General Principle 5 and Rules 7 and 31. The Rule deals first with the steps to ensure that confidential, price-sensitive information is kept secret. This is the preventive aspect of the subject of insider dealing. It then goes on to prohibit dealings during the confidential preliminary stages of a take-over offer, with a limited exemption for the offeror. Being an ethical requirement, the conduct that is forbidden can be enforced without the qualifications required in defining a criminal offence. For example the prohibition on dealings by an insider is absolute and not qualified by reference to information that is price sensitive.[1]

The implication of the second paragraph of the Rule—it does not say so explicitly—is that after the announcement of talks those concerned are free to deal. However, if the offeror or his advisers had received price-sensitive information which was still confidential, then they would not be free to deal. Although the Rule in terms deals only with the situation up to the announcement of any offer, the Panel would regard General Principle 5 and the general intentions of the Code as governing later conduct where there was confidential information that an offer was about to be abandoned.

Practice Note 9 provides:

If, after an announcement has been made that take-over or merger discussions are taking place or that an approach or offer is contemplated, the discussions are terminated or the offeror decides not to proceed with an offer, no dealings in the securities of the offeree company by the offeror or by any person or company privy to the intention to terminate the discussions or to the decision not to proceed with the offer may take place prior to the announcement that the discussions have been terminated or that a decision not to proceed with an offer has been taken.

The restrictions on dealings in Rule 30 do not apply to the offeror. Practice Note 9 however contains a reminder:

The exemption of the offeror under Rule 30 from the prohibition on dealings does not apply to cases where the offeror would be precluded from dealing under ordinarily accepted standards of business behaviour, e.g., where the offeror has been supplied by the offeree company with confidential price-sensitive information in the course of take-over or merger discussions.

The exemption of the offeror does not extend to subsidiaries that are not wholly owned by the offeror or to his staff or his advisers or to persons acting in concert with him. The exemption is restricted strictly to the offeror.

Much consideration has been given to the position of a person who receives a tip from an insider but who is not himself a party or adviser involved in a bid—in American parlance a tippee. The Rule prohibits dealings by anyone who 'is privy to the preliminary take-over ... discussions ...'. While the generality of this definition is preserved

---

[1] Panel statement of 2 October 1972 on dealings in shares of Rowan and Boden Limited.

specific mention is made of 'information . . . received in the context of a confidential relationship' where 'it was necessary that he received such information'. The Panel held that an individual, who was asked to call at a merchant bank about a possible directorship and who was then told that an offer for the company in question was imminent and that there might be no directorship, offended against the Rule when he went out and bought shares in the company.

Cases coming within any legal provisions against insider dealing will be prosecuted by the Department or the police; but there may be cases coming within Rule 30 but not within the law which would continue to be handled by the Panel.

Rule 31

Save in so far as appears from the Code, it is considered undesirable to fetter the market. Accordingly, all parties to a take-over or merger transaction (other than to a partial offer) and associates are free to deal subject to daily disclosure to The Stock Exchange, the Panel and the Press (not later than 12 noon on the dealing day following the date of the relevant transaction) of the total of all shares of any offeror or the offeree company purchased or sold by them or their respective associates for their own account on any day during the offer period in the market or otherwise and at what price.

In addition all purchases and sales of shares of any offeror or the offeree company made by associates for account of investment clients who are not themselves associates must be similarly reported to The Stock Exchange and to the Panel, but need not be disclosed to the Press.

Furthermore, dealings by any person, who is not an associate, in the shares of an offeror or the offeree company during an offer period which would have to be notified to the company by reason of Section 26 of the Companies Act 1976 and Section 33 of the Companies Act 1967 must be disclosed to The Stock Exchange, the Panel and the Press not later than 12 noon on the dealing day following the date of the relevant transaction. The disclosure must name the person dealing and the resultant holding.

(Previous references at pages 46, 56, 64, 83 and 144)

The Rule applies to the offeror, offeree and their associates (a wider term than persons acting in concert). This is the only use of the term 'associate' in the Code and the definitions at the beginning of the Code contain an interpretation of the term. Dealings by directors and senior employees of companies involved in bids have to be disclosed, also dealings by directors of advisers and employees of these advisers involved in the work of the bid. It should be observed that 10 per cent remains in 5(b) of the definition, notwithstanding the use of 5 per cent in section 26 of the Companies Act, 1976. The term 'associate' does not apply to a banker whose sole relationship with a party to a take-over or merger transaction is the provision of normal commercial banking services or such activities in connection with the offer as confirming that cash is available, or handling acceptances and other registration work.

An associate must disclose dealings on behalf of discretionary investment clients, and that includes individuals and funds for whom the associate is accustomed to make investment decisions without prior reference. Deals by or on behalf of persons acting in concert with the offeror should be disclosed, and their names given, although they may not fall within the definition of 'associates'. They are parties to the bid. In competitive bids, dealings by one offeror or persons acting in concert in the shares of the other offeror should be reported, as from the date of the announcement of the second offer.

A difficult question is where a group of people decide to build up a strong position in a company by individual purchases and then subsequently make a bid through a syndicate or company. The better opinion seems to be that only the syndicate or company would be reported as the offeror. The others could not deal once a bid was in contemplation. In the case of deals by an associate, it need only be said that the purchase has been made by an associate of one of the principals to the offer. If, however, the associate in such a case holds 10 per cent of the equity capital of the offeror or offeree his name should be given. Associates should identify the principal with whom they are associated even when dealing on behalf of clients. The Rule applies to all dealings, whether undertaken through The Stock Exchange or outside the market.

The taking or granting and the exercise of an option during the offer period should be disclosed. This includes the purchase or sale of a traded option contract. The sale and subsequent purchase of a block of shares, undertaken near the end of the fiscal year for capital gains tax purposes ('bed and breakfast' deals) should normally appear in the offer document and be reported during the offer period. They would not trigger off a liability under Rule 34.

If it is uncertain whether an announced offer will proceed—for example, if the offeror has said that he may not proceed if the offeree board are hostile and the board have indicated opposition—dealings should be disclosed until it is clear that the offer is being abandoned. The offer period does not continue through the period of reference to the Monopolies and Mergers Commission and subsequent consideration by the Department, since the bid is formally dropped on a reference. In a scheme of arrangement, there is no need to report dealings after the statutory meeting of shareholders but before the final ratification by the Court. The Rule applies where a company is public but not listed (including cases where the listing has been suspended or cancelled). The Stock Exchange should be informed of dealings. Offeree shareholders who have accepted a bid are thereby precluded from selling these shares (except as assented shares) thereafter in the market during the offer period. This is one of the reasons why shareholders tend to accept towards the very end of the offer period. Section 33 of the Companies Act 1967 can be useful in any difficulties about the meaning of 'disclosure'.

If a bid has failed, the offeror may not approach accepting shareholders and repeat the same or a similar offer. If allowed, this would nullify the requirement under Rule 21 than an offer cannot go unconditional until the offeror has 50 per cent of the voting rights. He can make market purchases of the offeree's shares, subject to the conditions laid down in Rules 34 and 35. All this binds persons acting in concert with the offeror, as well as the offeror. A number of detailed points on the operation of Rule 31 are dealt with in Practice Note 7:

(1) As a matter of mechanics, it is enough (for an associate) to inform The Stock Exchange by letter or telex of dealings, since The Stock Exchange, as well as publishing deals on the floor of The Stock Exchange sends copies of such announcements to the Panel and the Press.
(2) Similarly, it is enough for an associate to inform The Stock Exchange by letter or telex of dealings on behalf of investment clients, since The Stock Exchange sends a copy to the Panel. Such announcements are not published on the floor of The Stock Exchange nor sent to the Press.
(3) An offeror or offeree or an associate may disclose dealings through a merchant bank or stockbroker who acts on their behalf. Where there is more than one agent (a merchant bank and a stockbroker or a London broker or a country broker) responsibility to disclose should be agreed.

Rule 32

If the offeror or any person acting in concert with it purchases securities during the offer period at above the offer price (being the then current value of the offer) then it shall increase its offer to not less than the highest price (excluding stamp duty and commission) paid for the securities so acquired. An announcement of any such purchase and the consequent increased offer must be made immediately.

If the offer involves a further issue of already listed securities, the current value of the offer should normally be established by reference to the mean of the prices quoted by all those jobbers dealing in such securities at the time the purchase is effected. The same method should normally be used to calculate the value of such securities for the purpose of ascertaining what minimum increased consideration should be offered.

If the offer involves the issue of securities which are not already listed, the value shall be based on a reasonable estimate of what the price would have been had they been listed.

If there is a restricted market in the securities of the offeror, or if the amount of already listed securities to be issued is large in relation to the amount already listed, the Panel may require justification of prices used to determine the value of the offer.

Shareholders of the offeree company must be notified in writing of the increased price payable under this Rule at least 14 days before the offer closes.

(Previous references at pages 64, 79 and 110)

For the purpose of this Rule the price at which securities are purchased is the price at which the bargain between the purchaser (or his broker) and the vendor (or jobber) is struck. In deciding what price should be offered to shareholders as a consequence of a purchase, the commission and stamp duty are ignored. Where an offer is made for a security on terms that the acceptor may retain an accruing dividend or interest payment, the price, for determining whether purchases in the market or elsewhere exceed the offer price, is the cum dividend equivalent of the offer price. Later, when a shareholder has become entitled to the dividend and the market price has gone 'ex-div', it is the 'ex-div' price that is used to test market and other purchases.

The 'then current value of the offer' means the value of the offer at the moment at which the purchase of shares is made. In computing the value of the existing offer, the 'mean of the prices quoted by all those jobbers . . .' means the mean of the jobbers' spreads, not the mean of the jobbers' buying prices. It is accepted that, where an offer involves the offeror's shares, as all or part of the consideration, the offeror is allowed to pay a higher price in the market when his shares are riding high than when his shares are standing at a lower figure. If the offer is part shares and part cash, possibly with a cash alternative in respect of the share element, the value of the offer is not the total cash available but the value of the share element at the time of purchase plus the cash element. In formula bids for investment trusts, the offer is a cash payment equal to x per cent of the net asset value per share on the day on which the offer becomes unconditional. In respect of purchases of shares by the offeror during the currency of the offer, the ceiling price (above which a higher offer must be made) is the value of the formula on the day on which the purchase is made. Any revised offer that resulted from purchases would continue to be expressed as a percentage of net asset value.

The valuation of unlisted securities offered as consideration in an offer presents considerable problems. The Rule simply says that the value must be based on a reasonable estimate of what the price would have been if the securities had been listed, and that the Panel may require justification of prices used to determine the value of the offer (normally from the offeror's broker) if

(a) there is a restricted market in the securities of the offeror: which would include unlisted securities; or
(b) the amount of already listed securities to be issued is large in relation to the amount already listed.

The Rule can be met (provided that a cash offer is not required under some other Rule) by the addition of cash or extra securities to the consideration in the offer. If extra securities are offered but the cash consideration remains unchanged, then each acceptor of cash should have the opportunity to change his acceptance to securities. Similarly, if cash is offered at a later stage, acceptors of securities should have the opportunity to take it. If there is a cash offer and a share offer, and the share offer alone is extended, and purchases take place above the value of the share offer, then the share offer must be increased. Those who had accepted cash should have the opportunity to accept the increased share offer. If a new holding company has been created to make an offer for two companies, then to decide whether prices are being paid above the offer price it may well be necessary to look at the price of the shares in the two companies and pro-rate them in the proportion in which the shareholders of each company will get shares in the new holding company.

The combined effect of the Rules that an offer should not be open beyond 60 days and that a revised offer must be open for 14 days is that purchases of shares at a price which might make a higher offer necessary cannot be made after the 46th day from the issue of the offer document, unless the purchase is sufficiently large to take the offeror over 50 per cent and he can go unconditional. As an offer then normally remains open for 14 further days under Rule 23, the requirement that a raised offer must remain open for 14 days is met. Purchases of convertible securities currently convertible or warrants currently exercisable may in certain circumstances be relevant to this Rule in the context of the offer price for the underlying shares. Before such purchases are made the Panel should be consulted.

The sequence of events should be:

(a) shares purchased above the offer price;

(b) immediate announcement of the price paid and the fact that a raised offer will be made at the increased price;

(c) by 9.30 a.m. on the following day at the latest an announcement on the lines indicated by Rule 24.

As pointed out in the note on General Principle 8, problems may arise if an offeror buys in the market above the offer price after an offer has become unconditional but the offer is still open.

Rule 33

If (1) the shares of any class under offer in the offeree company purchased for cash by the offeror and any person acting in concert with it during the offer period and within 12 months prior to its commencement carry 15% or more of the voting rights of that class,

or (2) in the view of the Panel there are circumstances which render such a course necessary in order to give effect to General Principle 8

then, except with the consent of the Panel in cases falling under (1) above, the offer for that class shall be in cash or accompanied by a cash alternative at not less than the highest price (excluding stamp duty and commission) paid for shares of that class purchased during the offer period and within 12 months prior to its commencement.

If the offeror considers that the highest price (as define above) should not apply to a particular case, the offeror should consult the Panel which will have discretion to agree an adjusted price.

(Previous references at pages 73, 78, 90, 110 and 178)

This Rule dates from 1971. Unlike Rule 34 the Rule does not require a bid but if a bid is made it must be in cash or accompanied by a cash alternative.

If the offeror has had dealings in the shares of the offeree company before he contemplated making an offer, the 15 per cent in (1) is treated as referring to net purchases (i.e. purchases less sales). After the offeror has seriously in mind to make a bid and during the offer period purchases count without any deduction for sales. In a statement dated 8 October 1979 the Panel upheld a long-standing practice that for the twelve month period a net figure is used in respect of purchases and sales not obviously linked with the offer. In calculating the 15 per cent irrevocably committed shares, convertibles (unless conversion is effected) or share options are not normally included. The Rule refers to any class of share under offer and to purchases for cash of shares carrying 15 per cent or more of the voting rights of that class. The implication is that offers for other classes need not be for cash. Where however there are voting and non-voting ordinary shares, not greatly different in price, and the whole of the voting shares are purchased, the question may arise whether the cash offer should not extend to all the ordinary shares. The Rule is not regarded as applying to share transfers between a parent company and a subsidiary or to shares subscribed under rights issues or in consideration of the acquisition of assets.

If a cash offer has been closed and a share offer extended, any cash purchases thereafter at a higher price would mean that the cash offer has to be re-opened at that higher price. The cash offer would not, however, have to be renewed, if the cash purchases were not at a higher price.

If an offeror has committed itself not to revise an offer or not to repeat a cash alternative, it must not make purchases which will require it under Rule 33 to go against its earlier commitment. The material date for purchases is the date on which beneficial ownership passes. The fact that payment may be made by instalments is irrelevant.

If the offeror makes a paper offer worth much more than the price he paid for shares purchased for cash, the Rule 33 cash offer may be substantially less valuable than the paper offer.

If an offeror making a formula bid for an investment trust comes within Rule 33 or Rule 34 by purchases of shares, the price to be paid under the offer is the higher of (i) the formula price as at the date when the offer goes unconditional and (ii) the highest cash price paid in respect of the purchases.

The Rule applies to minority bids but the 15 per cent relates to the whole share capital in the class. Factors which the Panel would take into account when considering an application for an adjusted price include the size and timing of the relevant purchases, the attitude of the offeree board, whether shares had been purchased at high prices from insiders and the number of shares purchased in the preceding twelve months.

The Panel normally would operate under (2) only where the vendors were either directors of the offeror or offeree companies or otherwise closely connected with them. Thus (2) would apply if the chairman of a company held 10 per cent of the equity and sold all of his holding for cash. The definition of cash purchases should be borne in mind.

Rule 34

(1) Except with the consent of the Panel, where

    (a) any person acquires, whether by a series of transactions over a period of time or not, shares which (together with shares acquired

by persons acting in concert with him) carry 30% or more of the voting rights of a company, or

(b) any person who, together with persons acting in concert, holds not less than 30% but not more than 50% of the voting rights and such person, together with persons acting in concert, acquires in any period of 12 months additional shares increasing such percentage of the voting rights by more.than 2%,

such person shall extend an offer on the basis set out below to the holders of any class of share capital which carries votes and in which such person or persons acting in concert hold shares. In addition to such person, each of the principal members of the group of persons acting in concert may, according to the circumstances of the case, have the obligation to extend an offer. A comparable offer shall be extended to the holders of any other class of equity share capital whether such capital carries voting rights or not.

(2) Any offer under this Rule must, if appropriate, contain the provision as to reference to the Monopolies and Mergers Commission required under Rule 9. Apart from the foregoing and the provisions of paragraph (3) below, except with the consent of the Panel, any acquisition of shares which might give rise to a requirement for an offer under the provisions of this Rule must not be made if the implementation of such offer would or might be dependent on the passing of a resolution at any meeting of shareholders of the offeror or upon any other conditions, consents or arrangements.

(3) Offers made under this Rule shall be conditional upon the offeror having received acceptances in respect of shares which, together with shares acquired or agreed to be acquired before or during the offer, will result in the offeror and persons acting in concert holding shares carrying more than 50% of the voting rights but shall be subject to no other conditions, except as required by paragraph (2) above. It follows that the offer shall be unconditional as to acceptances where the offeror and persons acting in concert hold shares carrying more than 50% of the voting rights before such offer is made.

(4) The offer required to be made under the provisions of this Rule shall, in respect of each class of share capital involved, be in cash or be accompanied by a cash alternative at not less than the highest price (excluding stamp duty and commission) paid by the offeror and persons acting in concert for shares of that class within the preceding 12 months; where any such shares have been acquired for a consideration other than cash General Principle 8 may be relevant and the Panel should be consulted. The Panel should also be consulted as to the offer to be made for any class of share capital in respect of which no acquisitions

have taken place within the preceding 12 months or where there is more than one class of share capital involved. If the offeror considers that the highest price (as defined above) should not apply to a particular case, the offeror should consult the Panel which will have discretion to agree an adjusted price.

(5) Immediately upon an acquisition of shares which gives rise to an obligation to make an offer under this Rule, the offeror shall make an announcement of his offer giving the information required by the Code.

The announcement of an offer under this Rule should include confirmation by the financial adviser or by another appropriate independent party that resources are available to the offeror sufficient to satisfy full acceptance of the offer.

(6) Except with the consent of the Panel, no nominee of the offeror or persons acting in concert shall be appointed to the board of the offeree company, nor shall the offeror and persons acting in concert transfer, or exercise the votes attaching to, any shares held in the offeree company, until the offer document has been posted.

(Previous references at pages 75, 78, 79, 86, 93–7, 98–9, 103, 107, 108–9, 110 and 178)

Rule 34, taken with the definition of persons acting in concert and with the long Practice Note 8 on the interpretation of Rule 34, is almost a code in itself. Because of the serious financial consequences that follow from its operation, the interpretation of Rule 34 occupies the attention of the Panel executive and of practitioners more than any other provision of the Code.

The typical take-over bid involves a transaction between the offeror and the individual shareholder of the offeree company. Rule 34 requires anyone who has either (i) acquired shares carrying 30 per cent or more of the voting rights of a company or (ii) having between 30 per cent and 50 per cent of the voting rights, acquired more than 2 per cent in twelve months to extend an offer to other shareholders with voting rights at the highest price he paid for those shares in the previous twelve months. 'Anyone' includes persons acting in concert. The bidder has to make an offer to the holders of any class of share capital which carries votes and in which the bidder or persons acting in concert with him hold shares. If for example the bidder holds both ordinary shares and preference shares which have votes (either always or because the dividends on the preference shares are in arrears) then he must make an offer for the preference shares as well as for the ordinary shares. Shareholders cannot waive this right. They cannot say, either unanimously or by a majority, that they are content that someone should hold 30 per cent of the shares and that he does not need to make an offer for the remaining shares. The shareholders may reject the offer but the offer has to be made. There are certain limited circumstances in which shareholders can set aside a Rule 34 obligation, but they are cases in which shareholders are performing acts in the name of the company, not cases in which shareholders are acting simply as shareholders. The Rule is notable for the discretion vested in the Panel to settle a number of issues.

ACQUISITIONS THAT TRIGGER A BID

The Rule is concerned with acquisitions. It does not impose any obligation to make a bid as a consequence of the mere holding of shares. There are many companies where persons, or persons acting in concert, hold more than 30 per cent, either because they already had this holding before the Code obligation arose or because of partial offers or other reasons.

Rule 34(3) refers to shares acquired or agreed to be acquired. The latter part is intended to allow an offeror to include shares which he has contracted to purchase in the market but for which he has not yet paid. It is not intended in the ordinary course to include irrevocable commitments to acquire.

Logically it could be argued that, if effective control is already secured at 30 per cent, then no obligations should attach to a person who already has 30 per cent and goes on to acquire further shares. In fact, the figure of 30 per cent is necessarily arbitrary. What percentage of shares gives effective control depends in any individual case on the disposition of the remaining shares. If the shares are dispersed among many small holders, 10 per cent might give effective control: whereas 30 per cent would not give control against a block of 35 per cent or more. The Panel might relieve the acquirer of 30 per cent of shares of his obligation to make a bid, if he was faced with a 51 per cent holder who said that in no circumstances would he sell. Experience has shown that there are cases—sufficiently numerous to matter—where the holder of 30 per cent is prepared to pay a premium to secure shares that increase his holding and so his degree of control. It was for this reason that in 1974 anyone holding between 30 per cent and 50 per cent became liable to make a mandatory bid if he acquired a further 1 per cent in any period of 12 months—a figure which was increased to 2 per cent in 1976. When someone is already in possession of more than 50 per cent of the voting rights, or has acquired more than 50 per cent as a result of a bid, further acquisitions do not give rise to an obligation to make a mandatory bid. This situation often exists in old-established family businesses.

If a mandatory offer under Rule 34 has lapsed owing to lack of enough acceptances or for some other reason, the purchase of more than 2 per cent (which would spark off an obligation to make a further offer) runs from the date when the offer lapsed. Purchases before that date do not count. A major shareholder who joined a company board and brought the total per cent holdings of board members above 30 per cent would not create an obligation to make a bid. An offeror proceeding under Rule 21 may render himself liable to a mandatory bid under Rule 34 by reason of the acquisition of shares during the offer period. Where this happens, the offer must normally be recast to comply with Rule 34—there must be an immediate announcement, a circular to shareholders and there can be no conditions other than the need to secure at least 50 per cent of the voting shares and clearance in respect of reference to the Monopolies and Mergers Commission. The acquisitions considerably alter the position of the offeree shareholder since he is now faced with an offeror in control of the company. Accordingly the offer has to remain open for at least 14 days from the notification of the acquisitions that triggered off the Rule 34 obligation and this means that acquisitions triggering off Rule 34 cannot be made after the 46th day of a Rule 21 bid. The offeror, having incurred the Rule 34 obligation, can acquire as many further shares as he wishes, though the price at which he buys may affect his bid price.

PERSONS ACTING IN CONCERT

As pointed out in the definition of acting in concert, this is of great importance in the application of Rule 34.

Directors. As indicated in the definition, a company is presumed to be acting in concert with any of its directors (together with their close relatives and related trusts); but a director is not necessarily assumed to be acting in concert with other directors in relation to the company of which he is a director. Practice Note 8 says:

> Directors of a company are not presumed to be acting in concert in relation to control of the company of which they are directors, but their position may need to be closely examined by the Panel. Directors who are not acting in concert would be free, subject to other general restraints, to deal in shares of their company subject to the normal application of Rule 34 to the holdings each controls.
>
> However, during the course of an offer, or even before the date of the offer if the directors of the company have reason to believe that a *bona fide* offer might be imminent, the directors of that company would normally be presumed to be acting in concert if shares were then purchased and the normal provisions of Rule 34 would apply.
>
> If shareholders, who have indicated their support for the offeree company's directors against an offer, thereafter buy shares to frustrate the offer, the Panel would have to consider their position in relation to the directors and also in the context of Rule 37 (frustration of offers by persons with commercial

interests). The directors of companies defending against an offer, their supporters or their advisers, should consult the Panel before the purchase of any shares which might lead to a frustration of that offer.

Shareholders. In regard to offeror shareholders, Practice Note 8 points out:

Acting in concert requires the co-operation of two or more parties. Where a party has purchased shares without the knowledge of other shareholders or potential shareholders, but subsequently joins together with other shareholders to co-operate to obtain or consolidate control of a company and their existing shareholdings amount to 30% or more of that company, the Panel would not normally require a general offer to be made under Rule 34. Such parties having once joined together, however, the provisions of Rule 34 would apply so that

(a) if the combined shareholdings amounted to less than 30 per cent of that company, an obligation to make an offer would arise if any member of that group bought further shares so that the total shareholdings reached 30%,
(b) if the combined shareholdings amounted to between 30% and 50% of that company, no member of that group could buy shares which would result in the purchases of the group amounting to more than 2% of that company in any 12 month period without incurring a similar obligation.

Where a group of offeree shareholders indicate that they support the offeree directors in opposing a bid, that does not bring them within Rule 34, even if their holdings exceed 30 per cent. There could, however, come a point, e.g. through the acquisition of shares, where such shareholders were to be regarded as acting in concert with the board and the group would then become offerors by virtue of the Rule. Practice Note 8 summarizes the position as follows:

The Panel would not normally regard the action of shareholders voting together on particular resolutions as action which of itself should lead to an offer obligation, but it might in certain circumstances hold that such joint action indicated that there was a group acting in concert with the result that subsequent purchases by any member of the group could give rise to such an obligation.

Acquisition of Further Shares. If there is no change of controller, no Rule 34 obligation arises. Thus one wholly owned subsidiary can transfer a holding to another wholly owned subsidiary without thereby incurring an obligation to make a bid. Practice Note 8 sets out the general position as follows:

While the Panel accepts that the concept of persons acting in concert recognises a group as being the equivalent of a single shareholder, the membership of such groups may change at any time. This being the case, there will be circumstances when the acquisition of shares by one member of a group acting in concert from either another member or from a person who is not a member will result in the acquirer of shares have an obligation to make an offer. Whenever the holdings of a group acting in concert total 30% or more and as a result of a transfer or acquisition of shares a single member of the group acting in concert comes to hold 30% or more or, if already holding over 30% has acquired more than 2%, these are the factors which the Panel will take into account in considering whether to grant a dispensation from the requirement to make an offer:

(a) whether the leader of the group or the largest individual shareholder has changed and whether the balance between the shareholdings in the group has changed significantly;
(b) the price paid for the shares acquired;
(c) the relationship between the persons acting in concert and how long they have been acting in concert.

Where the group holds between 30% and 50% there will be an offer obligation if there are purchases of more than 2% by members of the group from non-members in any 12 month period. Where the group holds over 50% no obligations arise from purchases by any member of the group.

For the purpose of calculating the highest price paid in the event of an offer under Rule 34 the prices paid for shares transferred between members of a group acting in concert may be relevant, where, for example, all shares held within a group are transferred to that member making the offer or where prices paid between members are materially above the market price.

Sale of Part of Holding. Cases that give rise to considerable difficulty are where a shareholder with a controlling interest, sells part of his holding (up to 29 per cent) to another person. Are they acting in concert, so that a bid should now be made? The manner in which the Panel handles these cases was clarified in a revision of Practice Note No. 8 issued in December 1978.

Shareholders sometimes wish to sell part only of their shareholding or a purchaser may be prepared to purchase only part of a shareholding. This arises particularly where a purchaser wishes to acquire just under 30%, thereby avoiding an obligation under Rule 34 to make a general offer. The Panel will be concerned to see whether in such circumstances the vendor is acting in concert with the purchaser in such a way as effectively to allow the purchaser to exercise a significant degree of control over the retained shares, in which case a general offer would normally be required. A judgment on whether such significant degree of control exists will obviously depend on the circumstances of each individual case but by way of guidance the Panel would regard the following points as having some significance:

(a) there would be less likelihood of a significant degree of control over the retained shares if the vendor was not an 'insider';
(b) the payment of a very high price for the shares would tend to suggest that control over the entire holding was being secured;
(c) if the parties negotiate options over the retained shares it may be more difficult for them to satisfy the Panel that a significant degree of control

is absent. On the other hand, where the retained shares are in themselves a significant part of the company's capital (or even in certain circumstances represent a significant sum of money in absolute terms) a correspondingly greater element of independence may be presumed;

(d) it would be natural for a vendor of part of a controlling holding to select a purchaser whose ideas as regards the way the company is to be directed are reasonably compatible with his own. It is also natural that a purchaser of a substantial holding in a company should press for board representation and perhaps make the vendor's support for this a condition of purchase. Accordingly these factors, divorced from any other evidence of a significant degree of control over the retained shares would not lead the Panel to conclude that a general offer should be made.

Responsibility for making offer. In the normal case, where a potential offeror is operating with persons acting in concert, there is an obvious leader on whom lies the obligation to make a bid. But this is not always so. Before 1976 Rule 34 placed the obligation to make a bid simply on the person who acquired 30 per cent, though the Panel interpreted the Rule as placing some responsibility on persons acting in concert. Sub-paragraph (1) of the present (1976) Rule assumes that there is a leader on whom the obligation falls, but it adds 'In addition to such person, each of the principal members of the group of persons acting in concert may, according to the circumstances of the case, have the obligation to extend an offer.' The reference to 'principal members' excludes not only small shareholders but also wives, relatives and others brought within the net of persons acting in concert who could not reasonably be expected to accept the responsibility if the principals fell away. The reference to 'the circumstances of the case' is a pointer in the same direction.

Strictly speaking, the responsibility rests with the person who makes the acquisition, however small, that takes the holding beyond 30 per cent. Practice Note 8 puts the matter as follows:

The prime responsibility for making an offer under Rule 34 normally attaches to the person who acquires those shares, the acquisition of which imposes the obligation to make an offer. If such acquirer is not a principal member of the group of persons acting in concert, then the obligation to make an offer may attach to the principal member or members and, in exceptional circumstances, to other members of the group acting in concert. This could include a member of the group who at the time when the obligation arises does not hold any shares.

Experience has shown that circumstances vary so much that it is not possible to be more precise than in the 1976 Code. This illustrates the difficulty that would arise in dealing equitably with the responsibility for making a bid, in all possible circumstances, if the matter had to be handled by statute law with a precise statement of liabilities.

SPECIAL CLASSES OF SECURITIES

In general, the *acquisition* of convertible securities, warrants and options does not give rise to an obligation under Rule 34 to make a general offer. If, however, the acquisition of an option were to be accompanied by an agreement that the holder of the shares would meantime act as the option-holder wished, then an obligation under Rule 34 would probably arise. *The exercise of any conversion or subscription rights* would be an acquisition of shares for the purpose of Rule 34 and the Panel is reluctant to give any dispensation from the obligation to make a bid in such cases.

However, the purpose of the Rule is to protect the rest of the shareholders and if they have approved the issue of convertible stock or warrants or a share option scheme for (say) senior management and the board, then conversion or the exercise of subscription rights by those who obtained them when the issue was made would not trigger off a bid. This would not apply to stock subsequently acquired: and if stock is subsequently acquired the total holding of the person concerned is considered.

If a shareholder holds between 30 per cent and 50 per cent and there is an issue of new shares, he can take up sufficient of his rights to maintain his percentage holding without triggering a bid. He cannot, however, do this by purchases, in the market or otherwise, beyond 2 per cent per annum, without having to make a bid. Further detail about convertible securities, warrants and options in relation to Rule 34 is contained in Practice Note 8.

PLACINGS

The Panel is sometimes asked whether it is possible for a purchaser to acquire 30 per cent or more on condition that he undertakes to sell sufficient shares within a reasonable period of time to reduce his holding to below 30 per cent. Practice Note 8 summarizes the attitude of the Panel as follows:

Only in the most exceptional circumstances will the Panel consider granting such a dispensation. The Panel would, however, consider waiving the requirements of Rule 34 where arrangements have been made for the placing of sufficient shares to reduce the holding to below 30% prior to the purchase of 30% or more. In such cases the Panel will be concerned to ensure that none of the placees is acting in concert with the purchaser; for example, an obligation under Rule 34 would not be avoided by placing the shares with a number of persons having a common link, e.g. the discretionary clients of a bank or stockbroker, where that bank or stockbroker is acting in concert with the purchaser.

If a holding involving a mandatory bid has been built up by inadvertence, the Panel may waive the obligation on the understanding that the holding is reduced below 30 per cent. The dispersal must, of course, be to unconnected parties. If the offeror has decided to restrict his holding to some figure, the names of any placees who have agreed to accept the shares offered above the figure should be named in the offer document and details of the arrangements should be given.

WHITEWASH BY SHAREHOLDERS

The object of Rule 34 is to ensure that all shareholders have an opportunity to share in the extra value that shares possess which give the holder control of a company (taken to be 30 per cent or more). Rule 34 gives this opportunity to every shareholder and in the ordinary way a shareholder cannot be deprived of this right, even by a majority vote of his fellow-shareholders. There are, however, certain limited circumstances, in which it is thought to be reasonable, before control is obtained, to allow a majority of votes to approve what is proposed: and thereafter the Panel may waive the requirement to make a general offer. The common feature in all these cases is that they involve decisions by shareholders on company business. Thus they can arise as a result of the issue of new shares as consideration for an acquisition or for a cash subscription. Also in cases involving the underwriting of a rights issue and the underwriting of shares issued as consideration for an acquisition. Also loans given by finance houses on condition that there is an option to acquire equity capital at a later stage. The exercise of options may lead to a Rule 34 obligation unless the grant of the option was approved by a general meeting of shareholders. Of these, the most important is clearly the issue of shares as consideration for the acquisition of assets.

In these cases there must be prior consultation with the Panel by the parties concerned or their advisors; and a proof of the document to be sent to shareholders, before the general meeting to approve a transaction of this kind, has to be submitted at an early stage to the Panel.

The Panel will normally expect the circular to comply with Rules 13 to 17 and 19, references to offeror and offeree being interpreted to refer respectively to the potential controlling shareholder and to the company he will control. The circular should contain full details of the potential shareholding, which (if less than 50 per cent) cannot be further increased before the shareholders' meeting. Where the potential controlling shareholding may exceed 50 per cent of the voting rights, specific reference should be made to this possibility and to the fact that the controlling shareholder may increase his shareholding without incurring any further obligation under Rule 34 to make a general offer. The circular should also give competent independent advice on the proposal which the shareholders are being asked to approve, also a statement (if it be the case) that subject to shareholders' approval the Panel has agreed to waive any consequential obligation under Rule 34 to make a general offer.

The Panel's consent to a waiver of the Rule 34 requirement is subject to the approval of the proposals by the independent vote, on a poll, at meetings of the holders of any relevant class of share or loan capital, whether or not such meetings need to be convened to approve the issue of the securities in question. The Panel's consent is also subject to the disenfranchisement at such meetings of the prospective controller, those acting in concert with him and any other interested party.

Shareholdings in a company may be diluted following the issue by that company of new shares and normally the shareholding may not be restored to its original level without incurring an obligation to make a general offer if it has been reduced below 30 per cent or, if not, where restoration results in the acquisition of more than 2 per cent of the voting capital as enlarged taking into account any shares purchased during the previous 12 months. The Panel is, however, prepared to consider waiving the requirements of the Rule if an arrangement is made whereby shareholders, when authorizing the issue of new shares, approve the restoration of a diluted holding by purchases from those to whom new shares are issued. The purchase of further shares may invalidate a waiver given by the Panel in these circumstances.

Practice Note 9 contains the following statement: 'The approval of independent shareholders to the transfer of existing shares from one shareholder to another may on occasion, with the consent of the Panel, justify waiving the requirement for a general offer.' This is intended to cater for highly exceptional cases, such as a transfer following a death. Over a period of years it has in fact been used only in one or two cases.

TWO STAGE ACQUISITION OF CONTROL

Control of a company may be secured by the purchase of shares until the purchaser has just short of 30 per cent of the voting rights to be followed shortly thereafter (in agreement with the board of the company) by the issue of shares to that purchaser (or to persons acting in concert) in exchange for assets or funds injected into the company. Notwithstanding that the issue of the new shares is made conditional upon the prior approval of a majority of the shareholders independent of the transaction at a general meeting of the company and that the purchase of the original shareholding was not in any way conditional upon the issue of the new shares, the Panel will normally only extend the exemption from the obligation to make a general offer under Rule 34 if it is satisfied that there were no negotiations or understandings with the directors of the company relating to the asset or fund injection and the issue of the new shares before the most recent share purchase.

THE CHAIN PRINCIPLE

Where an offeree company holds 30 per cent or more of another company, or holds shares in another company which when added to the shares of that other company held by the offeror would result in the offeror's holding being more than 30 per cent, or, if over 30 per cent already, would increase the holding by more than 2 per cent, the Panel will not normally require an offer to be made under Rule 34. An offer would be required, however, if the holding of the offeree company constituted a substantial part of the assets of the offeree company or when the acquisition of the offeree company's holding was the main purpose of the acquisition of the offeree company itself. Thus in 1977 when Caparo Investments which owned 28 per cent of Singlo Holdings made a bid for Empire Plantations and Investments which owned 23 per cent of Singlo, Caparo was told that if the bid for Empire was successful (which it was not) it would have to make an offer to the remaining shareholders of Singlo. The Panel has to be consulted in all such cases to establish whether any obligation arises under the Rule in the circumstances.

RESCUE OPERATIONS

There are occasions when a potential offeree company is in such a serious financial position that the only way it can be saved is by an urgent rescue operation which involves the issue of new shares not to be approved by an independent vote of shareholders or the acquisition of existing shares by the rescuer which would otherwise fall within the provisions of Rule 34 and normally require a general offer. The Panel will, however, consider waiving the requirements of the Rule in such circumstances and particular attention will be paid to the comments of the directors and advisers of the potential offeree company.

The requirements of the Rule would not normally be waived, however, in a case where a major shareholder in a company rather than that company itself is in need of rescue. The situation of that shareholder may have little relevance to the position of other shareholders and therefore the purchaser from such major shareholder can expect to be obliged to extend an offer under this Rule to all other shareholders.

RULES

REFERENCE TO MONOPOLIES AND MERGER COMMISSION

The effect of Rule 9 is that any offer made under Rule 34 which is referred to the Monopolies Commission must lapse immediately. However, the obligation under this Rule to make an offer does not lapse on the reference and accordingly, if thereafter the decision of the Government is to allow the merger, the offer must be reinstated on the same terms and at the same price as soon as practicable. If the decision of the Government is not to allow the merger, the offer cannot be made and, if the Government has not so ordered, the Panel will have to consider whether to require the offeror to reduce his holding to below 30 per cent or to its original level before the obligation to offer was incurred if that was 30 per cent or more. The Panel would normally expect an offeror, whose offer has been referred to the Monopolies Commission, to proceed with due diligence before the Commission. However, if, after a reference, with the consent of the Panel, an offeror sells to parties unconnected with it within a limited period those shares, the acquisition of which caused it to incur an offer obligation, the Panel will regard the offer obligation as having lapsed.

If an offeror under this Rule requires prior clearance, for example, under the Treaty of Paris, before he can proceed with his offer, the Panel will require the offer document to be posted as soon as clearance has been received. If clearance is not given, the same consideration will apply as if the Government did not allow a merger to proceed. The Code does not forbid an offeror acquiring without such prior clearance shares which will give rise to an obligation to make a general offer under this Rule.

EXTENT OF OFFER

Where a person acquires shares with voting rights of 30 per cent or more, or adds more than 2 per cent if the holding is between 30 per cent and 50 per cent, then he has to make

(1) an offer for any class of share capital
   (a) which carries votes and
   (b) in which the person in question of any person acting in concert holds shares;
   at not less than the highest price (excluding stamp duty and commission) paid by the offeror and persons acting in concert for shares of that class within the preceding twelve months.
(2) a comparable offer for any other class of equity share capital whether such capital carries voting rights or not.

Practice Note 9 contains the following passage: 'If a general offer under Rule 34 has been made during the previous 12 months, shares purchased before or during that offer period will not be included in the calculation of the 2%.'

OFFER IN CASH

The offer must be in cash, or, if in paper, be accompanied by a cash alternative at the highest price (excluding stamp duty and commission) paid by the offeror and persons acting in concert for shares of that class within the preceding twelve months. One of the objects of Rule 34 is to enable the offeree shareholder to get completely clear of the offeror and this would not be achieved if the sole consideration consisted in whole or in part of the offeror's paper. Any offer consisting only of paper would involve the Panel in the invidious task of determining the exact value of the paper.

In some cases, the obligation is not as onerous as might seem. The most that has to be offered for the remaining shares is the highest price that was paid for 30 per cent. Rule 21 assumes that the full premium price for voting control is not reached till you buy 50 per cent or more of the shares. Purchases in the market during the currency of the bid are compared with the cash offer, not with any alternative paper offer even if the latter has a higher value.

CONDITIONS OF OFFER

The Rule endeavours to ensure that anyone who has incurred an obligation to make an offer cannot escape by hedging his offer with conditions that may not be fulfilled. In fact, before 1974, offers had to be unconditional in respect of the number of acceptances received. Rule 9 applies: i.e. there should be a condition that the offer will lapse if there is a reference to the Monopolies and Mergers Commission and the offer document should not be dispatched until there is a clearance, if that is relevant, under the Treaty of Paris. If the offer is referred to the Commission and is subsequently allowed, then the offer has to be implemented.

Difficulty has arisen in the past where a mandatory bid involved an increase in authorized capital by the offeror, a matter which normally requires shareholders' approval. If the offeror board was no longer keen on the bid, the shareholders' meeting provided an opportunity for killing it. Save with the consent of the Panel, the Rule does not allow acquisitions of shares which would give rise to a mandatory bid, if the implementation of the offer depends on a subsequent authorization of an increase in share capital by the offeror shareholders. The only other condition allowed, and indeed compelled, in a mandatory bid is that the offer will be conditional on the offeror and persons acting in concert ending up with more than 50 per cent of the voting rights. It follows that if the offeror and his friends already have more than 50 per cent the offer must be unconditional as to acceptances from the outset.

WITHDRAWAL OF MANDATORY OFFERS

The strong line taken by the Panel in 1974 (p. 85) that announced bids and particularly mandatory bids must be proceeded with resulted in General Principles 13 and 14 and a continuing tough attitude on this subject. Occasionally a case arises where it is manifest that the offeror is not able to proceed with a bid. The history of the Ashbourne case illustrates how reluctant the Panel is to accept this state of affairs. In 1975 a private investment company, Alco Metropolitan Properties, which held 33.2 per cent of the voting shares in Scotia Investments acquired a block of shares amounting to a further 26.9 per cent and announced that they would make a Rule 34 offer for the remaining shares. Subsequently they found that in such circumstances holders of Scotia convertible loan stock could require repayment at par and Alco were unable to meet this further commitment. The Panel in a statement dated 15 May 1975 censured the directors of Alco for not having considered the loan stock position. They were required to sell the 26.9 per cent block of Scotia shares, to offer them in the first instance to the rest of the Scotia shareholders and to have this offer underwritten for cash.

Rule 35

Except with the consent of the Panel, where an offer has been announced or posted but has not become unconditional in all respects the offeror and persons acting in concert with it may not within 12 months from the date on which such offer is withdrawn or lapses either

(1) *make an offer for the offeree company,*
or
(2) *acquire any shares of the offeree company if the offeror or persons acting in concert with it would thereby become obliged under Rule 34 to make an offer.*

(Previous reference at page 97)

This is one of several provisions in the Code designed to ensure that a company is not kept under prolonged siege by take-over bids. It should be noted that the Rule applies to announced offers that are withdrawn as well as to posted offers that are withdrawn or fail. The application to announced offers is sometimes overlooked. In the past Rule 22 was interpreted to mean that an offer which had not become unconditional in the offer period could not be replaced by a new offer except with the permission of the Panel. The practice had been to say that a failed offeror should not make a further offer for at least six months. This was extended to twelve months and put into Rule 35 in April 1976. The second part of the Rule is older and dates from the Code revision of June 1974. A failed offeror might be allowed to make a fresh offer within twelve months if someone else made an offer within that period or if the offeree board agreed with the new offer. An offeror who made an offer that went unconditional can, after the expiry of his original offer, make a fresh offer to the remaining shareholders. The terms can be an improvement on the terms previously accepted by the other shareholders and the new terms are not of course open to the acceptors of the original offer. Or, if the market has turned down, he can give less favourable terms.

The reference of a bid to the Monopolies and Mergers Commission raises some problems under the Rule. The offer will have lapsed on the announcement of the reference but can be reinstated if the Commission gives a clearance. The Rule would apply if after a clearance the offeror did not proceed within a reasonable period (normally within three weeks) to renew his bid. He would be given a rather longer period in which to enter the field again, if another offer appeared. In the ordinary case, if it looks as though the offer is going to fail, an offeror may not tell accepting shareholders that they can withdraw their acceptances and sell their shares to the offeror if they so wish. Immediately after the failure of his offer, an offeror may not offer to buy shares from those who accepted. If, on the other hand, the offer has gone unconditional, the offeror can buy shares from any remaining minority shareholders.

Rule 36

Except with the consent of the Panel, the offeror or persons acting in concert with it may not enter into arrangements to deal or make purchases or sales of shares of the offeree company, either during an offer or when one is reasonably in contemplation, if such arrangements to deal, purchases or sales have attached thereto favourable conditions which are not being extended to all shareholders.

(Previous reference at page 101)

This Rule is the application to a particular set of circumstances of General Principles 8 and 9. The words 'except with the consent of the Panel' were introduced in 1976. The application of the Rule was analysed at some length in the Panel's 1978/9 report. A common case with which the Rule was intended to deal was referred to in the Panel's reports for 1969/70 and 1973/4, namely an arrangement by which the offeror or potential offeror promises to make good to a vendor of shares (usually a large holder of shares) any difference between the sale price and the price of any subsequent successful offer or increased offer. The Panel frowns on this, even if an offeror purports to be willing to pay the offer price to all other shareholders from whom they acquire shares after the date of the special deal. Even if the arrangement purports to be given to all shareholders, this cannot in fact happen since there would be other vendors selling shares at the same time or later without the benefit of the condition. Not only are these other vendors being treated unfairly, but the removal of a block of shares on special terms could discourage a potential competitive offeror who might make a better offer. It has proved to be difficult to stop efforts to resort to this practice. Cases arise from time to time. In the spring of 1977 the Panel agreed that the attention of institutional shareholders should be drawn to the fact that the practice was contrary to Rule 36.

There are many variants which offend against the Rule. Thus a potential offeror would not be allowed to make an arrangement with the holder of a substantial block of shares that the latter will accept any public offer that the potential offeror may make and the potential offeror undertakes to buy the shares at the future offer price if the offer fails. This is contrary to the Rule and has the additional objection that it is the same as an attempt by an offeror to buy shares from acceptors of an unsuccessful offer. In effect that would be akin to allowing an offer to go unconditional at below 50 per cent acceptances.

Likewise an arrangement would not be allowed where a potential offeror obtained commitments from offeree shareholders to accept an offer at or above a stated figure, with the understanding that they could put their shares on the potential offeror if the bid was withdrawn, nor one in which the advisor to an offeror bought offeree shares as a principal, with an indemnity from the offeror against any loss but with the chance of taking any profit there might be. If a purchase of shares takes place when there is no bid on the horizon, the purchaser may enter into an agreement to pay the difference between what he paid and what he would have got under some future offer. There is no offer and none is reasonably in contemplation, so the Rule does not apply, but the Panel has here to be convinced that the purchaser was not contemplating a bid.

The Rule covers cases where a favour, exclusive to the vendor, is part of the transaction. These favours may not easily be quantifiable in money terms. In considering what are favourable conditions, attention is focused on the position of the other shareholders of the offeree company rather than on the vendor of the shares. There have been cases where a benefit restricted to the vendor has been allowed because it was not obvious that the other shareholders were being damnified. One such case was where a shareholder had assisted a company by guaranteeing a loan. When an offeror bought his shares and it was a condition of the sale that he should be relieved of his guarantee it was agreed that the shareholders had benefited from the guarantee and it would be hard to say that they should also benefit from its cancellation. There have been cases of agreed offers where some of the offeree company's assets were of no interest to the offeror and arrangements had to be made for their prior disposal, often to an existing shareholder. These have been allowed provided that the independent advisers to the offeree company under Rule 4 publicly stated that the terms were fair and reasonable and that the transaction was put to a vote of a shareholders' meeting. At that meeting the vote must be on a poll and interested parties disenfranchised.

The Rule also covers cases where a shareholder in an offeree company is to be remunerated for the part he has played in promoting the take-over. This was examined in a statement issued by the Panel on 19 July 1978 in the bid of Moolaya for Customagic. The level of remuneration should be no greater than the shareholder would have been entitled to receive for the same services if he had not been a shareholder.

The offeror may wish to arrange for the management of the offeree company to remain financially involved in the business. The methods by which this may be achieved vary; but the point of principle that the Panel tries to observe in considering such a scheme is that the risks as well as the rewards associated with an equity shareholding should apply to the management's retained interest. Thus the Panel would not normally find acceptable an option arrangement which guaranteed the original offer price as a minimum.

Rule 37

Since dealings in the market or otherwise by a person with a commercial interest in the outcome of an offer may result in a bona fide offer being frustrated or may affect the outcome of an offer, such person must consult the Panel in advance and be prepared to justify his proposed action as not being prejudicial to the interests of the shareholders as a whole.
(Previous references at pages 74 and 79)

As was pointed out by the Panel in its public statement of 6 January 1972 on the Venesta case, the Rule is intended to prevent the frustration of a bone fide offer by a third party whose interests are not shared by the general body of shareholders of the offeree company. Where the third party purchases shares to protect his investment or in the hope of securing an increased offer or a better competing offer his interest is identical with that of the other shareholders. Where, however, his purchases are intended either wholly or partly to protect or promote some other interest—for example an existing trading relationship with the offeree company which he suspects might be detrimentally affected by any transfer of control—the position is different. That is an ulterior purpose in which the rest of the shareholders have no interest and the achievement of which would not necessarily bring them any benefit.

The typical case with which the Rule is intended to deal is where a company with a trading connection with a company which is the subject of a bid fears that, if the bid succeeds, the trading link may be broken and buys shares in the offeree company with the intention of not accepting the bid. Other examples are a company which for its own commercial reasons does not wish to see the offeree company coming under the control of a competitor, and a company which does not wish to see the offeror company enter into the industry or business in which the offeree company is active.

The value of the shares to a purchaser with a commercial interest may bear no relation to the value of the same shares to an ordinary investor. The Rule provides that the Panel should be consulted as difficult problems can arise in some cases. If the company already has a substantial trade investment in the offeree company it may not always be easy to decide whether the company, in buying shares, is endeavouring to protect its investment (which does not come within the Rule) or to further its commercial interest. The need to determine whether the proposed purchase would be 'prejudicial to the interests of the shareholders as a whole' may sometimes involve a difficult value judgement.

The Panel has been reluctant to endeavour to quantify in general terms either the extent of the commercial interest or the size of the share purchase which brings the Rule into operation. Much depends on the circumstances of the individual case. The Rule does not, of course, apply to an offeror or persons acting in concert with him whatever their commercial interest. Although the Rule is generally regarded as operating in relation to the shares of the offeree company, it also applies to dealings in the shares of the offeror.

Rule 38

During the course of an offer, or even before the date of the offer if the board of the offeree company has reason to believe that a bone fide offer might be imminent, the board must not, except in pursuance of a contract entered into earlier, without the approval of the shareholders in general meeting, issue any authorised but unissued shares, or issue or grant options in respect of any

unissued shares, create or issue or permit the creation or issue of any securities carrying rights of conversion into or subscription for shares of the company, or sell, dispose of or acquire or agree to sell, dispose of or acquire assets of material amount or enter into contracts otherwise than in the ordinary course of business. Where it is felt that an obligation or other special circumstance exists, although a formal contract has not been entered into, the Panel must be consulted and its consent obtained.
(Previous references at pages 39, 56, 108 and 141)

This Rule has remained unaltered—save for a small verbal change—since 1969. It was designed to prevent the various devices by which some boards of offeree companies endeavoured to thwart bids and indeed in some cases to prevent a bid coming before their own shareholders or circumvent a decision of their shareholders in favour of a bid. The requests for advice come from offeree boards, wishing to ensure that the offeror will not be able to argue that Rule 38 has been broken. Most of the rulings relate to the disposal of assets of the offeree company or to the granting of service contracts to directors and staff. The offeree board may have decided, before they knew of the bid, to pay a larger dividend than usual or to have a rights issue—how that would be treated would depend on the circumstances of the case. The issue of capital to dilute the holding of the offeror would not be allowed, nor the use of funds to redeem preference shares, even if they were non-voting shares, not covered by the offer.

There are problems of interpretation. When might an offer be imminent? (Here an effort is made to keep in step with the administration of Rule 30.) What is the ordinary course of business? (Much depends on the nature of the business.) When are assets of material amount? (A guideline of 10 per cent of gross assets is useful but each case depends on its individual circumstances.)

The Rule deals with a variety of specific transactions that are regarded as unethical. An offeree board is entitled to oppose a bid by all the means in its power, provided that it acts fairly. The spirit of Rule 38 might be invoked in appropriate cases to prevent unethical conduct. For example (i) An offeree board might provide an offeror with a register of shareholders which is known to be defective or out of date. (ii) As part of its defences, an offeree board may distribute a large interim dividend with a view to showing how profitable the business is under their management and possibly with a view to raising the share price. In certain circumstances this might be regarded as contravening the spirit of Rule 38. In addition, it might create problems for the offeror, if he is successful in his bid. He might find that cash has been depleted and he might be paying too high a price for the remaining assets. He might also be regarded as failing to give effect to a statement that he did not intend to increase his offer, if shareholders are allowed to retain a special dividend declared after that statement. Occasionally a bidder may say that the amount he is offering per share will be reduced by the amount of any interim dividend.

Where a bid is referred to the Monopolies and Mergers Commission, Rule 38 is regarded as applying during the time occupied by the reference and by the subsequent consideration by Ministers. If, at any time during the offer period, before the posting of the offer document, the offeree company passes a resolution in general meeting, as envisaged by the Rule, the offeror may consider that the situation has been changed to his disadvantage. In such circumstances, the Panel may allow the offeror not to proceed with the offer.

Rule 39

The board and officials of an offeree company should take action to ensure during a take-over or merger transaction the prompt registration of transfers so that shareholders can freely exercise their voting and other rights. Provisions in Articles of Association which lay down a qualifying period after registration during which the registered holder cannot exercise his vote are highly undesirable.

This Rule has remained unchanged since the first edition of the Code in 1968.

The need for prompt registration flows from the desire not to fetter the market in shares.

There may be delays in registration from special causes, but the cases are few. Where there are partly-paid shares the board may require purchasers to produce evidence that they could meet a call for the unpaid part. In the case of a large purchase of such shares as a launching pad for a bid, Counsel advised one offeree board to 'look for indubitable and unimpeachable guarantees'. The rarity, these days, of partly-paid shares makes the matter of small practical importance. Again, public but unlisted companies may have an article that the transfer of shares is subject to the approval of the board.

As regards delays in allowing registered holders to vote, the articles of a few companies do not give newly registered shareholders an immediate right to vote. A period of three months was mentioned in one case. In the fifties, when companies were trying to fend off bids, a delay of six months between registration and the exercise of a vote was one of the devices canvassed (and sharply criticized in the financial press).

APPENDIX A

The Ashbourne Case

THE Ashbourne case was not of great intrinsic importance, but it occupied the time of the Panel more than any other case and over a longer period of time. Points of interest in the interpretation of the Code and the working of the Panel arose in the course of the lengthy proceedings: and the Panel's experience in the case led to amendments of the Code. Inspectors appointed by the Secretary of State for Trade in July 1975 investigated the affairs of Ashbourne. Their report, published in July 1979, contains a detailed history of the proposed bid by Crest and Corporate for Ashbourne and the subsequent events. The present note is a summary of the facts as they became known to the Panel and of the issues concerning the Code that arose.

On 6 December 1973 Brandts Limited issued a statement that Crest International Securities Ltd., Corporate Guarantee Trust Ltd., and their associates (the Consortium) had that day acquired 1,748,122 ordinary shares in Ashbourne Investments Ltd. from certain directors of Ashbourne at 46p per share and that these shares, added to 2,044,977 shares already held, resulted in the Consortium then holding 43.15 per cent of the ordinary share capital of Ashbourne. Brandts, on behalf of the Consortium, would be making an unconditional cash offer for the balance of the ordinary shares at 46p per share. an offer was also being made for convertible unsecured loan stock.

The directors of Ashbourne, when they sold their shares to Crest and Corporate, accepted the chairman of Crest as chairman of Ashbourne and allowed Crest and Corporate to assume management control of Ashbourne and its subsidiaries. The directors of Ashbourne who had sold their shares on 6th December had an obligation under Rule 10 (now 11) to obtain an undertaking from the Consortium that they would make an offer for the remaining shares at the same price and in any event the Consortium incurred an obligation under Rule 35 (now 34) to make a bid for the remaining shares. Crest and Corporate did not have the resources to implement this obligation.

APPENDIX A

The other principal member of the Consortium, later revealed to be Mr Bernard Glazer, a South African citizen, regarded his liability as limited in scope. Crest and Corporate relied mainly on Wilstar Securities (a private company owned by Mr William Stern) but also on Brandts to provide the funds, at least at the outset.

All this happened on the eve of the collapse of the property boom and many others, besides those involved in the Ashbourne saga, failed to read the signs of coming events. When Wilstar's difficulties manifested themselves in May 1974, the main prop for the bid had gone and Brandts expressed its inability to see how the bid was to be financed. The statement of 6 December had referred to the intention of the Consortium to merge the banking subsidiary of Ashbourne with the banking companies associated with Crest and Corporate and had said that details of the plans for the future of Ashbourne would be included in the offer document. In the early months of 1974 this and a later plan to merge Crest with Corporate were given as the reasons for delay in the issue of the offer document.

The Take-over Code, as it then existed, said that, if an offeror who had announced his intention to make an offer did not proceed with the formal offer within a reasonable time, he must be prepared to justify the delay to the Panel. As a matter of practice it was usual to expect the offer document to be published within three or four weeks of an announcement but it was accepted that there might be good reasons for delay. It was not till April 1976 that the Code provided that the offer document should normally be posted within twenty-eight days of the announcement. In the spring of 1974 the Panel executive began to press Brandts to get Crest and Corporate to issue the offer document to Ashbourne shareholders. The Panel executive rejected an application for the offerors to be allowed to make a bid at less than 46p per share.

The draft of the offer document went through many revisions but was in a final form by 29 March 1974. It was, however, never issued. On 4 April 1974 a Crest shareholder (Mr David Tannen) started an action in the High Court to restrain Crest from making a general offer for Ashbourne until the Crest shareholders had considered the matter at a general meeting. The Department of Trade Inspectors in their report reached the conclusion that Mr Tannen was giving effect to Mr Casper's wishes in initiating the legal action. The Panel arranged to be entered as joint defendants of the Tannen action, in order to ensure that the case for the bid to proceed would be adequately presented. Crest and Corporate started an action in the High Court against the Ashbourne directors who had sold them 1,748,122 Ashbourne shares, claiming rescission of the purchase on the grounds of misrepresentation of the financial position of Ashbourne at the time of the purchase.

On 21 June 1974 the Court adjourned these latter proceedings *sine die*, in order that the parties might continue negotiations with a view to settlement. These negotiations proved abortive.

At the beginning of April 1974 The Stock Exchange suspended dealings in Crest, Corporate and Ashbourne at the request of these companies, because of the uncertainties facing the bid. The Panel met to consider the Ashbourne situation on 15 July 1974. The Panel took the view that, as negotiations between the parties had broken down, it was essential in the interests of all shareholders that the proceedings against the Ashbourne directors should be restored to the Court list and prosecuted with the maximum possible speed. Mr L. I. Casper, the chairman of Crest, gave an undertaking to the Panel that this would be done. In the meantime, in a statement dated 23 July 1974, the Panel considered that the proper and fairest course, pending the outcome of such proceedings, was for it to direct that the Consortium and the board of Ashbourne should take immediate steps to procure that:

(1) The Consortium's representatives on the Ashbourne board be reduced from four to two.
(2) Mr L. I. Casper stood down as chairman of Ashbourne in favour of a director not associated with the Consortium.
(3) A representative of the Ashbourne Shareholders' Action Committee (which represented some 12 per cent of the issued share capital and which had requisitioned a general meeting of the company for the purpose of removing all the directors) be invited to join the board.
(4) The Consortium should not exercise the voting rights attached to 19.9 per cent of the ordinary shares in Ashbourne (being the shares purchased by them on 6 December 1973) and the Consortium should exercise the voting rights attached to any other shares held by any of them in such a manner as might be appropriate so as to preserve the composition of the board on the above lines.

The Panel reserved its final consideration of the conduct of the parties and the obligations under the Code until the Court proceedings had been concluded.

On 23 July 1974 the Consortium applied for and obtained *ex parte* an interim injunction restraining the Panel from publishing a statement of its findings, but this was not sustained by Mr Justice Kilner Brown when the matter was argued out on 24 July. The Court found that the Panel was activated by concern for the Ashbourne shareholders and not by criticism or condemnation of the Consortium. The Panel was, therefore, free to issue its statement and to see that the steps indicated in it were taken. The argument that the Panel was interfering with property rights beyond its powers was tacitly rejected.

On 24 July solicitors to the Consortium sent a letter to the Panel's solicitors in which they indicated a clear intention on the part of the Consortium not to comply with the provisions of the statement. In particular, they said: 'The statement and directive were ones which our clients, anxious as they have been and still are to co-operate with the Panel, were quite unable to accept. . . . As to voting of shares, our clients could not possibly undertake not to vote their shares . . .'

On 1 August four directors of the Consortium companies, Messrs L. I. Casper, S. H. Ross, S. J. Barry, and B. Simmons, issued a circular to all Ashbourne shareholders which again clearly indicated that the Consortium did not intend to comply with the requirements of the statement. The circular included the following paragraph: 'The Consortium . . . believe that it would be fundamentally contrary to the interests of Ashbourne shareholders and their own shareholders, for the reasons set out in more detail below, to reconstitute the board of Ashbourne as proposed by the Panel and to accept a restriction on the voting rights attached to their shareholding in Ashbourne.'

The non-Consortium directors of Ashbourne, who had a majority on the board, substituted Mr K. F. Suggett for Mr Casper as chairman, added a representative of the Action Committee to the board, and made certain management changes. As indicated above, the Consortium, however, failed to comply with ruling (1) and indicated an intention not to comply with ruling (4).

On 9 August 1974 the Panel rejected an application by the Consortium for leave to appeal to the Appeal Committee against the findings in the statement of 23 July. The findings related to an interpretation and application of the Code and could not be the subject of an appeal because they did not impose serious hardship on the Consortium. The Panel then considered a disciplinary charge which had previously been formulated and given to the Consortium. The Panel found that the Consortium were in breach of the Code and indicated that they would recommend that the facilities of the securities markets should be withheld from the Consortium companies. Faced with this decision, the Consortium decided to comply with the Panel's directions of 23 July. The threat that the Panel would employ its ultimate weapon had prevailed.

On 13 September 1974 the Consortium lodged with the Ashbourne board a requisition for an extraordinary general meeting of Ashbourne to consider various resolutions which would have fettered the authority of the board. On 18 September the Panel announced its ruling that the intention of their statement of 23 July was that the reconstituted Ashbourne board should continue to exercise the powers conferred on them by the Articles of Association in the normal way. Accordingly, the Consortium should vote the shares held by them (other than those purchased on 6 December 1973 which could not be used) against all the proposed resolutions. In the event the EGM was not proceeded with.

A meeting of the Panel was called on 31 October 1974 to consider an application by the parties for the Panel to approve the terms of an agreement to end the litigation between the Consortium and the Ashbourne directors who had sold shares to them. The Panel ruled that it was no part of its function to intervene in litigation and that it could not therefore express an opinion. It was announced on 6 November 1974 that the Consortium had withdrawn their claim in respect of misrepresentation against the Ashbourne directors who had sold shares to them and the Ashbourne directors had withdrawn a counter-claim.

On 21 November Mr Casper addressed a circular to the Ashbourne shareholders attacking the Ashbourne directors and saying that the future prosperity of Ashbourne would be materially improved if the company were again managed 'by those having the greatest interest in its prosperity'. The Panel was advised that the Panel could not consider the Consortium's outstanding obligation to bid for Ashbourne while the Tannen proceedings against Crest and the Panel were still pending. Accordingly, on 27 November 1974 the Panel applied to the Court for an order for a speedy trial of the Tannen actions. It was clear that Mr Tannen had no wish to proceed unless the Panel's measures against Crest were severe. It was explained to Mr Justice Templeman that the Panel were unable to conduct their investigation because of the rules of contempt of Court. The Judge therefore directed that the Panel could hold a hearing (in private, as was its custom) without being in contempt of Court and, depending on the findings and any penalties proposed, it would then be for Mr Tannen to decide whether or not he wished to pursue his action. 'So far as the Court is concerned there is no objection and every advantage in the Panel conducting such investigations as the Panel think fit'. The Panel was not, however, to issue any statement without reference to the Court. Mr Tannen could then decide whether he wanted to continue with the action.

The Panel held meetings in December 1974 in the presence of all the parties to discuss whether a bid obligation still existed, the position of Brandts and the possible courses of action open to the Panel. The annual general meeting of Ashbourne was held on 31 December 1974 and the result was that no Consortium directors were elected to the board, although the Panel had ruled that two should remain. A

Consortium representative was later added to the board at the request of the Panel.

By 25 March 1975 the Panel had drawn up and circulated to all the parties a lengthy statement of the position as the Panel saw it. The Panel decided to hear evidence early in 1975 from Mr Glazer. Mr Glazer had not appeared before the Panel but had sent written statements claiming that his financial obligations were limited to his original commitment. At this stage, the Panel did not know that in November 1973 Mr Casper had entered into an agreement to give Mr Glazer effective control over Ashbourne if the contemplated bid was successful. The Panel considered that there was a joint and several obligation on the members of the Consortium to make the general offer and each was fully liable for its discharge. Mr Glazer and his associated interests had bought some of the original shares, had bought all the shares purchased on 6 December 1973 and had made later purchases. Mr Glazer had, in the Panel's view, been at all material times a member of the Consortium. Under the arrangements made before the bid announcement was made, Mr Glazer, Wilstar, and Brandts were to provide the cash for the Ashbourne shares proffered by shareholders under the proposed general offer. The Panel considered that Wilstar and Brandts had continuing financial obligations, but were not part of the Consortium and not each liable under the then Code to make a general offer in the event of default by Crest, Corporate, or Mr Glazer.

Brandts claimed that they had no outstanding legal obligations and that they had discharged their ethical obligations by the endeavours they had made to get an acceptable offer on its feet. Mr Glazer reiterated the limited extent of the liabilities he had knowingly undertaken and claimed that he could not, in any event, provide further funds because of exchange control difficulties. The Ashbourne directors and other Ashbourne interests pressed the liabilities of Mr Glazer and of Brandts as they saw them.

The Panel met, without witnesses, on 7 May 1975 to consider the position. There had also appeared the first proposals by outsiders that they might make a bid for Ashbourne, though at a less figure than 46p a share. On 12 May 1975, the Panel had a meeting with all the main parties concerned, other than Mr Glazer who had written that he could not attend. No statement was issued, pending a further effort to secure the attendance of Mr Glazer. The Panel had to consider the proposed sale by Ashbourne of a trade investment and the desire of creditors of Crest and Corporat to sell Ashbourne shares held as security. Crest also called for an extraordinary general meeting of Ashbourne to change the board and direct its policy in various respects. On this last point the Panel reiterated in a statement issued on 7 August 1975 that its direction of 23 July 1974 was still binding and that it saw no useful purpose in the calling of an EGM. The Panel then required Crest to vote all the shares it held in Ashbourne against each of the resolutions tabled by Crest at an EGM of Ashbourne on 5 September 1975. The chairman of Crest agreed to this but later declined to confirm his undertaking. The Panel then issued a statement on 27 August 1975 that any failure of a member of the Consortium to comply fully with the statement of 7 August would be regarded as a breach of the Code.

The latter part of 1975 saw a number of developments that substantially altered the situation with which the Panel had to deal. Corporate became insolvent and went into liquidation. Crest, between 15 August and 2 September 1975, sold all its Ashbourne shares to Topview Ltd., acting on behalf of a Mr L. Faust. As a result of representations by Crest, the Department of Trade in July 1975 appointed inspectors under the Companies Act to enquire into the affairs of Ashbourne. Efforts were made by various interests to mount take-over bids for Ashbourne.

The Panel announced on 4 September 1975 that Topview had given assurances that the votes attached to the shares it had acquired from Crest would be exercised at the Ashbourne EGM in favour of the existing composition of the board. Mr Glazer and his associates also agreed to abstain. The EGM was held and the resolutions that had been tabled by Crest defeated. A further complication was introduced in an already very tangled business when the Department of Trade, at the instance of the inspectors investigating Ashbourne, suspended all rights, including those of transfer or voting, relating to 465,500 shares (5.3 per cent of the equity) held to the account of an overseas bank. The inspectors had been unable to discover who were the beneficial owners.

The Panel finalized its views on the case in a statement dated 14 November 1975. Mr Glazer appealed to the Appeal Committee against the findings in relation to him and appeared before the Committee. The statement, amended to take account of the Appeal Committee's views, was cleared with the High Court (because the Tannen action was still outstanding) and finally issued on 14 April 1976. The statement reiterated that where a number of persons made a bid there was a liability on each to make the bid if the others were unable to participate. As regards Mr Glazer, documents produced at a late stage showed that he was involved in the Ashbourne bid at a very early stage and the Panel was satisfied that he was a member of the Consortium. Mr Glazer was unable to implement his obligations, because of exchange control difficulties. In the special circumstances of an exceptional case, Mr Glazer was released from his obligation to make a bid at 46p; but he was directed not to buy Ashbourne shares nor to sell Ashbourne shares or loan stock to the Consortium. Moreover, he was not to frustrate any bid for Ashbourne acceptable to those holding the shares which would have received the original bid announced on 6 December 1973.

As regards Brandts, the Panel were satisfied that Brandts did all they reasonably could both to ensure that the Consortium complied with the Code and to promote with their own support new methods of enabling the Consortium to bid. Later they endeavoured to interest others in Ashbourne. In all the circumstances, the Panel decided that Brandts could not be required to provide the funds they had promised to the Consortium, still less the cost of the whole bid, independently of a bid from a member of the Consortium. The Panel noted that Brandts recognized that they had a certain moral commitment in the affair and had agreed to provide funds so that a bid by an outsider could incorporate a cash alternative.

Various proposed bids having fallen through, Ashbourne was eventually acquired in May 1976, with the agreement of the Ashbourne board, by Incentive Investments Ltd. which offered 21p in cash for each ordinary share. The directors of Incentive were Lord Mancroft, Mr Normal Castle and Lord Fisher of Camden. Mr Glazer and Mr Leon Faust agreed to accept the offer in respect of their shares and joined the board of Incentive. At the end of the day, Mr Norman Castle was chairman of Ashbourne and the directors included Mr Glazer and Mr Faust. On 15 December 1977 Mr Justice Templeman ruled that Incentive Investments Ltd. were entitled to acquire the 465,500 shares in Ashbourne which had been frozen by the Department of Trade but that the purchase price should be paid into a bank account and held there till further order.

What conclusions can one draw from this long-drawn-out affair? The Panel failed to secure that the remaining Ashbourne shareholders had a bid at 46p per share. The other lessons from the case cannot conceal the lack of success in the Panel's main objective. It is of course impossible to say whether heavy pressure by the Panel at the early stages could have led to the issue of the offer document, against the many factors that were militating against its issue. The case showed that the threat to employ that ultimate sanction at the disposal of the Panel—that the Panel would recommend that the facilities of the securities markets should be denied to a breaker of the Code—could be used to ensure that Panel directions were carried out.

The existence of legal proceedings slowed down the operations of the Panel. At the same time, the fact that the Panel was able to weave its way through a legal thicket showed that the fears that the Panel would find itself in conflict with the Courts were exaggerated. The truth is that the Courts recognize that the Panel, in administering the Code, is engaged in work of public importance and endeavour to facilitate its task. Difficulties arose because the City Working Party in writing the Code, and the Panel in interpreting it, had found it difficult to pinpoint responsibility when several are operating together to organize a bid. The Panel considered that, in a consortium, each major participant had an individual responsibility to make the whole bid if his partners were unable to do their part. It was not easy to enforce this if a participant claimed that he had understood his liability to be strictly limited.

Since the Code did not spell out the precise obligations of financial advisers, the final statement discussed the subject in some detail, and the Panel finally concluded that, although Brandts had been involved well beyond the role of adviser, they could not be required to finance the entire bid. The case, however, provided lessons that have not been lost on merchant banks. They could not unilaterally relieve themselves of obligations undertaken in mandatory bids. There was need for more precise specification and documentation of liabilities than had happened in Brandts' handling of the Ashbourne case. The Panel at various stages of the long saga resisted the temptation to call it a day and leave the Ashbourne shareholders to fend as best they could. This meant a long and exceedingly tedious case: but the lesson has perhaps not been lost on those who might hope that the Panel would weary in well-doing.

A number of changes in the Code flowed directly from Ashbourne. An addition was made to Rule 11 that, save with the consent of the Panel, directors who sell shares to a purchaser who has to make a mandatory bid must not resign from the board until the offer closes. Again it was provided in Rule 34(6) that, save with the consent of the Panel, the offeror should not nominate anyone to the board of the offeree company or exercise voting rights on shares until the offer document had been posted. It was also made clear in Rule 34 that the obligation to make a bid could apply to any principal member of a group acting in concert. A Practice Note explained that the Panel would not regard the underwriter of a mandatory bid, by virtue of his underwriting alone, as being a member of the group acting in concert and therefore responsible for making the offer.

APPENDIX B

Contents of Offer Document

Stock Exchange

1. As a heading the words 'If you are in doubt about this offer you should consult your stockbroker, bank manager, solicitor, or other professional adviser' or similar wording;

2. The date when the document is dispatched, the name and address of the offeror and if appropriate of the person or company making the offer on behalf of the offeror;

3. Precise terms of issue of the securities for which the offer is made, whether they will be transferred *cum* or *ex* any dividend or interest payment, the total consideration offered, the period within which and the method by which any cash consideration will be paid, how any securities issued will rank for dividends or interest, capital, and redemption, and when and how the documents of title will be issued, and how such offer may be accepted, and within what period;

4. If the offer is for the exchange of securities particulars of the first dividend or interest payment in which the new securities will participate and a statement indicating the effect of acceptance on the capital and income position of the offeree company's shareholders. If the new securities are not to be identical in all respects with an existing listed security, full particulars of the

rights attaching thereto and whether application for listing has been or will be made to The Stock Exchange;

5. The middle market quotations (if any) for any securities to be offered in exchange and in addition for the securities to be acquired, which quotations in the case of listed securities should be taken from The Stock Exchange Official List;

Rule 18

6. Where the offer is for cash or includes an element of cash, confirmation by the financial adviser or by another appropriate independent party that resources are available to the offeror sufficient to satisfy full acceptance of the offer;

Legal Requirement

7. A statement of all conditions attaching to acceptances and in particular whether the offer, by reason of the provisions of the Take-over Code or otherwise, is conditional upon acceptances being received in respect of a minimum number of securities, and, if that is so, that minimum number;

Stock Exchange

8. Particulars of all documents required to be lodged for valid acceptance. (If the offer lapses all such documents must be returned within fourteen days thereafter);

9. In the case of a partial offer, the reason for not making a full offer. (Any such partial offer must be on a *pro rata* basis);

10. In respect of the offeror company, the names of its directors, the nature and particulars of its business, financial and trading prospects, and in the case of an offer by a listed company which, if successful, would result in an acquisition falling within Class 1 of Chapter 4 of the Yellow Book, group borrowings and other indebtedness at the latest date reasonably practicable;

Stock Exchange and Practice Note 9

11. In respect of both the offeror and the offeree company:

APPENDIX B

(i) details for each of the last five financial years of turnover, net profit or loss before tax, the rate per cent of dividends paid and the total amount absorbed thereby;

(ii) a statement of the assets and liabilities shown in the last published audited accounts; and

(iii) particulars of all publicly known material changes or a statement that there are none.

Rule 26

12. Specific statements of the obligations of the offeror and the rights of the offeree company shareholders under Rules 21–5. (Where an offer is unconditional as to acceptances from the outset, Rule 21 is inappropriate and Rules 22–5 should be applied as necessary.)

Rule 17

13. The following particulars in respect of shareholdings (including, where appropriate, holdings of securities convertible into equity share capital and any rights to subscribe for such capital):

(i) the shareholdings of the offeror in the offeree company;

(ii) the shareholdings in the offeror (in the case of a share exchange offer only) and in the offeree company in which directors of the offeror are interested;

(iii) the shareholdings in the offeror (in the case of a share exchange offer only) and in the offeree company which any person acting in concert with the offeror owns or controls (with the names of such persons acting in concert);

(iv) the shareholdings in the offeror (in the case of a share exchange offer only) and in the offeree company owned or controlled by any persons who, before the posting of the offer document, have irrevocably commit-

ted themselves to accept the offer together with the names of such persons;
(v) if in any of the above categories there are no shareholdings then this fact should be stated;
(vi) if any party referred to above has dealt for value in the shares in question during the period beginning twelve months before the beginning of the offer period and ending with the latest practicable date before the posting of the offer document, the details, including dates and prices, must be stated. If no such deals have been made this fact should be stated.

Rule 19   14. Except in the case of a cash offer, whether its directors' emoluments will be affected by the acquisition of the offeree company;

Stock Exchange   15. Any payment proposed for compensation for loss of office. (No offer may be made conditional on such payment);

Rule 13   16. A statement whether or not any agreement, arrangement or understanding exists between the offeror or any person acting in concert with it and any of the directors, or recent directors, shareholders or recent shareholders of the offeree company having any connection with or dependence upon the offer, and full particulars of any such agreement, arrangement, or understanding.

Rule 13   17. A statement whether or not any securities acquired in pursuance of the offer will be transferred to any other person, together with the names of the parties to any such agreement, arrangement, or understanding, and particulars of all securities in the offeree company held by such persons, or a statement that no such securities are held.

Rule 9   18. Where an offer comes within the statutory provisions for possible reference to the Monopolies and Mergers Commission, a statement that it will lapse if there is a reference before the first closing date or the date when the offer becomes or is declared unconditional as to acceptances, whichever is the later.

Rule 15   19. The offeror will normally be expected to cover the following points in the offer document:

    (i) its intentions regarding the continuation of the business of the offeree company;

    (ii) its intentions regarding any major changes to be introduced in the business, including any redeployment of the fixed assets of the offeree company;

    (iii) the long-term commercial justification for the proposed offer; and

    (iv) its intentions with regard to the continued employment of the employees of the offeree company.

Rule 16   20. If a profit forecast is included, the requirements of Rule 16 should be met.

Rule 28   21. If an offer is being made for more than one class of share (involving separate offers for each class) and if the offeror intends to resort to powers of compulsory acquisition under section 209 of the Companies Act 1948, a statement that the section will be used in respect of each class separately.

Rule 14   22. A statement that the directors of the offeror and where appropriate of the offeree company (including any who may possess delegated detailed supervision of the document) have taken all reasonable steps to ensure that the facts stated and opinions expressed therein are fair and accurate and that no material facts have been omitted: also that they jointly and severally accept responsibility accordingly.

Stock Exchange
(Experts opinions)

23. If the offer document or any circular issued in connection therewith, whether by or on behalf of the offeror company or the offeree company, includes expressly or by implication a recommendation or an opinion by a financial adviser or other expert for or against acceptance of the offer, the Stock Exchange Council may require the document, unless issued by the expert in question, to include a statement that the expert has given and not withdrawn his written consent to the issue of the document and the inclusion therein of his recommendation in the form and context in which it is included.

(Inspection of documents)

24. The offeror company and the offeree company respectively must make available at a named place in the City of London (or such other place as the Council may agree) during the currency of the offer copies of the following documents; its memorandum and articles of association; its audited accounts for the last two financial years; all directors' service agreements of more than one year's duration (within the meaning of the Listing Agreement); any report, letter, asset valuation or other document any part of which is exhibited or referred to in any document issued by it or with its authority in relation to the offer; written consents of experts; and all material contracts (not being contracts entered into in the ordinary course of business) entered into not earlier than two years before the commencement of the offer period.

The document notifying availability for inspection must set out the dates and parties to the material contracts, together with a summary of the principal contents of each contract.

Advice Issued by Board of Offeree Company

These requirements apply to documents of the offeree company advising its shareholders on an offer (whether recommending acceptance or rejection of the offer).

Rules 10 and 17

1. The views of the board not only on the main offer but also on any alternative forms of consideration offered;
2. The shareholdings of the offeree company in the offeror;
3. The shareholdings in the offeree company and in the offeror in which directors of the offeree company are interested;

   If in any of the above categories there are no shareholdings then this fact should be stated.
4. Whether the directors of the offeree company intend, in respect of their own beneficial shareholdings, to accept or reject the offer.
5. If any party referred to above has dealt for value in the shares in question during the period commencing twelve months before the beginning of the offer period and ending with the latest practicable date before the posting of the offer document, the details, including dates and prices. If no such deals have been made, this fact should be stated.

   References to shareholdings in 2 and 5 above include, where appropriate, holdings of securities convertible into equity share capital and any rights to subscribe for such capital.

Rule 19

6. Particulars of all service contracts of any director or proposed director with the offeree company or any of its subsidiaries (unless expiring, or determinable by the employing company without payment of compensation, other than statutory compensation, within 12 months). If there are none, a statement to this effect. If such contracts have been entered into or have been amended within six months of the date of the document, particulars of the

	contracts amended or replaced. If there have been no such new contracts or amendments, a statement to this effect.
Rule 4	7. The substance of the advice given by the independent adviser asked by the directors of the offeree company to advise on the offer.
Rule 15	8. Comments on the offeror's statement of his intentions about the future of the offeree company, as set out in Rule 15.
Rule 16	9. If a profit forecast is given, the requirements of Rule 16 should be met.
Rule 14	10. A statement that the directors of the offeree company (including any who may have delegated detailed supervision of the document) have taken all reasonable steps to ensure that the facts stated and the opinions expressed therein are fair and accurate and that no material facts have been omitted: also that they jointly and severally accept responsibility accordingly.

INDEX

Aberdare Holdings 34
Acceptance forms 229
Acceptances of offer
  publication of details 26, 29, 251
Accepting Houses Committee 11, 19, 53, 57, 115, 129
Accountancy 148
Accountancy bodies, consultative committee 115
Accountancy profession 37, 129
Accountancy profession (US) 7
Accountants and profit forecast 55, 56, 233
Accountant 40
Accounting standards 37
Acting in concert 70, 97, 107, 108, 139, 191–2, 271–4
Adepton 70–3, 196
Advertisements 114, 211, 228–9
Advice, independent
  to offeree company 39, 120, 201–2, 216–8, 257–9, to offeror 218
Advisers at panel meetings 132
Allegheny Ludlum Industries 109, 217
Allied Breweries 67, 80
Allied Suppliers 66
Aluminium Company of America 14
American Tobacco 45, 205
Amey 66
Announcement of offers
  ability to implement 212, 215, condition of offer 222, disclosure of principal 215, 222, obligations of offeror 28, 212, press notice by offeree board 218, prior notification to offeree board 20, 214, responsibility for statements 212, statistics 111, terms of offer 44, 222, withdrawal of offer 55

Appeal Committee 57, 116, 135–6
Approach with view to offer 215–6
Argo Caribbean Group 71
Ashbourne Investments 91, 105, 149, 150–1, 227, 288–96
Asset stripping 12, 58
Asset valuations 236–7
Associated Electrical Industries 36
Association of Stock and Share Dealers 57
Associates 83, 192–3, 207–8, 261–3
  brokers as associates 207
Atholl Developments 13
Australia 102

Babcock and Wilcox 151, 246–7
Balance between offeror and offeree 80, 119
Baltic Exchange 6
Bank of England 6, 11, 19, 37, 54, 115, 141, 145
Banker as associate 262
Barber, Lord 85
Barclays Securities 69
Barings 36
Barrington, Sir Kenneth 37, 124
Beevor, A. R. 54
Belgium 180–1
Benston, Professor George J. 174
Berkeley Hotel 13
Blanden, Michael 63
Blaskey Wallpapers 77
Blue Sky laws (US) 177
Board of Trade 22, 28, 31, 53, 57, 61, 63, 137
Boots 89
Bovis 64

Bowater 66
BP 141
Braithwaite, Sir John 12
British Aluminium 14, 15
British American Tobacco 66
British Bankers Association 11
British Chambers of Commerce 19
British Insurance Association 19, 116, 129, 212
British Investment Trust 110
British Land 70
British Lighting Industries 36
British Match 100, 140
British Nylon Spinners 27
British Steel Corporation 224
Brokers giving information 208
BSQ Securities 213
BTR 112
Bucks, Michael 37, 41, 124
Burmah Oil 141
Butler, Lord 12

Cambridge Instruments 138
Cannon, Peter 38, 124
Capital Gains Tax 30
Carr, Sir William 47
Cash
  alternative offer, 111, 249, 251, confirmation that available 239, consideration in cash 30, 239, definition 193
Caverham 66
Cazenove 45, 46
Cementation 64, 196
Channel Islands 190
Chivers 16, 17
City Capital Markets Committee 115
City Company Law Committee 162, 164
City Solicitors Company 162
City Working Party 27, 37, 53, 73, 75, 76, 106
Clark, Sir Robert 38
Clay, J. M. 124
Clore, Sir Charles 9, 10, 13, 17, 21, 212
Cobbold, Lord 19
Code, Take-over 1968 38–41
  1969 55–6
  1972 78–80
  1974 95–7
  1976 106–8
Cohen Committee 157
Cohen, Manuel F. 174
Combined English Stores 88

Commercial Union 80
Companies
  listed 189, overseas 190, private 190, public unlisted 190
Companies Act 1948 25, 145, 146, 158
  1967 58, 69, 70, 158
  1976 143, 147, 168
Companies Bill 1973 139, 163, 167
  1978 164, 165, 166
  1979 164, 166
Comparable offers 243
Condren C. E. 41, 54
Confederation of British Industry 37
Conglomerate mergers 30
Considerations, analysis 111
Consolidated Gold Fields 66, 112
Consolidated Signal 71, 74
Control, acquisition 194, 211
Controlling shareholders 227
Convertible loan stock 242, 257–9, 265
Cook and Watts 33
Cooke, W. P. 41, 54
Coral, J. 77, 209
Corporate Guarantee Trust 91, 150, 288 et seq.
Corporation tax 31
Council for Securities Industry 6, 115–8, 129
Courage 66
Court Hotels 213
Courtaulds 26, 27, 33, 44–5
Courts and the Code 64, 147–54
Crane Freuhauf 214
Creditors 209–11
Crest International Securities 91, 150, 288 et seq.
Cross, Lord 135
Crosland, Rt Hon Anthony 49
CST Investments 95, 146
Customagic Manufacturing 106, 125, 284

Debenhams 17, 80
De La Rue 66
Dell, Rt Hon Edmund 50, 144
Department of Industry 142
Department of Prices and Consumer Protection 140, 141
Department of Trade 117, 122, 138, 144
Department of Trade inspections 145–6
Directors
  definition 194, documents to shareholders 218, frustration of bid 199–200, 286–7, legal duties and the Code

INDEX

149, 152, 197, 200, oppression of minority 202, personal interests 209–11, relations with shareholders 21, 23, 28, 149, 195, 197, 198, 206
Discretionary investment clients 262
Disciplinary cases 130–6, 154
Disclosure, meaning 263
Disposal of holdings of shares 91, 275
Distributive trades 9
Dividend restraint 9
Documents—standard of care 211
Dorland 69
Dufay Bitumastics 43–5
Dunford and Elliott 113, 152

Economist 12, 17, 19, 21, 28, 212
EEC 182–5
  code of exchange conduct 5, 117, 184–5, draft directive on take-overs 183, iron and steel undertakings 224
European Commission 149
European Court 150
Ely Breweries 18
Employees 84, 97, 121, 209–10, 230–2
Equity share capital 298
Exchange control 57, 112
Exchange offers (US) 171

Fair Trading Act 1973 7, 84, 140
Fair Trading, Director-General 7, 140, 146
False market 200–1
Faulks Committee on Defamation 162
Federal Trade Commission (US) 174, 224
Fifty-Shilling Tailors 11
Financial advisers 105–6, 198, 239–40
Financial Times 21, 125
Flemings 47
Formula bids 109–11, 267
France 179–80
Fraser, Ian 54, 68, 69, 127
Fraser, Lord of Allander 31
Frazer, P. R. 41, 54, 127, 128
Free market in securities 20, 26, 66
Fruehauf Corporation (US) 214
Frustration of bids 79, 285
Future intention of offeror 84, 97

Gaitskell, Rt Hon Hugh 12
Gallahers 45, 205
Gamages 70
General Electric Company 33, 36

General Mining (SA) 103
General Principles 107
  additions in 1976 195, purpose 122, 195, relation to rules 196, 204
General Telephones and Cables 36
General Undertaking 29
Germany 182
Gillum, John 95
Goch, Desmond 21
Gold Fields of South Africa (SA) 102
Government and Code 137–146
Graff Diamonds 152
Grand Metropolitan Hotels 81
Greencoat Properties 94
Green Paper—monopolies and merger policy (1978) 119
Greig, David 88
Grendon Trust 95
Grunwald, H. 18
Guardian 83, 100
Guest, Keen and Nettlefold 149–50

Hacking, Lord 12
Hambros 14, 15, 34, 47
Harris, Martin 127
Harrods 17, 18
Hart-Scott-Rodino Act (US) 224
Haverton Holdings 10
Haw Par 103
Hays Wharf 85, 86, 131, 149
Heath, Rt Hon Edward 82
Henshall, W. & Sons 210
Hill Samuel 36, 44, 47, 102
Holland, Sir Milner 54, 148
Hollom, Sir Jasper 129
House of Fraser 17, 189
Howe, Sir Geoffrey 139
Hull, John 127

Illingworth Morris 16
Imperial Chemical Industries 26, 27
Imperial Tobacco 55, 66
Independent advice to shareholders 120, 257–9, 284
Industrial Reorganisation Corporation 31, 138
Industry Act 1975 142
Information
  to potential offeror 227 to shareholders 206
Insider 166
Insider dealing
  civil remedies 162, 164, definition of

Inside dealer—*contd.*
  offence 165–7, EEC developments 167, grounds of objection 164–5, handling of cases 168, offeror 80, panel inquiries 98, 160–1, preventive measures 168–9, proposals for legislation 84, 162–4, rule 30 259–61, stock exchange inquiries 159, UK proposals 157–8, US practice 155–7, 1968 Code 159
Inspectors 63, 95, 145–6
Institute of Directors 19
Institutional investors 35, 121
Insurance brokers 5
Insurance companies 11
International Distillers and Vintners 35, 66
International Learning Systens 61
International Paints 43–5
International Stores 66
International Telephone and Telegraph (US) 36
International Registry Ltd 10
Investment trusts 109–11, 267
Investment Trusts, Association 19, 57, 115, 129
Irish Republic 105, 190
Isle of Man 190
Issuing Houses Association 11, 19, 26, 37, 38, 46, 47, 57, 116, 129, 133, 219
Italy 181–2

Jackson, Professor Derek 47
Jackson the Tailor 11
Jasper, H. & Co. 18
Jenkins Committee 11, 24–6, 69, 158, 165, 212, 257
Jenkins, Rt Hon Roy 12
Johnson Firth Brown 152
Johnston, Sir A. 129
Joint Review Body 144–5
Journal of Business Law 133
Justice report on insider dealing 162

Kearton, Lord 45
Kennington, I. G. 124
Kent, George Ltd 138
Kleinwort Benson 64, 65, 105
Knight, J. R. 116
Kripke, Professor Homer 173
Kuwait Investment Office 86

Land and General Developments 101
Land Securities Investment 13
Law and the Code 54, 147–154
Law Society 148
Lazards 14, 15, 127
Leach, Sir Ronald 63
Leases 60–3, 136, 159
Lee, T. P. 127, 128
Legal proceedings 83, 152, 200
Legal representations 133–5
Licensed dealers 3, 57, 137
Licensed Dealers (Conduct of Business) Rules 22–4, 25–6, 28, 31, 38, 40, 122–3, 137, 138, 214, 224, 254, 255, 256
Lintang Investments 18
Lloyds 5
Loan stock 242, 257–9, 266
London clearing banks 19, 57, 116, 129 213
London Tin 103
Lonrho 82, 115
Lowson, Sir Denys 82, 115
Loss, Professor Louis 156, 175
Lye Trading Company 224

Macaine 33
Macdonald D. C. 116, 124, 127
Maclehose 83
McMahon, J. H. G. 83
Mandatory bids
  acquisitions 91–7, 270–3, cash 280, chain principle 278, conditions 222, 280–1, controllers selling part 273, convertibles 275, directors selling control 43, 226, 271, increase in capital 277, offeree shareholders 269, 272, offeror shareholders 272, options 275, persons in concert 98–9, 271–5, placings 275–6, reference to Monopolies Commission 279, rescue operations 278, responsibility for bid 274, transfers between shareholders 273, two-stage acquisition of control 277–8, warrants 275, unconditional 280, US practice 178, whitewashes by shareholders 276–7, withdrawal 281
Marc Gregory 94
Market freedom 68
Market purchases of shares
  by merchant bank adviser 34, 48, 64, by offeror or offeree to be disclosed 39, 55, 261–3, effect on bids 66–9,

INDEX

70–6, 201–3, following on paper bid 70, reporting of substantial purchases 112, 143, standing in the market 72
Market Committee, CSI 117–18
Maxwell, Robert 47, 60, 62, 136
Meetings with selected shareholders 207
Menzies, Sir Peter 129
Merchant banks as advisers 197
'Mergers'—Board of Trade booklet 138
Merits of take-overs 190
Metal Industries 34
Metropolitan Estates and Property 80
Miles Druce 149–50
Minority shareholders, oppression 202
Mitford-Slade, P. B. 54
Monetary penalties 53
Monopolies and Mergers Commission 11, 31, 66, 67, 89, 135, 140, 141, 200, 223–4, 279, 282, 287
Montagu, Samuel 64
Montague Burtons 11
Moolaya Investments 106, 125, 284
Morgan Grenfell 34, 45, 47, 48, 102
Morris, Herbert 151
Morris, Philip (US) 45
Murdoch, Robert 47, 48
Mynors, Sir Humphrey 37, 41, 53, 54, 124

National Association of Securities Dealers (US) 7, 174
National Coal Board Pensions Funds 110
National Corporation of Malaysia 104
National Enterprise Board 142
Neill, F. Patrick 116
Netherlands 182
New York Stock Exchange 170
News (Australia) 47, 48
News of the World 47, 48
Nominee shareholdings 12
Non-equity capital 242, 244
Non-voting shares 11
Norbury Insulation 131
Norcros 74
Notes on Amalgamations 9, 19–21, 158

O'Brien of Lothbury, Lord 37, 47, 51–3
Offer
  ability to implement 212, 215, 239, acceptances 32, 40, 247–50, announcement of results 250–1, becoming unconditional 23, 32, 244–7, cash or paper 30, 67, 80, 205, conditions 23, 222, definitions 194, extension 244–7, identity of offeror 23, 40, 215, 222, lapsed 281, minimum and maximum period 244, not allowed after failed offer 281, numbers 119, offeree board to be informed 214, period open 21, 23, 28, 40, 247–50, price 28, 67, reasonably in contemplation 205, renewal after failed offer 282, revision 25, 29, 244–7, selected shareholders 205, separate classes 257, suspension of dealings 251–2, terms 39, 222, transfer of shares to outsiders 228, types of considerations 111, 50 per cent acceptances before unconditional 241–4
Offer document
  contents 23, 230–2, 252–3, copies to Panel executive 126, employees of offeree 97, 232, future intentions of offeror 97, 230–2, posting to shareholders 23, 225, 241, prospectus standard 228, resources available 238, rights and obligations to be stated 252–3, sent to Panel 241, shareholdings in offeror and offeree 237–9, submitted in draft to Stock Exchange 29, 126
Offer period 194
Offeree directors
  agreements with offeror 228, circulating views on offer 225, frustrating offer 21, 39, 286, information to potential offerors 227, informing shareholders of offer 218–20, receiving offer 20, 23, 216, remaining during offer period 226–7, responsibility for statements 230, selling controlling interest 226, shareholdings to be revealed 237–9, service contracts 240
Offeree documents 237–9, 240–1
Offeree shareholders 20, 108–9
Offeror
  agreements with offeree directors 227, approach to offeree shareholders after failed bid 263, definition 194, dealings 121, 259–61, holdings in offeree 222, 266–7, preliminary announcements 220, responsibility for statements 230

Offeror shareholders 121
Outrams 31
Overseas offeree companies 102–5, 190
Overseas offeror 102–3, 215
Ozalid 74

Panel
 alternate members 41, discretion under code 122, duration of rulings 101–2, first meetings 41, first year's operation 40–50, membership 37, 41, 129, powers 56, 57, 65, procedure 41, 42, 129–33, proposed by Bank 37, quarterly meetings 135, reorganisation of 1969 54–5
Panel's annual reports
 1968–9 42, 59, 1969–70 59, 107, 159, 282, 1970–1 59, 65, 203, 1971–2 79, 1972–3 82, 100, 231, 1973–4 282, 1976–7 106, 217, 1977–8 140, 205, 1978–9 250, 282
Panel executive 43, 54, 58, 125–9, 190
Paper offers 67, 68, 72, 98
Partial bids
 allowed in US 180, criticised in first code 40, licensed dealers rules 23, not allowed with full bid 103, 255, regarded as undesirable 21, 40, restrictions after bid 254–5, rules made tighter 56, rules relaxed 109, 253–7, switch to general offer 256
Pearce, Lord 57, 135
Pearson D. C. F. 62
Penalties for infringements 53
Pennington, Professor R. R. 148, 183
Pension Funds, National Association 57, 66, 115, 129
Pergamon Press 47, 60–3, 159
Pernas Securities 103, 104
Philips 32
Practice Notes 59–60, 78, 104
Preference shares 242
Preliminary announcements 218–21
Press 208–9
Press announcements 229–30, 241
Prevention of Fraud (Investment) Act 3, 22, 25, 145, 147, 157
Price/earnings ratio 67
Private companies 190
Private investors 118–9
Profit forecasts 36, 39, 44, 55, 113, 178, 232–7, 247
Property boom, collapse 85

Prospective legal actions 179
Prospectus 211
Purchase of shares
 after failed offer 281, by persons with commercial interest 284–5, from offeree directors 91, in previous year 266, with favourable conditions 282
Pye 32

Quarterly panel meetings 135
Quotations Committee 115
Quotations Department 126

Radio 113, 208
Ralli International 66
Rank Organization 66, 138
Raphael, Clive 101
Recession
 announced bids 84–91, price in bids 91, disposal of holdings 91
Regis Property 70
Registration of acquired shares 287
Representation of witnesses before panel 133
Reprimands, public or private 161
Responsibility statements 228–30
Restrictive trade practices—panel exemptions 144
Requirements by panel—duration 101–2, 104
Reverse take-over bids 121, 190
Review of monopolies and merger policy 119
Revised Notes on Company Amalgamations 26–9
Reynolds Metals (US) 14, 15, 16
Richard Thomas and Baldwin 27
Richardson, Rt Hon Gordon 116, 144
Rider, B. A. K. 157
Rockwell International Corporation (US) 201
Rodo Investment Trust 43
Rowland, David 71
Rules
 waiving by panel 197, spirit 196

St Martin's Preserving 16, 17
St Martin's Property 85, 86, 131, 149
Salt (Saltaire) 16
Samuel, H. 13
Sanctions 56, 57, 161, 189
Savoy Hotel 13
Schemes of arrangement 147, 153–4

INDEX

Schoders 14
Schweppes 16, 17
Scottish Australian 102
Scottish and Universal Investments 31, 160
Scottish Motor Traction 13
Sears Holdings 13, 17
Seers, J. & Co 10
SEC (US)
  comparison with Code 178, criticisms 173–4, effectiveness 173, fields of operation 171–2, inapplicability to UK 174–7, reasons for setting up 170–1, relations with self-regulatory bodies 174, state laws 177, take-over bids 173
SEC proposed for UK 45, 82
Secrecy before announcement of bid 221, 259–60
Securities Act (US) 171, 173
Securities Exchange Act (US) 155, 172, 174, 175
Security—1977 statement 168
Self-regulation 3–7, 65, 82, 126, 142–3, relation with State supervision 7, 144–5, 189
Selmes, C. 95, 146
Shares
  classes 203, 243–4, issues by offeree 39, issues by offeror 34, offeror shares 83, purchases by related companies 35, 36
Shareholders
  equality of treatment 202–5, 206–9, freedom under code 86, information and time 198
Shawcross, Lord 54, 59, 65, 82, 123–4, 129
Shore, Rt Hon Peter 142
Showerings 35
Shut-offs 120, 248–50
Shut-out bids 76–8, 79, 99–101, 108, 120, 276
Silentbloc 112
Sime Darby 104
Slater Walker 30
South Africa 102
Spirit of Code 55, 196–7
Stable R. O. C. Q.C. 63
Stag Line 12
State legislation (US) 177
Statutory powers for panel 3, 4, 53, 65
Statutory supervisory body 143

Sterling Guarantee Trust 70
Stewart and Lloyds 27
Stock Exchange
  acceptance of panel findings 56, American Tobacco/Gallaher 46, City Working Party 19, false markets 207, liaison with Bank 6, membership of CSI and of panel 116, 129 offeror's future intentions 84, operations left free 66, overseas companies 102, prevention of leakages 168, securities regulation 171, listed company's circulars 29, support for panel 57, work of first panel 57
Stock Exchange model code for companies 163, 167
Stock Exchanges (US) 7
Sunday Telegraph 95
Suspension of dealings 53, 221
Swedish Match 109

Take-over activity 9, 30, 31, 42, 58, 66, 98, 126
Take-over panel 6, 37, 125–135
Tangley, Lord 19
Telephone Rentals 33
Television 113, 208
Tender Offers (US) 171
Thomson, Lord 31
Thorn Electrical Industries 32, 34, 36
Thwarting of bid 2, 84–7
The Times 12, 18, 21, 35, 73, 84, 95
Town and Country Planning Act 9
Tradewinds (Malaysia) 103
Trafalgar House Investments 196
Transfers—registration 287
Treaty of Paris 279, 280
Treaty of Rome 182
Trust Houses Forte 80
Tube Investments 14, 15, 16

Underwriters 221
Underwritten offers 249
Unilever 67
Union Corporation 102
Unit Trust Association 54, 57, 116, 129
United Drapery Stores 11, 17, 80
Unlisted public companies 190

Venesta International 74
Volume of business 126
Voting rights 194

Walsh, Graham R. 128
Warburgs 14, 45, 85
Wareham W. S. 54
Warehousing 32, 69, 139, 143
Watney Mann 17, 35, 66, 81
Weidmann, H. A. G. 141
Weyburn Engineering 93, 94
White Papers
    Company Law Reform (1973) 139, 163
    Conduct of Company Directors (1977) 143, 163
    Future of Company Reports (1977) 143
    Prevention of Fraud (Investment) Act (1977) 143
    Changes in Company Law (1978) 143, 164
Whitehead Iron and Steel 27
Whiteley B. S. and W. 142
Whitewash of Rule 34 obligation 109, 276–7
Wilkinson and Riddell 33
Wilkinson Match 109, 217
Wilkinson Sword 100, 140
Williams, G. G. 118
Williams Act (US) 171–2
Williams Hudson 70–3
Wilmot Breeden 201
Wilson Committee 120, 144
Wilson, Rt Hon Sir Harold 49, 144
Withdrawal of announced offers 60, 83–90, 225, 281
Wood, W. and Son 77
Woodall-Duckham 247
Worcester Buildings 13